WATERFALL
LOVER'S GUIDE
NORTHERN CALIFORNIA

WATERFALL LOVER'S GUIDE
NORTHERN CALIFORNIA

MATT & KRISSI DANIELSSON

More than
300 Waterfalls
from the North
Coast to the
Southern Sierra

THE MOUNTAINEERS BOOKS

THE MOUNTAINEERS BOOKS
*is the nonprofit publishing arm of The Mountaineers Club,
an organization founded in 1906 and dedicated to the exploration,
preservation, and enjoyment of outdoor and wilderness areas.*

1001 SW Klickitat Way, Suite 201, Seattle, WA 98134

First edition, 2006

Manufactured in the United States of America

Acquiring Editor: Cassandra Conyers
Project Editor: Laura Drury
Copy Editor: Anne Moreau
Cover and Book Design: The Mountaineers Books
Layout Artist: Mayumi Thompson
Cartographer: Ben Pease
Photographer: All photographs by the authors unless otherwise noted.

Cover photograph: *Huntington Falls (Golden Gate Park)*
Frontispiece: *A seasonal cascade downstream from Dawn Falls near Larkspur.*

Library of Congress Cataloging-in-Publication Data
Danielsson, Krissi.
  A waterfall lover's guide to Northern California / Krissi and Matt Danielsson.-- 1st ed.
    p. cm.
  Includes bibliographical references and index.
  ISBN 0-89886-967-6 (pbk.)
  1. Hiking--California, Northern--Guidebooks. 2.
Waterfalls--California, Northern. 3. California, Northern--Guidebooks.
I. Danielsson, Matt. II. Title.
  GV199.42.C2D36 2005
  917.94--dc22
                    2005029008

CONTENTS

WATERFALLS QUICK-REFERENCE CHART

	FALLS TYPE	VISIBLE BY CAR	HIKE LENGTH (MILES)	DIFFICULTY	OFF-TRAIL HIKE	DOGS ALLOWED	POPULAR FOR BIKING	WHEELCHAIR ACCESSIBLE	STROLLER FRIENDLY	FEE CHARGED
North Coast										
1 Jedediah Smith Redwoods State Park										
Fern Falls ★★★	C		5	M						
2 Smith River and Highway 199										
Myrtle Creek Falls ★★★	C		5	H	•	•				
Grassy Flat Falls ★★★	C	•				•				
Madrona Falls ★	C	•				•		•		
Little Spout Falls ★	H	•				•				
Little Jones Creek Falls ★★	C	•				•				
Knopki Falls ★★★★	B		<1	FH		•				
Wilderness Falls ★★★★	C		19	FH		•				
3 Prairie Creek Redwoods State Park										
South Gold Bluffs Beach Falls ★★★	H		2	E			•		•	$
Gold Dust Falls ★★★	H		2	E			•		•	$
North Gold Bluffs Beach Falls ★★★	H		2	E			•		•	$
Fern Canyon Falls ★	C		1	E						$
John Baldwin Falls ★★	H		2	FE						$
4 Redwood National Park										
Trillium Falls ★★	C		2	FE						
5 McKinleyville										
Mill Creek Falls ★★★	B	•				•				
6 Humboldt Redwoods State Park										
South Fork Honeydew Falls ★	T	•								
7 Smithe Redwoods State Reserve										
Dora Creek Falls ★★	P		<1	E	•	•				
8 King Range Natn'l Conservation Area										
Lost Coast Falls ★★★	C		3–24	FE		•				
9 Russian Gulch State Park										
Russian Gulch Falls ★★	P		6	E			•		•	$
10 Jackson Demonstration State Forest										
Chamberlain Creek Falls ★★★	P		<1	M		•				
11 Yolla Bolly Middle Eel Wilderness										
Rattlesnake Creek Falls ★★	C					•				
Balm of Gilead Creek Falls ★★★★	P		12	M	•	•				
Shasta-Trinity Region										
1 Highway 299										
Green Point Ridge Falls ★★	B	•				•				
Willow Creek Cascades ★	C	•				•				
Willow Creek Falls ★★	P	•				•				
Gray Falls ★	C		1	E		•				
Schneiders Bar Falls ★★	C	•				•				
2 Somes Bar										
Ishi Pishi Falls ★	C	•				•				

Falls type:
P = plunge
H = horsetail
F = fan
B = block
T = tiered
S = segmented
C = cascades

Hike difficulty:
E = easy
FE = fairly easy
M = moderate
FH = fairly hard
H = hard

★ = Uninspiring
★★ = Modest
★★★ = Good
★★★★ = Very good
★★★★★ = Exceptional

	FALLS TYPE	VISIBLE BY CAR	HIKE LENGTH (MILES)	DIFFICULTY	OFF-TRAIL HIKE	DOGS ALLOWED	POPULAR FOR BIKING	WHEELCHAIR ACCESSIBLE	STROLLER FRIENDLY	FEE CHARGED
3 Happy Camp										
Ukonom Falls ★★★	P		1	FE						
Sheridan Falls ★★	B		5	E		•				
Twin Falls ★★	H	•								
4 Marble Mountain Wilderness										
Maple Falls ★★★	S		8	FE		•				
Sur Cree Falls ★★	C		6	M		•				
Shackleford Falls ★★	H		<1	E						
East Boulder Creek Falls ★★	H		4	M		•				
5 Seiad Valley										
Horsetail Falls ★★★	C	•								
Ponytail Falls ★	C	•								
6 Mount Shasta										
Whitney Falls ★★★★	P		6	FH						
Coquette Falls ★★★	C		2	FH	•					
Mud Creek Falls ★★★★	P		2	FE						
Ash Creek Falls ★★★★	T	•	2	FH						
7 McCloud										
Lower McCloud Falls ★★	H	•	<1	E		•		♿	•	
Middle McCloud Falls ★★★★★	B	•	2	E		•			•	
Upper McCloud Falls ★★★	C		<1	E		•				
Lower Squaw Valley Creek Falls ★★	C		5	M		•				
Upper Squaw Valley Creek Falls ★	C		7	M		•				
8 Dunsmuir										
Mossbrae Falls ★★★★★	S		3	FE		•				
Hedge Creek Falls ★★★	P		<1	M		•				
9 Castle Crags State Park										
Burstarse Falls ★★★	P		5	FH		•				
Sweetbriar Falls ★★	C	•	<1			•				
10 Trinity Alps Wilderness										
Grizzly Lake Falls ★★★★★	P		12	H		•				
Swift Creek Falls ★★	C		2	FE		•				
Canyon Creek Falls ★★★	C		8–15	M		•				
Kickapoo Waterfall ★★★	P	•				•				
11 Shasta Lake										
Potem Falls ★★★★	F		<1	E		•				
Lion Slide Falls ★★★	B		<1	E		•				
Montgomery Creek Falls ★★	T	•				•				
Shasta Dam ★★	P	•						♿	•	
12 Whiskeytown Lake										
Boulder Creek Falls ★★★★	T		7	M						$
Lower Brandy Creek Falls ★★	C		<1	FE						$
Brandy Creek Falls ★★★	B		3	M						$
Crystal Creek Falls ★★★★	C		<1	E				♿	•	$
Upper Crystal Creek Falls ★★★★	C		3	FH	•					$

Falls type: P = plunge H = horsetail F = fan B = block T = tiered S = segmented C = cascades	Hike difficulty: E = easy FE = fairly easy M = moderate FH = fairly hard H = hard ★ = Uninspiring ★★ = Modest ★★★ = Good ★★★★ = Very good ★★★★★ = Exceptional

	FALLS TYPE	VISIBLE BY CAR	HIKE LENGTH (MILES)	DIFFICULTY	OFF-TRAIL HIKE	DOGS ALLOWED	POPULAR FOR BIKING	WHEELCHAIR ACCESSIBLE	STROLLER FRIENDLY	FEE CHARGED
Lassen Region										
1 Modoc National Forest										
Mill Creek Falls ★★★	H		<1	E		•			•	
2 McArthur Burney Falls Memorial State Park										
Burney Falls ★★★★★	S	•	<1	E				♿	•	$
3 Fall River Mills										
Pit River Falls ★★	C	•								
4 Lassen Volcanic National Park										
Hat Creek Cascades ★★	C		3	FE						$
Kings Creek Cascades ★★★	C		2	FE						$
Kings Creek Falls ★★★★	C		3	FE						$
Mill Creek Falls ★★★★	P		3	M						$
Bluff Falls ★★★	P	•	<1	FE		•				$
5 Mineral										
Deer Creek Falls ★★	B	•				•			•	
Lower Deer Creek Falls ★★★	C		4	E						
Lower Canyon Creek Falls ★★★	S		10	H	•	•				
Upper Canyon Creek Falls ★★★	S		11	H	•	•				
Battle Creek Falls ★★	C	•								
6 Quincy										
Indian Falls ★★★	B		<1	E		•				
7 Graeagle										
Little Jamison Falls ★★★	H		3	M		•			•	
Hawsley Falls ★★	C		3	FE		•				
Frazier Falls ★★★★	T		1	E		•		♿	•	
Fern Falls ★★	C		<1	E		•				
8 Lava Beds National Monument										
Crystal Cave Falls ★★★★	C		<1	H						$
San Francisco Bay Area										
1 Sugarloaf Ridge State Park										
Sonoma Creek Falls ★★★	P		1	M						$
2 Santa Rosa										
Mayacama Retreat Falls ★★★	C		<1	E						$
3 Armstrong Redwoods State Reserve										
Armstrong Falls ★★	C	•								$
4 San Rafael and Fairfax										
Stairstep Falls ★★	T		3	E					•	
Little Carson Creek Falls ★★★	T		3	M		•			•	
Cascade Falls ★★	C		2	FE		•				
Plunge Pool ★★	C		1	FE	•	•				
Cataract Falls ★★★	C		3	M		•				
Dawn Falls ★★	P		<1	E		•				
5 Mill Valley										
Cascade Falls ★★	C		<1	E				♿		

Falls type:
P = plunge
H = horsetail
F = fan
B = block
T = tiered
S = segmented
C = cascades

Hike difficulty:
E = easy
FE = fairly easy
M = moderate
FH = fairly hard
H = hard

★ = Uninspiring
★★ = Modest
★★★ = Good
★★★★ = Very good
★★★★★ = Exceptional

	FALLS TYPE	VISIBLE BY CAR	HIKE LENGTH (MILES)	DIFFICULTY	OFF-TRAIL HIKE	DOGS ALLOWED	POPULAR FOR BIKING	WHEELCHAIR ACCESSIBLE	STROLLER FRIENDLY	FEE CHARGED
6 Stinson Beach										
Morses Gulch Falls ★★★	F		1	FE						
Steep Ravine Falls ★★	C		4	M						
7 Point Reyes National Seashore										
Alamere Falls ★★★★★	B		11	FE						
Phantom Falls ★★★	H		13	FE						
Horsetail Falls ★★	H		14	FE						
8 Walnut Creek										
Abrigo Falls ★	H		3	E		•				$
9 Mount Diablo State Park										
Mount Diablo Falls ★★★	C		6	FE						
10 Sunol-Ohlone Regional Wilderness										
Murietta Falls ★★	C		16	FE		•				$
Little Yosemite Falls ★★	P		3	FE		•		♿	•	
11 Vacaville										
Creek Walk Falls ★★	C		<1	E		•		♿	•	
12 San Francisco										
Martin Luther King Jr. Memorial Falls ★★★	B	•					•	♿		
Rainbow Falls ★★★	B	•				•				
Huntington Falls ★★★	P	•	<1	E		•		♿	•	
Tea Garden Falls ★★★	C		<1	E				♿	•	$
13 San Pedro Valley County Park										
Brooks Falls ★★★	T		2	FE						
14 La Honda										
Tiptoe Falls ★★	P		2	E						$
Pomponio Falls ★★	P		<1	E				♿	•	$
Upper Pomponio Falls ★	C	•								$
15 Edgewood County Park										
Sylvan Trail Falls ★	C		1	E					•	
16 Castle Rock State Park										
Castle Rock Falls ★★	P		2	FE					•	$
17 Big Basin Redwoods State Park										
Berry Creek Falls ★★★★	C		11	FE						$
Silver Falls ★★★	C		11	FE						$
Golden Cascade ★★★	C		12	FE						$
Sempervirens Falls ★★★	H	•	3	FE						$
18 Forest of Nisene Marks										
Five Finger Falls ★★	P		12	H						$
Maple Falls ★★★	H		13	M						$
19 Uvas Canyon County Park										
Granuja Falls ★★	C		<1	E		•			•	$
Black Rock Falls ★★★	C		2	FE		•			•	$
Upper Falls ★★	C		2	E		•			•	$
Basin Falls ★★	C		2	E		•			•	$

Falls type: P = plunge, H = horsetail, F = fan, B = block, T = tiered, S = segmented, C = cascades. Hike difficulty: E = easy, FE = fairly easy, M = moderate, FH = fairly hard, H = hard. ★ = Uninspiring, ★★ = Modest, ★★★ = Good, ★★★★ = Very good, ★★★★★ = Exceptional	FALLS TYPE	VISIBLE BY CAR	HIKE LENGTH (MILES)	DIFFICULTY	OFF-TRAIL HIKE	DOGS ALLOWED	POPULAR FOR BIKING	WHEELCHAIR ACCESSIBLE	STROLLER FRIENDLY	FEE CHARGED
Uvas Falls ★★	C		<1	E		•			•	$
Triple Falls ★★	T		3	M		•			•	$
Sacramento and San Joaquin Valley										
1 Snow Mountain Wilderness										
Stony Creek Falls ★★★	F		5	M		•				
2 Oroville										
Feather Falls ★★★★★	F		8	M		•	•		•	
Upper Frey Creek Falls ★	C		4	M		•	•		•	
Lower Frey Creek Falls ★	C		4	M		•			•	
Seven Falls ★★★★★	T		4	H		•				
Milsap Bar Falls ★★	C		4	FE		•				
Curtain Falls ★★★	P		5	H		•				
Chambers Creek Falls ★★★★	T		4	M		•			•	
3 Spenceville Wildlife and Recreation Area										
Lower Fairy Falls ★★	C		5	FE		•			•	
Upper Fairy Falls ★★★	P		5	FE		•			•	
4 North Table Mountain Ecological Preserve										
Coal Canyon Falls ★★★★	P		5	FE	•	•				
5 Auburn										
American Canyon Falls ★★★	H		4	M		•				
Knickerbocker Falls ★★	P		2	M		•			•	
Lake Clementine Falls ★★★	B	•				•				
Paradise Canyon Falls ★★	C	•				•				
Codfish Falls ★★★	C		3	FE		•				
6 Colfax										
Devils Falls ★★★	S	•				•				
Mexican Gulch Falls ★★	C	•				•				
Indian Creek Falls ★★	T		3	M						
Stevens Creek Falls ★★	C		3	M						
7 Nevada City										
Humbug Creek Falls ★★	H		3	M						
Rush Creek Falls ★★	C		2	E		•		♿	•	
Yuba River Falls ★★	S		1	E		•			•	
8 Sutter Buttes										
The Falls ★★★	C		1–7	E						$
Lake Tahoe Region										
1 Sierra City										
Loves Falls ★★★	B		<1	FE		•				
Big Springs Garden Falls ★★★	S	•								
2 Downieville										
Pauley Creek Falls ★★★	C		<1	E					•	
3 Sierraville										
Webber Falls ★★★★	T	•								

Falls type:	Hike difficulty:
P = plunge	E = easy
H = horsetail	FE = fairly easy
F = fan	M = moderate
B = block	FH = fairly hard
T = tiered	H = hard
S = segmented	
C = cascades	★ = Uninspiring
	★★ = Modest
	★★★ = Good
	★★★★ = Very good
	★★★★★ = Exceptional

	FALLS TYPE	VISIBLE BY CAR	HIKE LENGTH (MILES)	DIFFICULTY	OFF-TRAIL HIKE	DOGS ALLOWED	POPULAR FOR BIKING	WHEELCHAIR ACCESSIBLE	STROLLER FRIENDLY	FEE CHARGED
4 Washington										
Killer Fang Falls ★★	P		1	E		•			•	
5 Gold Run										
South Fork Deer Creek Falls ★★★	S	•								
6 Emigrant Gap										
Bear River Falls ★★	B		<1	E		•		♿	•	
Bowman Lake Falls ★★★	C		<1	M	•	•				
Faucherie Falls ★★★	P		<1	E	•	•				
7 Soda Springs										
Heath Falls ★★★	P		10	FH		•				
8 Foresthill										
Grouse Falls ★★★★★	S		1	E		•			•	
9 Pollock Pines										
Bassi Falls ★★★★★	C		1	E		•			•	
Bridal Veil Falls ★★	H	•								
Sly Park Falls ★★★	H		2	FE		•				
10 Placerville										
Pilot Creek Falls ★★	C		6	M		•			•	
11 Grizzly Flat										
Buttermilk Falls ★★	P	•	<1	E	•	•				
12 South Lake Tahoe										
Horsetail Falls ★★★★	C		3	M	•	•				$
Cascade Falls ★★★★	C		2	FE		•				
Upper Eagle Falls ★★★	C		<1	E		•			•	
Lower Eagle Falls ★★★★	C		2	M		•			•	
Upper Glen Alpine Falls ★★★	P		1	E		•			•	
Lower Glen Alpine Falls ★★★★	C	•				•				
13 Markleeville										
Hot Springs Creek Falls ★★★	S		3	FE		•				
Caples Creek Falls ★★	P		1	FE		•				
Hawley Grade Trail Falls ★★	S		<1	E		•			•	
14 Carson-Iceberg Wilderness										
Llewellyn Falls ★★	C		12	FE		•				
Carson Falls ★★	C		18	FE		•				
Yosemite Region										
1 Sonora Pass										
Leavitt Falls ★★★	P	•	<1	FE		•				
Cascade Falls ★★	C		13	M		•				
Sardine Falls ★★★★	S	•	2	E		•				
Sardine Creek Falls ★★	C	•				•				
Blue Canyon Falls ★★	H	•				•				
Deadman Creek Falls ★★	H	•				•				
Kennedy Meadow Falls ★★★★	C		2	FE		•				
Niagara Creek Falls ★★★	T		<1	E		•			•	
2 West Highway 120										

Falls type:
P = plunge
H = horsetail
F = fan
B = block
T = tiered
S = segmented
C = cascades

Hike difficulty:
E = easy
FE = fairly easy
M = moderate
FH = fairly hard
H = hard

★ = Uninspiring
★★ = Modest
★★★ = Good
★★★★ = Very good
★★★★★ = Exceptional

	FALLS TYPE	VISIBLE BY CAR	HIKE LENGTH (MILES)	DIFFICULTY	OFF-TRAIL HIKE	DOGS ALLOWED	POPULAR FOR BIKING	WHEELCHAIR ACCESSIBLE	STROLLER FRIENDLY	FEE CHARGED
Diana Falls ★★	C		1	E		•				
Rainbow Pool Falls ★★	B	•								
Little Nellie Falls ★★	T	•				•				
Jawbone Falls ★★	C		<1	E		•				
Preston Falls ★★	P		8	M		•				
3 Hetch Hetchy Reservoir										
Carlon Falls ★★	H		3	E		•				$
Madeleine Falls ★★	H		1	E					•	$
Hetch Hetchy Falls ★★	H		2	E						$
Tueeulala Falls ★★★	F	•	3	E						$
Wapama Falls ★★★★★	C	•	5	E					•	$
Rancheria Falls ★★★	C		13	M						$
4 Grand Canyon of the Tuolumne River										
Tuolumne Falls ★★★★	C		10	M						$
White Cascade ★★★	C		12	FH						$
California Falls ★★★	C		15	FH						$
LeConte Falls ★★★	C		17	H						$
Waterwheel Falls ★★★★	C		19	H						$
Cathedral Falls ★★	C		22	H						$
Register Creek Falls ★★★	H		25	H						$
5 El Portal										
Chinquapin Falls ★	C	•								
6 Yosemite Valley										
Silver Strand Falls ★★★	H	•								$
Widows Tears ★★	H	•								$
Tamarack Falls ★★★	T	•								$
Wildcat Falls ★★★	T	•	<1	E						$
The Cascades ★★★★	C	•	<1	E						$
Ribbon Falls ★★★★	P	•								$
El Capitan Falls ★★★★	H	•								$
Sentinel Falls ★★★★	T	•								$
Bridalveil Falls ★★★★★	P	•	<1	E				•	•	$
Yosemite Falls (upper) ★★★★★	F	•	7	H						$
Yosemite Falls (lower) ★★★★★	P	•	<1	E				•	•	$
Lehamite Falls ★★★	C	•								$
Snow Creek Falls ★★★★★	S		8	M						$
Tenaya Falls ★★★	C		4	M						$
Tanechka Falls ★★	P		4	M						$
Royal Arch Cascade ★★★	C	•								$
Staircase Falls ★★	T	•								$
7 Mist Trail										
Vernal Falls ★★★★★	B		3	M					•	$
Silver Apron ★★	C		4	FH						$
Glacier Point Falls ★★	P		4	FH						$
Nevada Falls ★★★★★	H		5	FH						$

Falls type:
P = plunge
H = horsetail
F = fan
B = block
T = tiered
S = segmented
C = cascades

Hike difficulty:
E = easy
FE = fairly easy
M = moderate
FH = fairly hard
H = hard

★ = Uninspiring
★★ = Modest
★★★ = Good
★★★★ = Very good
★★★★★ = Exceptional

	FALLS TYPE	VISIBLE BY CAR	HIKE LENGTH (MILES)	DIFFICULTY	OFF-TRAIL HIKE	DOGS ALLOWED	POPULAR FOR BIKING	WHEELCHAIR ACCESSIBLE	STROLLER FRIENDLY	FEE CHARGED
8 Merced Lake										
Echo Creek Falls ★★	C		20–22	M						$
Bunnell Cascade ★★	C		14–15	M						$
9 Foresta										
Foresta Falls ★★	C	•								$
10 Tioga Pass										
Yosemite Creek Falls ★★	C	•								$
11 Wawona										
Chilnualna Falls ★★★★★	T		8	FH						$
Alder Creek Falls ★★★	C		8	FH						$
Illilouette Falls ★★★★★	H		4	M						$
Pywiack Cascade ★★★★	C	•			•					$
12 Fish Camp										
Fish Camp Falls ★★	P		1	E		•			•	
Big Creek Falls ★	C		<1	E		•			•	
Eastern Sierra Region										
1 Lee Vining										
Ellery Lake Falls ★★	S	•								
Big Bend Falls ★★★	C	•	<1	E		•				
Aspen Falls ★★	C	•				•				
Lundy Canyon Falls ★★★★	C		3	FE		•				
2 Twin Lakes										
Horse Creek Falls ★★	C		4	FH		•				
Virginia Peak Falls ★	C		14	FH						
Buckeye Hot Spring Falls ★	C	•				•				
3 June Lake										
Rush Creek Falls ★★	C	•				•				
Gem Lake Falls ★★	C		9	FH		•				
Glass Creek Falls ★★★	C		4	M		•				
4 Devils Postpile National Monument										
Rainbow Falls ★★★★★	B		3	E				•		$
Lower Falls ★★★	C		4	E						$
Minaret Falls ★★★	C		2	E						$
Sotcher Lake Falls ★★	C		<1	E						$
5 Mammoth Lakes										
Twin Falls ★★★★	C	•	<1	E		•			•	
Mammoth Creek Falls ★★★	H		<1	FE		•				
Garnet Lake Falls ★★★	C		10–14	FH		•				
Shadow Lake Falls ★★★	T		6	M		•				
Upper Nydiver Lakes Falls ★★	P		11	FH		•				
Middle Nydiver Lakes Falls ★★	C		12	FH		•				
Lower Nydiver Lakes Falls ★★	H		12	FH		•				
6 Toms Place										
Rock Creek Lake Falls ★★	C		<1	E		•				
Horsetail Falls ★★	C		4	M		•				

Falls type:
P = plunge
H = horsetail
F = fan
B = block
T = tiered
S = segmented
C = cascades

Hike difficulty:
E = easy
FE = fairly easy
M = moderate
FH = fairly hard
H = hard

★ = Uninspiring
★★ = Modest
★★★ = Good
★★★★ = Very good
★★★★★ = Exceptional

	FALLS TYPE	VISIBLE BY CAR	HIKE LENGTH (MILES)	DIFFICULTY	OFF-TRAIL HIKE	DOGS ALLOWED	POPULAR FOR BIKING	WHEELCHAIR ACCESSIBLE	STROLLER FRIENDLY	FEE CHARGED
7 Bishop Creek										
North Lake Falls ★★	C	•				•				
Bishop Creek Falls ★★★	C	•	<1	FE		•				
Goldmine Falls ★★★	C	•				•				
Schoebers Falls ★★	P	•								
South Fork of Bishop Creek Falls ★★	C		<1	E		•				
8 Big Pine										
First Falls ★★	C		<1	E		•				
Second Falls ★★	C		3	FE		•				
9 Independence										
Golden Trout Falls ★★	P	•				•				
Robinson Lake Falls ★★	C	•				•				
Kings Canyon Region										
1 Oakhurst										
Bass Lake Falls ★	C	•				•				
Angel Falls ★★	C		1	E		•				
Devils Slide Falls ★★	C		4	FE		•				
Corlieu Falls ★★★	P	•	<1	FE		•				
Red Rock Falls ★★	B		3	FE		•				
2 North Fork										
Whisky Falls ★★	C	•				•				
Chiquito Falls ★★★	C		<1	E		•				
Jackass Falls ★★★★	C	•				•				
3 Huntington Lake										
Rancheria Falls ★★★	C			FE		•			•	
4 John Muir Wilderness										
Twin Falls ★★★	C		8	M		•				
Rock Creek Falls ★★	C	•				•				
5 Kings Canyon National Park										
Grizzly Falls ★★★★	T	•				•				$
Upper Tenmile Creek Falls ★★	T	•	<1	FE		•				$
Tenmile Creek Falls ★★★	C		4	M		•				$
Mist Falls ★★★★	C		8	M						$
Roaring River Falls ★★★	F		<1	E				♿	•	$
Silver Spray Falls ★★★★★	C		30	H						$
Blue Canyon Falls ★★★★★	C		31	H						$
Ella Falls ★★★	C		3	M					•	$
Viola Falls ★	C		3	M					•	$
6 Sequoia National Park										
South Fork Kaweah Falls ★★★	P		3	M						$
Black Wolf Falls ★★★	C	•								$
Tufa Falls ★★	C		<1	E					•	$
Crystal Creek Falls ★★★	C		2	E						$
Franklin Falls ★★★	C		4	E						$
Marble Falls ★★★★	C		7	FE						$

Falls type:
P = plunge
H = horsetail
F = fan
B = block
T = tiered
S = segmented
C = cascades

Hike difficulty:
E = easy
FE = fairly easy
M = moderate
FH = fairly hard
H = hard

★ = Uninspiring
★★ = Modest
★★★ = Good
★★★★ = Very good
★★★★★ = Exceptional

	FALLS TYPE	VISIBLE BY CAR	HIKE LENGTH (MILES)	DIFFICULTY	OFF-TRAIL HIKE	DOGS ALLOWED	POPULAR FOR BIKING	WHEELCHAIR ACCESSIBLE	STROLLER FRIENDLY	FEE CHARGED
Panther Creek Falls ★★★	H		6	M						$
East Fork Kaweah Falls ★★	C		4	FE						$
Middle Fork Kaweah Falls ★★	C		<1	E					•	$
Big Fern Springs ★★★	C	•								$
Granite Spring ★★	T	•								$
Pinewood Falls ★★	P	•								$
Cascade Creek Falls ★★	P		1	FE						$
Tokopah Falls ★★★★	C		3	FE						$
7 Monarch Wilderness										
Garlic Falls ★★★★	T		10	H	•					

WATERFALLS QUICK-REFERENCE CHART

Auto: The waterfall can be seen from the car or with a minimal walk from the parking lot.

Dogs allowed: Rules can change periodically and it is best to check with the ranger. "Dogs allowed" is marked for waterfalls within parks that have no rules prohibiting dogs. Dogs are generally not allowed on hiking trails in California state parks and in national parks.

Wheelchair-accessible: These falls are confirmed to be wheelchair accessible, but it is theoretically possible that additional trails may be accessible if a wheelchair has appropriate tires, and the person is traveling with a companion that can help through difficult parts. Waterfalls accessible by car have not been marked as wheelchair-accessible but should be assumed to be so.

Stroller-friendly: These trails have terrain compatible with an off-road, light, easily maneuverable jogging stroller. These trails may include shallow creek crossings and moderately difficult sections not friendly to a traditional city-style stroller. Refer to the wheelchair-accessible trails for suitable choices for a stroller without off-road style wheels.

Popular for Biking: These trails are amenable to mountain bikes, but other trails may also allow biking. Contact park rangers for current information.

DEDICATION

For our daughter Madeleine,

who we hope will always have a love

of nature and the outdoors.

ACKNOWLEDGMENTS

Special thanks to the following for generously letting us use their images in this book:

Andrew Sawadisavi (*www.andeys.com*), Annemarie Fiorella, Henry Lomeli, Jason Kling, Kevin Gong (*www.kevingong.com*), Michael Lockert, Rick Nieves, Russ Weatherbee, Shari Harral, Sonja Steidlmayer, Tim Burkhart, Yen-Wen Lu (*www.yenwen.net*).

We'd also like to extend our thanks to the following who helped us in our research: Adrienne Freeman, Alethea Hatfield, Amber Scott, Andrew Uarley, Anthony Botello, Barbara Paolinetti, Bill Bonner, Bill Mentzer, Bob Conner, Bob Wick, Brian Neill, Brian Sanford, Carolyn Scott, Casey May, Catherine Eskra, Chich Goss, Cindy Beckstead, Claude Singleton, Cynthia Lusk, Dave Stockton, David Stough, David L. Moore, Dean Lutz, Debbie Cushman, Don Lane, Don Lee, Don Pass, Ed Moore, Eric Carter, Fay Yee, Fred Krueger, Gary Liess, Gary Rogers, Gay Baxter, Greg Scherr, Heather Noel, Henry Lomeli, Holly Huenemann, Jack Kenny, Jason Kling, Jan Drees, Jeanne Casten, Jeff Wiley, Jennifer Ebert, Jennifer White, Jeremy Olson, Jill Cargill, Jill Dampier, Jim Lasell, Joe Chavez, John Golda, John Hoffnagel, John Scull, Jonel Ishida, Judy Schaber, Ken DeCamp, Larry Randall, Katie Colbert, Leon Turnbull (*www.waterfallswest.com*), Lindsey Pulliam, Marty Steidlmayer, Mary August, Mary Furney, Matthew Tews, Mia Monroe, Michael Swezy, Mike Stanley, Morgan Ziegler, Nedra Martinez, Pandora Valle, Philip Messerschmitt, Ray Acker, Ricardo Trejo, Rich Gibson, Rob Mason, Robert Wetzel, Robin Ishimatsu, Ron Hancock, Russ Weatherbee, Sarah Hill, Shannon Taylor, Shari Harral, Stephen Riley, Steve Noverr, Steve Zachary, Susan Burkindine, Tim Burkhart, Todd Barto, Tom Gunther, Tony Smithers, Tracy Becker, Trudy Tucker, Wayne Deese.

INTRODUCTION

For outdoor enthusiasts, California is one of the best places in the world to be. Where else can you hike through giant redwood trees, have lunch by the foot of a majestic waterfall, and make it back to the parking lot by the beach in time to catch a picture-perfect sunset over the Pacific Ocean?

This book has been written as a comprehensive field guide to the best waterfalls in the northern half of the state. You will find small, picturesque 10-foot drops, roaring giants, and plenty of waterfalls somewhere in between. Some falls only require pulling over and stepping out of your car to enjoy their beauty. Others are the reward of all-day hikes or backpacking trips through extreme terrain. Whether you are a rugged backpacker in search of a challenge or a family looking for a nice place to have a picnic, we hope this book will help you find the kind of waterfall you are looking for.

REGIONAL FORMAT

This guide is organized into nine geographic regions. We have tried to order these based on how the major highways are laid out and what general areas you would typically consider for a day trip or weeklong vacation in each region. The regions are further broken down into smaller areas containing waterfalls in relative proximity to one another.

WATERFALL ENTRIES

Names. Some waterfalls have official names; some even have two or more names, both official and unofficial, from different sources; and some names are used too frequently to be of any help. For example, the official USGS maps of northern California contain painfully many instances of "The Falls" scattered along the many streams. In these cases we have used the names used by local rangers, visitor center employees, park volunteers and the like. Where locals know a fall by multiple names, we have tried to include all known names. Those falls for which we found only unofficial names (or for which we have made our best guess at naming ourselves) are marked (u) for "unofficial" after the waterfall name.

Rating. We've attempted to include a universal rating system for all waterfalls in the northern part of the state; however, bear in mind that the ratings for almost all waterfalls in this book are heavily dependent on what time of year you visit. What may be a three-star rating in April can be a one-star rating by September, when the mighty flow has shrunk to a dinky trickle down the bedrock surface. Conversely, if you visit a waterfall in late summer that appears unimpressive, it might knock your socks off in spring during snowmelt. Here is our basic rating system:

★ **Uninspiring.** Primarily interesting to die-hard waterfall enthusiasts and for viewing through the car window on the way past.

★★ **Modest.** Nice background scenery for picnics or other outings.

★★★ **Good.** Pretty enough to make a special trip.

★★★★ **Very good.** Outstanding scenery worth snapping several photos.

★★★★★ **Exceptional.** Awe-inspiring and memorable.

Waterfall Form. The forms defined below are those most commonly seen in the falls listed in this guide. Falls may possess elements of multiple forms, blurring the lines from one to the next. Remember that the form may change dramatically throughout the year depending on the flow—an April block can easily become a plunge or a segmented waterfall by August.

Plunge. Descends vertically from its river or stream, losing contact with the rock surface.

Horsetail. Descends vertically or almost vertically, maintaining contact with the surface for most of its length.

Fan. Similar to a horsetail, but the breadth of the spray increases toward the bottom of the falls.

Block. Descends as a wide, block-shaped drop from a broad water flow (commonly found in river waterfalls).

Tiered. Descends as a series of several falls, with distinct starts and stops and at least two tiers visible from a single point.

Segmented. Descends in multiple threads, with at least two visible from a single point.

Cascades. Descends down a slope with a series of stairsteps along a surface.

Best Season. Just like it sounds—the time of year you're most likely to catch the waterfalls at their best. Some waterfalls flow year-round but have distinct peak seasons. Some waterfalls will actually dry up when viewed outside their peak seasons. When in doubt over whether a waterfall is flowing enough to merit a visit, call the ranger station for the latest information.

Access.

Located next to a road accessible by a passenger vehicle, usually visible from the car. May require a short, easy walk to get the best view.

Located next to a road, but the road is rough enough that it is best reached by a high-clearance (4WD) vehicle.

Reaching the falls requires between a five-minute and a six-hour trek along a well-established path or trail (i.e., your typical day hike). These trails range from a quarter mile to ten miles in round-trip length.

Getting to the waterfall may require overnight or multiple-night camping. These hikes follow established trails that are greater than ten miles in round-trip length.

No developed trail leads to the falls, but you can get there with a trusty compass and backcountry experience. Wear a strong pair of hiking boots and bring appropriate supplies. These hikes are not recommended for young children and may be risky for inexperienced adults and those with physical limitations. We recommend consulting with a local ranger before attempting these hikes.

 Access is possible only by canoe, boat, or raft.

 Wheelchair accessible.

 Bicycle accessible.

Difficulty. When the trip requires a hike, we have rated the trails and off-trail hikes on a simple scale:

 Easy   Fairly Hard

 Fairly Easy   Hard

M Moderate

Please note that trail length is far from the only determining factor in this rating. A half-mile climb up a steep mountainside is rated as more difficult than a 3-mile hike along a flat beach, for example. Other factors include rocks and other debris covering the trails, rock hopping or wading across streams, and overall trail condition.

Keep in mind that these ratings are merely general indications and that your fitness level will have the final say on whether a trail is Easy or Fairly Hard. If you are not sure of your current fitness level, we recommend starting with short hikes rated Easy and Fairly Easy to gauge your reaction. If you are in poor health or are not currently exercising regularly, consult with your doctor before hitting the trails.

Elevation. These are approximations of the waterfall's altitude above ocean level. Again, let us stress that these are not exact figures; they are merely included to give you a basic idea of the altitude.

Trail Length. All estimates are round trips or completed loops. Note that in many cases you can choose different routes and loops to reach the same waterfall. Unless otherwise noted, the default is to show the length of the shortest route.

USGS Quad. The U.S. Geological Survey (USGS) offers the most widely known topographical maps, covering all of the United States. This entry simply indicates the quadrant (map) on which the waterfall can be found. You can contact USGS directly to purchase maps, but they are also typically available at big libraries. Make note, however, that not all waterfalls are actually marked on the map; in these cases we have the annotation (ns) for "not shown" or (nl) for "not labeled"; it's usually just called "falls."

Contact. Try as we might to include everything of importance about each waterfall, there is a chance you will want to contact someone about additional details. Or perhaps it's early spring and you want to check to make sure the road isn't closed due to snow. Whatever your reason, we've included brief information on where to turn for more information about each waterfall.

SEASONS

Before we go into specifics about each area, let's talk about the seasons in general terms. Northern California is extremely diverse, for good and for bad. The good part is that it's one of the few places where you can surf in the morning and go skiing in the afternoon. The bad news is that you can get caught unprepared if you are going someplace with a climate different from what you're used to.

In the southwestern and central part of the north state, summer is hot and dry. That means most waterfalls will shrink down to a meager trickle or dry up altogether. As you can see from a few of the pictures in this book, bad timing can rob you of much of the "oomph" of an otherwise great fall.

As a rule, aim to hit the San Francisco Bay Area, Sacramento and San Joaquin Valley, western North Coast and southern Shasta-Trinity area in winter and spring. Since it rarely snows, all precipitation will be in the form of rain. As a bonus, winter and spring hikes are much cooler and more pleasurable than late-summer hikes when the temperatures hit three digits. For snapping the best pictures, try to hit the trails a day or two after heavy rains.

Snow and ice is a big issue when you look at the Sierra Nevadas and the other mountainous areas up north. Many roads and parks are closed all winter and don't open until May or June. Such closures should be respected at all times, as there is usually a good reason for them.

The good news is that everything opens up right around the time the action starts as far as waterfall lovers are concerned. During winter, all precipitation is stored in a thick snow blanket—and when it starts melting all at once, you can catch some truly spectacular sights.

The bottom line is that waterfall enthusiasts in northern California are lucky enough to have options all year round. By the time the winter rains end and the lowland areas start drying up, the falls in the mountains start flowing. And by the time the snow is done melting and the streams have slowed to a trickle, the next round of winter rains isn't too far off—starting the cycle anew. Yeah, California is great, isn't it?

SAFETY AND COMMON TRAIL SENSE

Many trails in this book will take you through wilderness areas, which are potentially dangerous by nature. Despite safety rails, warning signs, and modern technology, your best defense will always be good ol' common sense. Getting a good angle of a waterfall is a strong siren song that can lure otherwise smart people into making stupid mistakes. People have died trying to lean just a little too far out over the edge to get that perfect picture. Don't let your hobby cost you your life.

Entire books are dedicated to hiking "how-to," and we strongly encourage you to read more on this issue if you intend to make long, strenuous, or potentially hazardous journeys. For shorter hikes, follow these basic guidelines:

- Tell a friend or relative about your plans and when you expect to be back.
- Wear sturdy boots and rugged pants when hiking in poison oak or snake country.
- Don't stray from the trails if you can help it.
- Know the limitations of everyone in your party and do not exceed them.
- Keep children under close supervision at all times.
- Avoid sloping, bare areas, especially during rainy season.
- Never attempt to climb up or down a waterfall.
- Never lean on rails to get a better look, no matter how secure they look.
- Always respect signs and follow park personnel instructions.
- Study the map beforehand and familiarize yourself with the area.
- Turn back if you are unsure about the route ahead.
- When in doubt, talk to a ranger or other park service personnel.

In addition, there are some items you should always bring along on a day hike.

❏ This book.
❏ Compass and detailed map, preferably topographical.
❏ Plenty of water or reliable water filtration system.
❏ High-energy snacks, such as peanuts and protein bars or energy gel packs.
❏ First-aid kit.
❏ Knife.
❏ Matches in waterproof container.
❏ Flashlight with extra batteries.
❏ Extra clothes or blanket.
❏ Sun protection, such as hats and sunscreen.
❏ (Optional) GPS receiver.
❏ (Optional) Bug spray.
❏ Emergency shelter for longer hikes.

For overnight stays, you have several additional items to consider; get a book about backpacking to get more information on proper preparation.

Some of the waterfalls in this book have paved paths that lead straight to the destination. But more commonly, you will have to "rough it" a little. To make sure your presence does not disturb the landscape more than necessary, keep these ground rules in mind:

- Stay near the center of the trail and walk on durable surfaces whenever possible. This is especially important if you travel in a group; try to leave as few footprints as possible behind you.
- Bring all of your trash back home with you. If you have spare space in your pockets, pick up any trash you encounter.
- On the flip side, leave rocks, plants, and other features where they are. If you need a memento, snap a picture.
- Do not "improve" nature. Constructing a makeshift chair next to the

trail or breaking off branches to allow for unobstructed views of a nice valley may seem harmless, but it's not.

- Wash yourself and your dishes at least 200 feet away from any water source.
- Use backcountry toilets where possible. Bury human waste at least 200 feet away from water sources.
- Never feed wild animals, no matter how cute they are.
- If you bring your own pet along, make sure that it is under strict control at all times. Some parks and forests allow pets only in designated areas—always respect posted signs. If you are planning to hike and are not 100% sure Fido can come along, leave your pooch at home.
- Be extra careful around sensitive times for wildlife, such as mating and nesting season.
- Obtain permits, when required, for overnight camping or trail access. Some parks and forests, especially designated wilderness areas, prohibit anything with wheels—and that includes strollers. When in doubt, contact a local ranger station to check the rules and regulations.
- Lastly, respect private property. Landowners may allow hikers to pass through their property as long as hikers stay on the trail and behave responsibly. Disturb the landowners and they may fence off their property, cutting off access to the waterfall for you and countless other waterfall enthusiasts.

Again, hiking and waterfall hunting is a mostly safe and enjoyable activity, but there will almost always be some element of danger. Always take proper precautions. No guidebook can alert you to every hazard or predict changes that may happen between its writing and the time you head out there. When you visit any of the waterfalls in this book, you assume responsibility for your own safety. Be sure to check road and trail conditions and weather reports before hitting the trails. Staying informed about current conditions and exercising common sense are the keys to a safe, enjoyable outing.

Matt and Krissi Danielsson

A NOTE ABOUT SAFETY

Safety is an important concern in all outdoor activities. No guidebook can alert you to every hazard or anticipate the limitations of every reader. Therefore, the descriptions of roads, trails, routes, and natural features in this book are not representations that a particular place or excursion will be safe for your party. When you follow any of the routes described in this book, you assume responsibility for your own safety. Under normal conditions, such excursions require the usual attention to traffic, road and trail conditions, weather, terrain, the capabilities of your party, and other factors. Keeping informed on current conditions and exercising common sense are the keys to a safe, enjoyable outing.

The Mountaineers Books

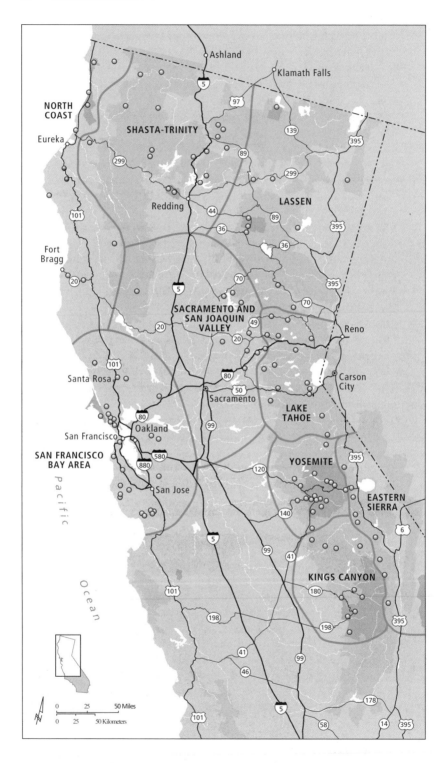

Map Legend

━━━━━━━ Interstate Highway	River or Creek
━━━━━━ Highway	Minor Creek
──────── Local Road	Waterfall
======= Dirt Road	Lake/Body of Water
--------- Featured Trail	Glacier
········· Other Trail	Park or Forest
(680) (5) Interstate	Wilderness
(101) (97) U.S. Highway	Park Boundary
(299) (96) State Highway	Other Land
[43N21] [5] County or Forest Road	

℗ Parking	
▲ Campground	
ᚦ Picnic Area	
■ Point of Interest	
△ Peak	

North

0   .5   1 Mile
0   .5   1 Kilometer   Scale

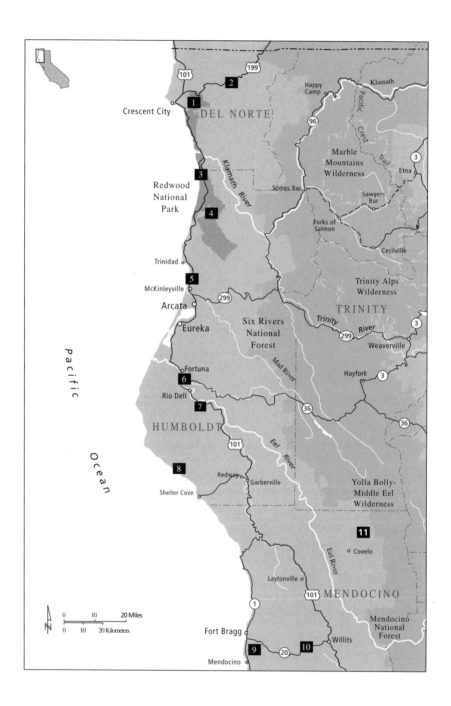

NORTH COAST

The picturesque coastal area north of San Francisco is temperate and wet. In the summer, the temperatures stay cooler than anywhere else in the state, thanks to the fresh gusts and frequent fogs rolling in from the ocean. Winter is mild with little chance of snow (unless you go to the mountains in the east), but hikers should be prepared for dramatic downpours that can close off roads. Some areas of the north coast reportedly hit 100 or more inches of annual precipitation. If you will be viewing these winter waterfalls, don't forget to pack a raincoat!

While a few waterfalls in this area run all year, the prime season for most is December through May due to the heavy rainfall. Along Highway 199, some "surprise" waterfalls spring to life seemingly at random during the winter, only to disappear without a trace as spring arrives. Keep your eyes peeled for these bonus sights as you look for the more established waterfalls described in this book.

In addition to creating waterfalls, the rain and fog foster a perfect environment for the famous coast redwood (*Sequoia sempervirens*) trees. Combining the old-growth redwood forests of Prairie Creek Redwoods State Park, Del Norte Coast, Jedediah Smith Redwoods State Park, and the National Park Service's Redwood National Park, you have 45 percent of California's total remaining redwood population right here.

These majestic trees provide picture-perfect backgrounds to the north coast's many waterfalls, making the hike to and from each site a truly humbling experience. The world's tallest redwood is also located in this region, just southeast of Orick. (See the Redwood National Park entry for more details.)

In addition, the north coast is home to not one, but three different drive-through trees. These are in Klamath (Terwer Valley exit in town), Myers Flat (Avenue of the Giants exit), and Leggett (follow signs off Highway 101). Each site charges admission, but it is worth the detour for the unforgettable experience of driving through a living tree.

1 JEDEDIAH SMITH REDWOODS STATE PARK

This peaceful state park was named after pioneer Jedediah Stong Smith, commonly believed to be the first white man to explore the interior of northern California. Starting out in 1826, Smith's two-year journey took him from the Great Salt Lake in Utah, across the Mojave Desert, and into California by way of the San Bernardino Mountains down south.

This park features 10,000 acres of majestic old-growth redwoods, with occasional patches of Douglas-fir, western hemlock, Sitka spruce, and Port Orford

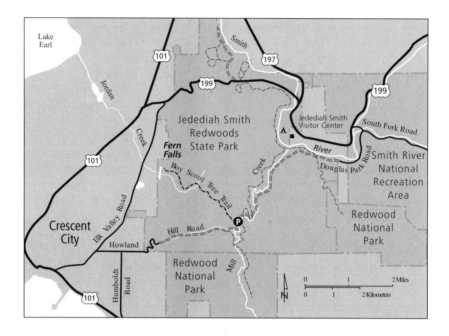

cedar sprinkled in. The park is just east of coastal Highway 101 near Crescent City, where you take the Highway 199 exit and almost immediately enter the park. For maps and other information, keep going a few miles and stop at the visitor center on your right.

FERN FALLS ★★★

BEST SEASON: December–May
ELEVATION: 450 ft
TRAIL LENGTH: 5.5 miles
USGS QUAD: Crescent City (ns)
CONTACT: Jedediah Smith Redwoods State Park; 707-464-6101 ext. 5112

Fern Falls is a 20-foot cascade on Jordan Creek. While Fern Falls is pretty, even the most avid waterfall enthusiast will likely conclude the waterfall is not the best part of this hike. This trip traverses an intensely green, untouched redwood forest that will have you realizing the true sound of silence. Given the roughly 6-mile round-trip hike to reach the falls and the lack of major metropolitan areas nearby, you will probably be alone on the trail.

To reach Fern Falls, take Highway 101 to the Elk Valley Road exit. After a mile, turn right on Howland Hill Road, continuing until you reach the Boy Scout Tree Trail on your left. Look for a sign on a fence. Hike about 2.75 miles to the falls, passing the namesake Boy Scout Tree on your way.

2 SMITH RIVER AND HIGHWAY 199

Tired of the crowded parks and recreation areas in more "civilized" areas? Come here for a breath of fresh air. The Smith River National Recreation Area is a vast 300,000-acre sanctuary of pristine woodlands where you can literally hike an entire day without meeting another human being—even in peak waterfall season. The park's crown jewel is the Smith River itself, a majestic body of water so clear you almost have to dip your hand in it to believe that it is actually there. Famous for its abundance of giant salmon and steelhead trout, the Smith River is also the only river in the state that remains free of human meddling. Not a single dam or construction impedes the natural flow of any part of the river system, completing the image of the last bit of completely untouched Californian wilderness.

Highway 199 stretches northeast from coastal Highway 101 near Crescent City to the Oregon border, clipping the northwestern corner of California. The area is home to a whole slew of waterfalls in the rainy season, although many dry up over summer.

MYRTLE CREEK FALLS ★★★

BEST SEASON: December–May
ELEVATION: 700 ft
TRAIL LENGTH: 5 miles
USGS QUAD: Hiouchi
CONTACT: Six Rivers National Forest; 707-457-3131

Myrtle Creek Falls is a 60-foot drop on Myrtle Creek, roaring powerfully during peak flow season. The hike to reach Myrtle Creek Falls is anything but easy. It starts out simple, following the Myrtle Creek Botanical Trail, but the trail leads you in less than half of the 2.5-mile one-way trip to the falls. The rest of the trip consists of scrambling along the creek, a route that lacks any established trails. Expect to climb rocks and muddy slopes. Trying to catch the peak season of the waterfall means you are also in the peak season for mudslides. In other words, attempt this hike at your own risk. Despite the need for caution and experience, the trip is rewarding and the waterfall is worth the trouble. Look for the trail near milepost 7 off Highway 199 about 1.5 miles past Hiouchi and 10 miles east of Crescent City.

GRASSY FLAT FALLS (U) ★★★

BEST SEASON: December–May
ELEVATION: 700 ft
USGS QUAD: Gasquet (ns)
CONTACT: Six Rivers National Forest; 707-457-3131

Cascades by Grassy Flat

At Grassy Flat Campground near Gasquet, you will find twin cascades pouring down the hillside into the Smith River. The falls are very pretty and easy to access by car. From Crescent City, head east on Highway 199 past Gasquet to Grassy Flat Campground on the right. The campground is often closed in winter and the sign covered, but if you pass the sign for river access at Madrona, Grassy Flat is the turn before that, and Madrona is a great place for a U-turn if needed. At the Grassy Flat Campground turnoff, look for an immediate dirt road heading off to the left. Turn on this road and head to the end, where you will find Grassy Flat and the best view of the falls.

MADRONA FALLS (U) ★

BEST SEASON: December–May
ELEVATION: 700 ft
USGS QUAD: Gasquet (ns)
CONTACT: Six Rivers National Forest; 707-457-3131

This small, unnamed waterfall is about 30 feet tall and sits on the north side of the highway. Catch a distant glimpse of it when walking under the bridge at the Madrona turnoff near Grassy Flat Campground. Or, park and walk back up beside the highway for the best view.

LITTLE SPOUT FALLS (U) ★

BEST SEASON: December–March
ELEVATION: 700 ft
USGS QUAD: Gasquet (ns)
CONTACT: Six Rivers National Forest; 707-457-3131

This is a series of unnamed, unspectacular falls just past the Madrona turnoff along Highway 199. Heading north, look for two to three very thin, spout-like waterfalls in the pullout area on the right side of the highway. They will be in a round gravel area a few hundred yards past the sign for Madrona.

LITTLE JONES CREEK FALLS (U) ★★

BEST SEASON: December–May
ELEVATION: 900 ft
USGS QUAD: Hurdygurdy Butte (ns)
CONTACT: Six Rivers National Forest; 707-457-3131

The cascade on Little Jones Creek is about 20 feet high and definitely worth a look. Unfortunately, the best place to view it is out the car window as you cross over a bridge with no immediate pullouts and only a minimal shoulder. The bridge is 8.5 miles past Gasquet when approaching from the west and 0.8 mile past the turnoff for Patrick Creek. Look to the right while crossing the bridge. Brave waterfall seekers can park in a pullout on the eastern side of the bridge and walk back to look at this lovely cascade, though we wouldn't recommend it.

KNOPKI FALLS (U) ★★★★

BEST SEASON: December–May
ELEVATION: 1600 ft
TRAIL LENGTH: 0.25 mile
USGS QUAD: Broken Rib
Mountain (ns)
CONTACT: Six Rivers National Forest; 707-457-3131

Knopki Falls is the unofficial name of a striking, powerful 25-foot fall on the Middle Fork of the Smith River. It is probably the most impressive of the Highway 199 waterfalls, leaving viewers breathless both from its beauty and from the trek to its base. It may only be a quarter-mile round-trip scramble, but be aware that part of the trip includes descent by rope down a vertical rock slab. The surfaces can be slippery, so only fit hikers should attempt the trip.

Knopki Falls

To reach the trailhead, drive 15 miles past Gasquet to the turnoff for Knopki Creek Road (misspelled as Knopti on some maps). Follow Knopki Creek Road just over 2 miles, crossing three bridges. During winter, the road is sometimes covered in snow, and plows do not reach the whole way to the falls. Bring tire chains.

WILDERNESS FALLS ★★★★

BEST SEASON: May–August
ELEVATION: 2700 ft
TRAIL LENGTH: 19 miles
USGS QUAD: Devils Punchbowl
CONTACT: Six Rivers National Forest; 707-457-3131

Wilderness Falls is a 50-foot free fall and cascade on Clear Creek. It is accessible only via a long backpacking trip, so the trip is not for inexperienced hikers. There are a few different routes to access the falls, but the best is the Young's Valley Trail, which offers a 19-mile round-trip hike. Take Highway 199 past Gasquet about 16 miles to the Knopki Creek

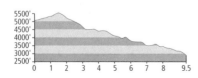

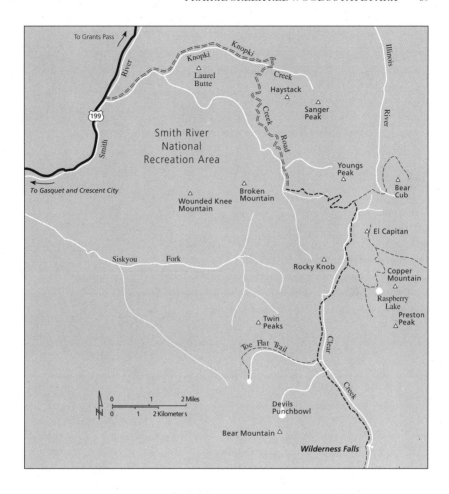

Road exit. Turn right and drive 14 miles to the trailhead. Once you begin hiking, you will reach the waterfall after 9.5 miles.

3 PRAIRIE CREEK REDWOODS STATE PARK

This 14,000-acre park has been off-limits to logging since the early 1920s. It was designated a World Heritage Site and an International Biosphere Preserve, in 1980 and 1983, respectively. The park is home to some of the world's tallest trees, most of which can be accessed through the park's 70-mile network of trails. Save-the-Redwoods League played a key role in preserving the park. Today, you will find more than 280 memorial groves scattered around the park funded by donations to the organization.

For the park's main entrance, look for the Newton B. Drury Scenic Parkway exit off Highway 101 right between Eureka and Crescent City. To reach the waterfalls, skip the main entrance and instead take the Davison Road exit. Head toward the ocean, 2.5 miles north of Orick off Highway 101. The narrow, bumpy road meanders through canopies of redwoods for 4 miles before reaching the park entrance. After paying the entrance fee, drive another 4.5 miles to the parking area for Fern Canyon, which is where you should begin your hike. You may face a few stream crossings with your car along the way. Be sure to watch out for Roosevelt elk—an enormous species often found grazing here. Davison Road, being unpaved, is often closed immediately after heavy rains, so call the park to confirm that you will be able to reach the falls.

SOUTH GOLD BLUFFS BEACH FALLS (U) ★★★

BEST SEASON: December–May
ELEVATION: 0 ft
TRAIL LENGTH: 2 miles
USGS QUAD: Fern Canyon (ns)
CONTACT: Prairie Creek Redwoods State Park; 707-464-6101 ext. 5301

This is the first of the three nearly identical waterfalls along the Coastal Trail at Gold Bluffs Beach. It is an 80- to 85-foot spout that trickles down from an unnamed creek. It has no official name; rangers usually refer to the cluster of falls at Gold Bluffs Beach as "the falls." Overgrown ferns and other plant life surround the waterfall. As you hike north on the Coastal Trail from the Fern Canyon parking lot, go just over a mile. Listen for the waterfall on your right; a short trail leads in toward its base.

GOLD DUST FALLS ★★★

BEST SEASON: December–May
ELEVATION: 0 ft
TRAIL LENGTH: 2.3 miles
USGS QUAD: Fern Canyon (ns)
CONTACT: Prairie Creek Redwoods State Park; 707-464-6101 ext. 5301

The middle waterfall on the Coastal Trail is the only one with an official name. It looks very similar to the first fall. About 0.2 mile past the first waterfall, listen for another and look for the offshoot trail.

NORTH GOLD BLUFFS BEACH FALLS (U) ★★★

BEST SEASON: December–May
ELEVATION: 0 ft
TRAIL LENGTH: 2.5 miles
USGS QUAD: Fern Canyon (ns)
CONTACT: Prairie Creek Redwoods State Park; 707-464-6101 ext. 5301

After taking in Gold Dust Falls, consider hitting still another just a skip away to the north. Like the first waterfall, this one has no official name and is part of "the falls" cluster. Listen for it and watch for another unmarked trail to reach it. Like Gold Dust Falls and the southernmost fall along the trail, it is a narrow spout in an enclave of ferns and green plants.

Gold Dust Falls

FERN CANYON FALLS (u) ★

BEST SEASON: December–May
ELEVATION: 100 ft
TRAIL LENGTH: 1 mile
USGS QUAD: Fern Canyon (ns)
CONTACT: Prairie Creek Redwoods State Park; 707-464-6101 ext. 5301

Not officially named, the 12-foot waterfall on Home Creek at Fern Canyon is relatively unimpressive; however, if you will be hiking through Fern Canyon anyway, be sure to take a look. Start north from the parking lot, and watch for the sign for Fern Canyon. The trail is not well maintained and is often difficult to follow in the winter. Hike along the banks of Home Creek; though depending on the water level, the path can sometimes be impassable. Call in advance to check the conditions if you plan to enter Fern Canyon. At the canyon's end, take a side detour into the canyon on your right to find the waterfall, which should be just over a half mile from the parking lot. Afterward, return through Fern Canyon, loop back on the James Irvine Trail, or continue onward for a longer hike.

JOHN BALDWIN FALLS (u) ★★

BEST SEASON: December–May
ELEVATION: 150 ft
TRAIL LENGTH: 2 miles
USGS QUAD: Fern Canyon (ns)
CONTACT: Prairie Creek Redwoods State Park; 707-464-6101 ext. 5301

The 25-foot waterfall into Home Creek on the James Irvine Trail also has no official name. Like Fern Canyon Falls, it is more worthy of a side note than as a destination in itself. It falls along the trail just above a bridge, near which you will find a plaque memorializing John Baldwin. There are two paths to reach it. You can take the James Irvine Trail from the Fern Canyon entrance and hike 1 mile south to the bridge; this may be wise if Home Creek is flowing too strongly to allow passage through Fern Canyon. Your second option is to traverse through the ferns and pick up the James Irvine Trail. In this case, you will reach the falls a half mile after leaving the canyon.

---

4 REDWOOD NATIONAL PARK

Boasting 112,500 acres, Redwoods National Park is home to a lot of old-growth redwoods. Chief among them is "The Tall Tree," the world's tallest redwood. At 367 feet and 600 years of age, it is an impressive sight that should not be missed. A good portion of Highway 101 south of Crescent City passes through the park.

Trillium Falls ★★

BEST SEASON: December–May
ELEVATION: 400 ft
TRAIL LENGTH: 2 miles
USGS QUAD: Orick (ns)
CONTACT: Redwood National Park; 707-464-6101

The Trillium Falls Trail loop is popular and much easier to access than Fern Canyon. Trillium Falls itself is fairly small, but the hike is worth it nonetheless for the scenery. From Highway 101, take the Davison Road exit a few hundred yards to the Elk Meadow Day Use Area on the left. Start hiking on the paved Davison Trail and watch for signs to direct you to Trillium Falls. Once you detour on the Trillium Falls Trail, it is about a half-mile climb to reach the falls. Stay on the main trail zigzagging up the hill. Upon reaching the falls, you can turn around and head back to the parking lot, or keep going up to form a 2-mile loop.

Trillium Falls

5 McKinleyville

McKinleyville was originally named Minorsville, but the town changed its name in 1901 in honor of the assassinated President McKinley. As you drive through town on your way to Mill Creek Falls, you will almost certainly notice a huge totem pole in the center of town. This is the tallest totem pole in the world; carved from a single redwood tree, the totem pole is 160 feet tall and weighs approximately 57,000 pounds. McKinleyville is located along Highway 101 just north of Arcata.

MILL CREEK FALLS ★★★

BEST SEASON: December–May
ELEVATION: 140 ft
USGS QUAD: Arcata North (ns)
CONTACT: Humboldt County
Visitors Bureau; 800-346-3482

This 15- to 20-foot waterfall in McKinleyville flows year-round but most impressively in winter. To reach it, turn west off Central Avenue at Turner Road. The road goes right past the waterfall. It will be on the left and is easy to miss when heading west, but you'll have no problems seeing it on the way back after making a U-turn at road's end a quarter mile away.

Mill Creek Falls in McKinleyville

6 HUMBOLDT REDWOODS STATE PARK

If you are among the many who are intrigued by the mighty, fog-engulfed redwoods of the Californian coast, you have hit the jackpot—this is the largest redwood state park around, featuring more than 17,000 acres of old-growth redwood forest on its roughly 53,000-acre area. To get here, take Highway 101 to the Myers Flat exit. Turn onto Avenue of the Giants, go through town and continue northeast another 4 miles to the park visitor center.

SOUTH FORK HONEYDEW FALLS (U) ★

BEST SEASON: January–April
ELEVATION: 400 ft
USGS QUAD: Weott (ns)
CONTACT: Humboldt Redwoods State Park; 707-946-2409

This small, unnamed waterfall is only about 6 feet high, but it is still pretty as a drive-by. It tumbles down a hillside into the Eel River. Heading south on Highway 101, take the South Fork/Honeydew exit, which is 40 miles south of Eureka. Pull over near the stop sign to find the waterfall. Coming off 101 heading north, turn left at the stop sign and park near the bridge. This waterfall is seasonal and disappears by summer.

7 SMITHE REDWOODS STATE RESERVE

This cozy 665-acre park, formerly known as Lane's Redwood Flat, used to be a private resort until the state took it over. Pretty as Dora Creek Falls may be, it is easy to see why the famous Lane's Tunnel Tree steals the show. This majestic redwood sits right next to the road, offering visitors a chance to walk through the extensive

South Fork Honeydew Falls at high flow in winter

tunnel in its trunk. The reserve is off Highway 101 about 4 miles north of Leggett and about 2.5 miles north of Standish-Hickey State Recreation Area.

DORA CREEK FALLS ★★

BEST SEASON: December–May
ELEVATION: 700 ft
TRAIL LENGTH: 0.25 mile
USGS QUAD: Piercy (ns)
CONTACT: Smithe Redwoods State Reserve; 707-247-3318

You can almost—but not quite—see this 60-foot waterfall from Highway 101. It plunges from Dora Creek into the Eel River near the Dora Creek Bridge. Look for the Frank and Bess Smithe Grove, which has a parking area on the west side of the highway. The waterfall is actually on the east side of the highway, but the best place to access it is from the west via a short, easy scramble down from the parking area. Cross under the bridge to get a better view.

---

8 KING RANGE NATIONAL CONSERVATION AREA

Those who travel along coastal Highway 1 expect magnificent ocean views pretty much the whole way. However, for a 35-mile stretch between Fort Bragg and Eureka, Highway 1 is pushed far inland. What gives? This is the Lost Coast—a clash between ocean and mountains so dramatic there was no hope of ever constructing a highway here. On the upside, it makes a recreational gem for those in the know. After enjoying the many small falls along the beach, find

Dora Creek Falls

a spot to watch the sunset and finish the day. Not all areas are accessible, but the fact that there is a 4087-foot peak just 3 miles inland from the ocean should give you an idea of the kind of spectacular views that can be had here. Take the Briceland Road exit off Highway 1 just north of Garberville and follow signs to Shelter Cove.

LOST COAST FALLS ★★★

BEST SEASON: December–May
ELEVATION: 0 ft
TRAIL LENGTH: 3 to 24 miles
USGS QUAD: Shelter Cove (ns)
CONTACT: Bureau of Land Management Arcata; 707-825-2300

After the rains, you can find a splendid collection of 15- to 20-foot waterfalls trickling down along the Lost Coast Trail. The waterfalls are most striking immediately after the winter rains but are usually nonexistent in summer. When they are active, you are unlikely to find a better hiking trail than this. On one side, you have cliffs and waterfalls, and on the other side, you have the Pacific Ocean. What could be better?

The Lost Coast Trail is 24 miles long; it stretches between Shelter Cove and the Mattole River mouth in the King Range National Conservation Area. Most of the small falls are between Buck Creek (1.5 miles north of Shelter Cove) and Big Flat (8.5 miles north of Shelter Cove). To get to the trailhead, go to the town of Shelter Cove. From Shelter Cove Road, turn north onto Beach Road, which ends in a parking lot for the trailhead at Black Sands Beach. For safety reasons, hike only during low tide. Additionally, there are no bridges: remember that some stream crossings may be difficult or impossible after heavy rains. The King Range coast is a wilderness setting with no facilities, so bear this in mind when planning a trip.

9 RUSSIAN GULCH STATE PARK

As the name implies, the first white explorers and settlers in this area were Russian. After building Fort Ross in 1811, they stuck around and were soon joined by a number of small lumber mill companies that enjoyed modest success at best. The park we see today was created in 1933 by joint private and county efforts to preserve this dramatic piece of California coastline. The park is relatively small at just 1162 acres, but it features 30 campsites and numerous day-use trails.

In addition to the waterfall, you may want to take a look at the famous "blowhole," a large hole some 200 feet inland that drops 60 feet to a tunnel leading out to the ocean. As the tide rises, water crashes into the tunnel all the way to the blowhole. To find Russian Gulch State Park, watch for the park sign 2 miles north of the town of Mendocino on Highway 1.

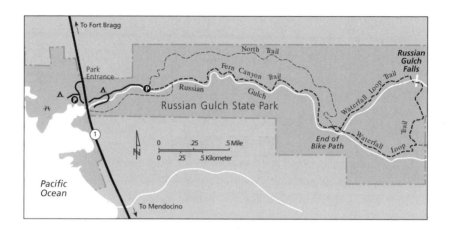

Russian Gulch Falls ★★

BEST SEASON: December–May
ELEVATION: 200 ft
TRAIL LENGTH: 6 miles
USGS QUAD: Mendocino (ns)
CONTACT: Russian Gulch State Park; 707-937-5804

Russian Gulch Falls is a 36-foot plunge in the Russian Gulch Valley. Like many other north coast waterfalls, the waterfall is usually not what draws park visitors. Most people take it as icing on the cake, a lovely side note to an enjoyable expedition through the redwood forest.

There are two routes to reach the falls. The easiest is to hike or bike along the Fern Canyon Trail from the parking lot, then upon reaching the Waterfall Loop, lock your bike and take the left side of the loop to reach the waterfall in 0.75 mile. At that point, you can turn back or continue around the loop to return to the Fern Canyon Trail. For the shorter route, the total mileage would be just over 2 miles of hiking and just over 3 miles of biking—or a 6-mile round trip on foot. It is also possible to hike in on the North Trail, which takes you on more of a tour through the forest.

---

10 JACKSON DEMONSTRATION STATE FOREST

This 50,000-acre piece of public land has long been a political battleground. Adversaries such as the Sierra Club and various grassroots organizations continue to butt heads with lumber companies and the California Department of Forestry about logging practices. Sure enough, as you hike the trails, you will see the impact of aggressive logging on these once pristine old-growth forests. The future remains unclear for Jackson Demonstration State Forest, but for now you can enjoy some trails without the noise and bare land patches that come with logging.

The forest is located just southeast of Fort Bragg where you go 6 miles on Highway 20 from its intersection with Highway 1. Coming from Willits, you go about 28 miles west on Highway 20 from Highway 101.

Chamberlain Creek Falls

CHAMBERLAIN CREEK FALLS
★★★

BEST SEASON: December–May
ELEVATION: 500 ft
TRAIL LENGTH: 0.5 mile
USGS QUAD: Comptche (ns)
CONTACT: Jackson Demonstration State Forest; 707-964-5674

This peaceful 50-foot plunge falls on Chamberlain Creek in the middle of an old-growth redwood grove. It is only a quarter mile each way to the falls, but the hike is very steep. To reach the falls, take Highway 20 east from Highway 101 at Willits. Continue 16 miles to Forest Road 200, which is an unsigned dirt road right before the bridge at Chamberlain Creek. Turn right and go 4.5 miles to a turnoff on the left, bearing left at the fork signed for Camp Mendocino. The turnoff is marked by rails and a set of steps leading down from the road. It is possible to create a longer loop hike that passes this waterfall; check at the forest office or visit the forest website for possible routes.

11 YOLLA BOLLY MIDDLE EEL WILDERNESS

This oval 150,000-acre area lives up to the name "wilderness" in the truest sense of the word. Flora and wildlife dominate the scene in the absence of humans, and the mountains and ridges are as steep as they come. As an example, the highest peak, Mount Linn (8092 feet), is just a few miles from Cottonwood Creek some 5500 feet below. There are areas here where few people—if anyone!—have ever set foot. Those who enjoy a challenge will love the raw ruggedness here. You may even decide to make an extra detour into the wild after tackling Balm of Gilead Creek Falls. Take the eastbound Highway 162 exit off Highway 101 about 10 miles north of Willits and continue to the town of Covelo. The Covelo Ranger Station is right off Highway 162, also known as Covelo Road.

Rattlesnake Creek Falls ★★

BEST SEASON: June–October
ELEVATION: 3500 ft
USGS QUAD: Willis Ridge (ns)
CONTACT: Mendocino National Forest; 707-983-6118

Rattlesnake Creek Falls is 15 to 20 feet high, falling on Rattlesnake Creek just off the road. From the Covelo Ranger Station, take Highway 162 northwest through the Round Valley Indian Reservation to where the highway becomes Mendocino Pass Road. Continue on Mendocino Pass Road to the Eel River Work Center, and then head northeast on M-1. After 25 miles, look for a bridge. The waterfall is right across from there, and it is an easy walk to get to the base of it.

Balm of Gilead Creek Falls ★★★★

BEST SEASON: July–September
ELEVATION: 4400 ft
TRAIL LENGTH: 12 miles
USGS QUAD: Wrights Ridge (ns)
CONTACT: Mendocino National Forest; 707-983-6118

The waterfall on Balm of Gilead Creek is only about 35 feet tall, but it is still a spectacular sight. It pours off a mountainside chute down into a swimming hole. Being located in the middle of beautiful countryside doesn't hurt its appeal either. The waterfall can be difficult to reach, however. To get there, follow Highway 162 to Road M-1 as described for Rattlesnake Creek Falls, but continue 7 miles past the first waterfall. Turn left on Rock Cabin Road and continue a mile to the trailhead parking lot. It is 6 miles to Balm of Gilead Creek, but you need to rough it a bit to get to the waterfall itself. Anyone attempting this hike should stop at the ranger station to pick up a map and discuss the route with a ranger before heading out.

SHASTA-TRINITY REGION

This area is sparsely populated compared to the rest of California, but that means there are ample opportunities to rough it to your heart's delight. There are trails on which you can hike for days without encountering another human being. In other words, this is a great place for outdoor enthusiasts—but it is also heavily populated by wildlife, including black bears. As always, it is wise to remain re-

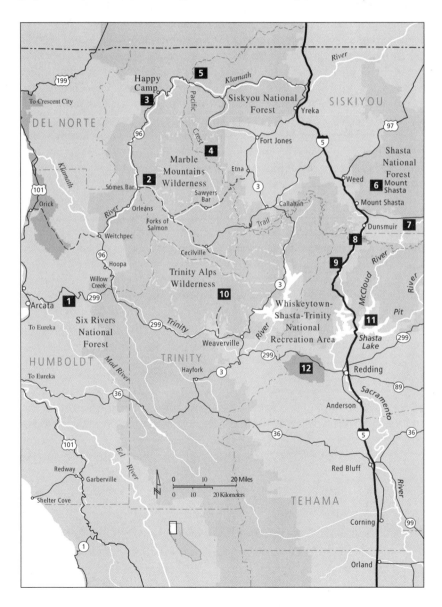

spectful of nature no matter how experienced you are. Out here, a small problem can become serious in a hurry if you are not properly prepared. When in doubt, ask local rangers for advice.

Those who do not appreciate strenuous hikes will be pleased to know that there are several top-notch waterfalls easily accessed by car. McCloud Falls, Hedge Creek Falls, Crystal Creek Falls, and many others require only an easy walk of a few hundred feet to reach the outlook points.

The most notable landmark you will see here is Mount Shasta, a slumbering volcano dominating the landscape at 14,162 towering feet over sea level. The top remains snowcapped almost all year and can be seen over 100 miles away from surrounding areas if the skies are clear. In cloudy conditions, however, you might drive right past the mountain and never know it was there. Another distinct feature of Mount Shasta is its frequent and odd cloud formations around the top. Many local stores offer postcards and posters of the most spectacular ones, but keep your eyes open. You may get an unexpected treat, especially at sunset when the saucer-shaped clouds shine bright red and pink.

Visual impact aside, Mount Shasta has great spiritual importance to local tribes and remains one of the most important sources of "cosmic energy" around, according to several New Age groups. If you are curious about this phenomenon, stop by one of the bookstores in Mount Shasta City and browse.

In addition to the picturesque mountain towns, the Gold Rush left its marks on these hillsides and a legacy that lives on today. One of the more intriguing stories is that of the buried gold at Castle Crags. Back in the 1800s, a gang of bandits pulled off a magnificent stagecoach robbery, scoring a huge treasure in gold. Unfortunately for them, there simply was no way to transport all the gold while evading the law, so they buried the treasure. They fled and never returned, leaving the bounty for whoever is lucky enough to start digging in the right spot.

This is but one of the many quirky stories and legends of the area. Simply put, this is a great spot for vacationers looking to round out the waterfall viewing with fascinating stories of California's colorful history.

---

1 HIGHWAY 299

Highway 299 is this region's parallel to Highway 199 in the north coast region, running from Arcata toward Redding in the east. Highway 299 carries you from

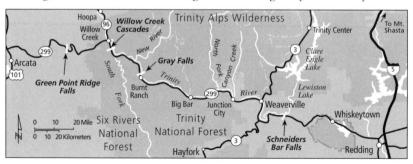

Green Point Ridge Falls at high flow in winter

the coast-hugging Highway 101 to flat-and-dry Sacramento Valley. In between the two, you cross over a hundred miles of mountains with plenty of seasonal waterfalls that can be seen from the road. Most of these are small and many are temporary, but if you happen to be in the area after heavy rains, keep your eyes peeled and your camera ready to catch some nice "bonus" waterfalls in addition to the ones listed below.

GREEN POINT RIDGE FALLS (U) ★★

BEST SEASON: December–May
ELEVATION: 1600 ft
USGS QUAD: Lord-Ellis Summit (ns)
CONTACT: Humboldt County Visitors Bureau; 800-346-3482

The waterfall on Green Point Ridge is a roaring block visible off in the distance from the highway. There may be a trail leading to its base from which you can obtain a better view, but heed signs indicating private property. Bring binoculars and look for the falls on the south side of the highway 2 miles west of the eastern-most exit for Chezem Road.

WILLOW CREEK CASCADES (U) ★

BEST SEASON: December–March
ELEVATION: 700 ft
USGS QUAD: Salyer (ns)
CONTACT: Six Rivers National Forest; 530-629-2118

A series of thin, unnamed cascades runs on the south side of Highway 299 a mile west of the Boise Creek Campground. The cascades are 20 to 30 feet high, but fairly unspectacular. Watch for them as you drive past.

Willow Creek Falls (u) ★★

BEST SEASON: December–May
ELEVATION: 600 ft
USGS QUAD: Salyer (ns)
CONTACT: Six Rivers National Forest; 530-629-2118

Along Highway 299 near the town of Willow Creek, you will find a surprisingly pretty 20-foot plunge tucked away in a little enclave on the south side of the highway. The fall sits on the eastern side of Willow Creek about a half mile past Friday Ridge Road, for travelers heading west.

Willow Creek Falls

GRAY FALLS ★

BEST SEASON: December–May
ELEVATION: 800 ft
TRAIL LENGTH: 1.2 miles
USGS QUAD: Ironside Mountain
CONTACT: Six Rivers National Forest; 530-629-2118

Gray Falls is spelled differently on different topographical maps, sometimes being called Grey Falls; the Forest Service website refers to it as Gray's Falls. Regardless of spelling, this neat little waterfall of less than 10 feet is nice to check out if you are camping in the area. It is at peak flow after winter rains. Take Highway 299 2.5 miles east from the Burnt Ranch Campground to a turnoff on the right for the Gray Falls Campground. It is just over a half-mile walk to the falls. The campground is closed year-round but there is a day-use area at the trailhead. If you have trouble finding the falls, look for GPS coordinates 40.85388N, 123.48116W.

Schneiders Bar

Schneiders Bar Falls (u) ★★

BEST SEASON: December–May
ELEVATION: 1060 ft
USGS QUAD: Del Loma (ns)
CONTACT: Shasta-Trinity National Forest; 530-623-6106

Several small cascades pour into the Trinity River as it runs alongside Highway 299, but one of the prettiest is near Schneiders Bar. It is a roughly 40-foot vertical cascade emerging from the forest and plunging down to the river below. View it from the pullout 2.4 miles west of Hayden Flat Campground.

---

2 Somes Bar

Somes Bar is located at the confluence of the Salmon and Klamath Rivers, far away from the hustle and bustle of Highway 101. Although the coast is 40 miles to the west, it is still an 80-mile drive to Somes Bar due to the winding mountain roads. Somes Bar originated in the early 1860s as a store built a mile and a half up the Salmon River to supply miners seeking their fortune in the area. Unfortunately, the town was off to a rocky start when unprepared miners (and everyone else in the Salmon River area) got cut off by snow in spring 1851, causing great difficulty for everyone in the Salmon River area. By the time the snow melted and supplies were again made available, many miners had eaten their mules and even their own shoes to survive. Due to flooding, the store was relocated a half mile downstream in 1936 and then again after the 1964 flood to its current location, where Ishi Pishi Road meets Highway 96.

To reach Somes Bar and Ishi Pishi Falls from the south, take Highway 299 to Willow Creek, then take Highway 96 north for approximately 40 miles. To get to Somes Bar from the north, take the Klamath River/Highway 96 exit from I-5 and follow Highway 96 for 105 miles to reach Somes Bar.

Ishi Pishi Falls ★

BEST SEASON: March–August
ELEVATION: 600 ft
USGS QUAD: Somes Bar
CONTACT: Klamath National Forest; 530-493-2243

Ishi Pishi Falls is more of a white-water cascade on the Klamath River than an actual waterfall. Dropping 30 feet over 300 yards of river, it looks like a large rapid with house-size boulders interspersed throughout. This section of the river holds a Class VI white-water rating, indicating extreme danger. For the waterfall enthusiast who is going to be in the area, taking a peek at the waterfall could be an interesting side trip.

You can view Ishi Pishi Falls from Highway 96 about 100 yards up the river from Somes Bar. Coming from Happy Camp, there are pullouts between the Elementary School and the Salmon River Outpost/post office. Be respectful when visiting the land; this is a site of spiritual significance to the Karuk Tribe.

3 HAPPY CAMP

Try to resist the temptation of being witty—there's no variation on "being a Happy Camper" puns that the locals haven't heard a hundred times already. The name originates from the Gold Rush days. Sometime in the mid- to late 1800s, the story says, after a particularly good day of prospecting, some miners began celebrating their good fortune in camp by passing around a bottle of whiskey. As the night wore on, they decided it was a good time to name their camp. Being in an extremely happy state, they settled on the name Happy Camp.

Happy Camp boasts several buildings that have large mural paintings highlighting different key historical episodes. The town is where the State of Jefferson meets Bigfoot, both names of scenic byways. A 15-foot-tall metal sculpture of Bigfoot stands watch over the junction of the two byways. Happy Camp is also the administrative center for the Karuk Tribe, a respected self-governing tribe. A visit to the Karuk Cultural Center and Museum allows for a glimpse into their rich cultural history. Happy Camp is located about halfway between Highway 101 and I-5 along Highway 96.

Ukonom Falls ★★★

BEST SEASON: March–August
ELEVATION: 1000 ft
TRAIL LENGTH: 1 mile
USGS QUAD: Ukonom Mountain (ns)
CONTACT: Klamath National Forest; 530-493-2243

Ukonom Falls is a pretty pair of 25-foot twin waterfalls in the forests near the Marble Mountain Wilderness, one of the most underrated areas in all of California. The falls are only accessible by boat; followed by a short hike up Ukonom Creek, so check with a ranger or river rafting tour guide for the best way to reach them.

Sheridan Falls ★★

BEST SEASON: April–June
ELEVATION: 2100 ft
TRAIL LENGTH: 5.5 miles
USGS QUAD: Huckleberry Mountain (ns)
CONTACT: Klamath National Forest; 530-493-2243

Sheridan Falls is a 10-foot drop on an unnamed tributary to Elk Creek. It came into being during the floods of 1997 and became a permanent waterfall. It runs year-round but the peak flow is in late spring. Sheridan Falls is accessible from the Elk Creek Trail, which begins at the Sulphur Springs Campground. Follow the Elk Creek Trail for approximately two and a half miles to a gentle, flat path that leads to the fall's base. To reach Sulphur Springs Campground, take Elk Creek Road located off Highway 96 in the town of Happy Camp. It is a 14-mile drive to the campground.

TWIN FALLS ★★

BEST SEASON: November–June
ELEVATION: 960 ft
USGS QUAD: Ukonom Mountain (ns)
CONTACT: Klamath National Forest; 530-493-2243

Twin Falls is a 15-foot drop on Twin Falls Creek near a picnic area. The waterfall is visible from the highway and is located 17 miles downriver from Happy Camp.

4 MARBLE MOUNTAIN WILDERNESS

The Marble Mountain Wilderness is a 242,000 square-mile wilderness established first as a "primitive area" in 1931, then as a "wilderness" in 1953. It was finally included in the national wilderness preservation system in 1964. You will find plenty of water here, with 89 "official" lakes ranging in size from less than an acre to more than 65 acres, plus a number of smaller lakes that are best described as seasonal. This, coupled with an ample supply of steep mountainsides, makes this prime hunting ground for "bonus" waterfalls that only run after rains or rapid snowmelt. Marble Mountain itself, with its curious red-and-gray marbled peak, is also worth a look. Marble Mountain Wilderness is located in the region between Highway 101 and I-5, just south of the Oregon border.

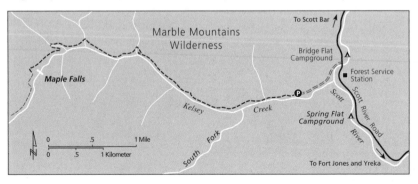

Maple Falls ★★★

BEST SEASON: April–July
ELEVATION: 4100 ft
TRAIL LENGTH: 8 miles
USGS QUAD: Grider Valley
CONTACT: Klamath National Forest; 530-493-2243

Maple Falls is a 60-foot free fall on Kelsey Creek. It is a lovely waterfall and worth the 8-mile round-trip hike to reach it. The trail provides several awe-inspiring views, and you will pass multiple smaller waterfalls along the way to the main attraction.

From Yreka, head west on Highway 3 for 16 miles to Scott River Road, then turn right and go 17 more miles. When you reach the bridge past the Forest Service Station, turn left on a dirt road and continue 0.6 mile, bearing right after the first quarter mile. Once you are on the trail, hike uphill for 4 miles until you hear and see the falls.

Sur Cree Falls ★★

BEST SEASON: April–July
ELEVATION: 2700 ft
TRAIL LENGTH: 6 miles
USGS QUAD: Salmon Bar (ns)
CONTACT: Klamath National Forest; 530-493-2243

Sur Cree Falls is a roughly 200-foot fall, but only a small portion is visible from the trail. From Sawyers Bar, drive west on Sawyers Bar Road for 4 miles to the Little North Fork Campground. From the picnic area, take the Little North Fork Trail 3 miles to the waterfall for a 6-mile round trip.

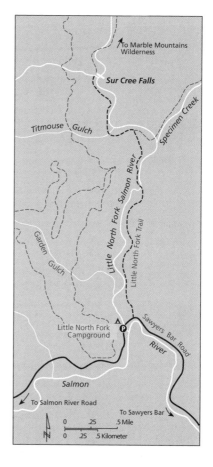

SHACKLEFORD FALLS (U) ★★

BEST SEASON: May–August
ELEVATION: 2400 ft
TRAIL LENGTH: 0.5 mile
USGS QUAD: Russell Peak (ns)
CONTACT: Klamath National Forest; 530-493-2243

Shackleford Falls sits on private property of the Fruit Growers Supply Company, although surrounded by Klamath National Forest. The company allows public use of the property; use good trail sense to make sure it stays that way. The waterfall is about 20 feet high. From Fort Jones, take Scott River Road right for 7 miles and bear left on Quartz Valley Road. Drive 4 more miles to Road 43N21 and turn right. Continue 1.2 miles until you cross over the creek. Hike upstream on the dirt road to reach the falls in a quarter mile.

EAST BOULDER CREEK FALLS (U) ★★

BEST SEASON: May–August
ELEVATION: 6200 ft
TRAIL LENGTH: 4 miles
USGS QUAD: Ycatapom Peak (nl)
CONTACT: Klamath National Forest; 530-493-2243

The waterfall on the East Boulder Creek near Boulder Lake is a 30-foot plunge. The trail has some spectacular views of the valley and Marble Mountain Wilderness scenery. From Callahan, head south on South Fork Road and bear right on Road 40N17 after 0.75 mile. Drive 5 miles farther, then watch for signs for the East Boulder Trail, which should be a left on Road 39N10. Drive 2 miles farther to the trail. You will reach the falls after 2 miles of uphill climbing.

5 SEIAD VALLEY

Seiad Valley is located about 50 miles west of Yreka, not too far from the Oregon border. While mostly famous for its fishing (unofficially named 'The Steelhead Capital of the World"), the steep mountains and winter precipitation add some nice waterfalls to the package. If you are hungry after seeing the waterfalls, consider stopping by the Seiad Valley Store and Cafe for their famous Pancake Challenge. The Travel Channel ranked this modest roadside cafe as third in its special "Gross Outs: The World's Best Places to Pig Out" (aired May 18, 2003), so bring loose-fitting pants. To get to Seiad Valley, take Highway 96 from I-5 and drive west until you reach the town.

Horsetail Falls ★★★

BEST SEASON: April–June
ELEVATION: 4100 ft
USGS QUAD: Kangaroo Mountain
CONTACT: Klamath National Forest; 530-493-2243

Horsetail Falls sits in a remote area of Siskiyou County. It is 40 to 50 feet tall, not counting the cascades that continue along Seiad Creek at the bottom of the falls. The waterfall is accessible by car if you take Highway 96 west 50 miles from I-5 and turn north on Seiad Creek Road. After 3.8 miles, Seiad Creek Road will fork. You want to take the left fork on Road 48N20, which will be a gravel road.

Ponytail Falls ★

BEST SEASON: April–June
ELEVATION: 4300 ft
USGS QUAD: Kangaroo Mountain
CONTACT: Klamath National Forest; 530-493-2243

Continue a half mile north of Horsetail Falls (see above) on Road 48N20 and look to the east up the creek to see another small cascade.

---

6 Mount Shasta

Nowhere along the entire length of I-5 will you find anything that so totally dominates the scenery as Mount Shasta. At 14,162 feet, this dormant volcano and its perennially snowcapped peak can be seen towering above the other mountains from many miles away. The Native American tribes considered Mount Shasta a sacred place, as do many New Age groups and cults today, because of its perceived cosmic energies. Some groups claim the mountain is home to the fabled underground city of Telos. Another version holds that it is home to the Lemurians, a species capable of transforming themselves between a material and spiritual state at will. Still others speak of UFOs and an extraterrestrial haven. There are plenty of other legends and theories surrounding Mount Shasta, but whether you buy into the spiritual side or not, it is one impressive mountain. I-5 passes right by, so you could not miss Mount Shasta even if you tried (that is, unless it is cloaked in fog as occasionally happens).

Topographic maps show multiple unnamed waterfalls on various creeks that flow down Mount Shasta's slopes, but only the following have established trails. Hiking off established trails is not recommended; it is very easy to get lost in the Mount Shasta Wilderness.

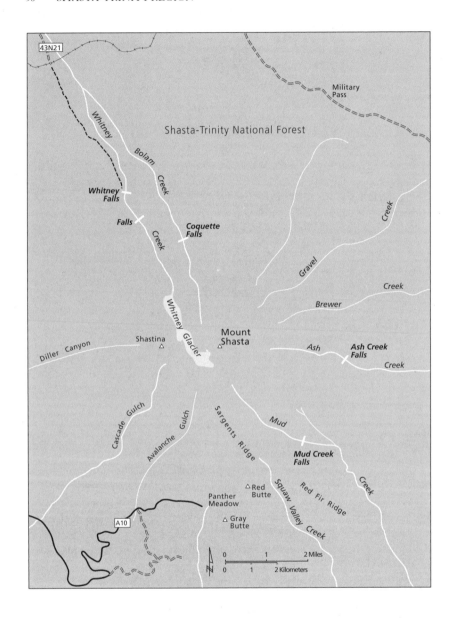

Whitney Falls ★★★★

BEST SEASON: April–May
ELEVATION: 6200 ft
TRAIL LENGTH: 5.5 miles
USGS QUAD: Mount Shasta
CONTACT: Shasta-Trinity National Forest; 530-926-4511

Whitney Falls is a dramatic 250-foot free fall into a beautiful canyon in the Mount Shasta Wilderness. The view is spectacular; you can see the waterfall as well as the Whitney Glacier and Mount Shasta's double peaks. It is a great hike, but the waterfall is very short-lived and can only be seen in early summer while the glacier melts or immediately after a heavy rain.

A 1997 flood buried much of the trailhead and it has not been restored, so access can be tricky. Only 18 inches of the trailhead sign sticks up out of the mud. It is still possible to hike the trail, but consult with a ranger on conditions before heading out. To get to the trailhead, go north from Weed about 12 miles on Highway 97 to Highway A-12. That is a landmark; make a U-turn back 0.2 mile and turn left on a dirt road (43N21). Go 1.7 miles, hang right in the forks, and then cross the railroad tracks and continue 2.1 miles farther to the trailhead. It is a 2.75-mile climb to reach the overlook to the falls, but as of this writing the first mile of the trailhead is buried in debris.

Coquette Falls ★★★

BEST SEASON: July–September
ELEVATION: 8100 ft
TRAIL LENGTH: 2 miles
USGS QUAD: Mount Shasta
CONTACT: Shasta-Trinity National Forest; 530-926-4511

At the time of this writing no established trail leads to Coquette Falls, another magnificent cascade on Bolam Creek. The Forest Service hopes to give the Bolam Trail a face-lift in the future, which will provide easier access to this waterfall. For now, the trek involves a mile of off-trail hiking into the Mount Shasta Wilderness. From Forest Road 41N21 turn onto 42N33 right after the railroad crossing and pull over along the road wherever you like. Contact the ranger station beforehand to discuss a route and alert the ranger to your plans. Visit in late summer or after heavy rains. The GPS coordinates to the falls are 41.44882N, 112.21431W.

Mud Creek Falls ★★★★

BEST SEASON: June–September
ELEVATION: 7000 ft
TRAIL LENGTH: 2 miles
USGS QUAD: Mount Shasta (nl)
CONTACT: Shasta-Trinity National Forest; 530-926-4511

Mud Creek Falls pours more than 200 feet off the Mud Creek Glacier on Mount Shasta. It falls amid some of the best scenery on the mountain. While it is not hard to reach the viewpoint, the view is distant and there is no trail to the fall's base. To view Mud Creek Falls, ironically, you will need to take the Clear Creek Trail, which can be complicated to find. From Highway 89 in McCloud, head east 2.9 miles to Pilgrim Creek Road and turn left at a sign for the Mount Shasta Wilderness. Go 5.2 miles to a sign for Forest Service Road 41N15. Turn left and drive 5 miles, then continue straight on 41N61 at the dirt intersection. Bear left on 41N25Y and watch for signs to direct you the rest of the way to the Clear Creek Trailhead. After reaching the trailhead, it is a mile-long climb. At the top, you will see a vast panoramic view of Mud Creek Canyon, including the waterfall.

Ash Creek Falls ★★★★

BEST SEASON: June–September
ELEVATION: 7500 ft
TRAIL LENGTH: 2 miles
USGS QUAD: Mount Shasta
CONTACT: Shasta-Trinity National Forest; 530-926-4511

Ash Creek Falls tumbles 320 feet from a cliff just under a beautiful shot of Mount Shasta. Like all the other waterfalls on Mount Shasta, it is a sight worthy of photographs. This one flows year-round, but the peak season is in summer while the glacier melts. Ash Creek Falls can be seen in two ways: the Black Fox Forest Service Lookout, or by roughing it.

For the Black Fox Forest Service Lookout: From I-5, take Highway 89 past McCloud. After 2.8 miles past McCloud, turn left onto Pilgrim Creek Road (Road 13). Go about 13 miles to a dirt road on the right (41N05). Continue another 2 miles, and then turn right again on 41N57. Go about 3 miles, turn on 41N07 and continue about 2 miles to the lookout. There should be signs. Bring binoculars.

By foot, the directions are the same up to Pilgrim Creek Road. Go 5.2 miles, then turn left on Widow Springs and go about 5 miles to the junction with Road 31. Turn right onto Road 31 for about 3 miles, then left onto 41N16, then left again onto 41N61. Stay on the main road through the forks and spurs. After 5 miles on 41N61, turn on 41N44 and stay on it for 2 miles until the road ends. Find your way about a mile upstream to the waterfall.

7 McCloud

McCloud is what you may call a purebred logging town; the McCloud River Lumber Company built the whole town in 1897 and owned pretty much all of it until 1963 when they sold it to another company. As it turned out, the U.S. lumber industry took a turn for the worse, and the business-owned town concept more or less collapsed. Fortunately, the town pulled itself together and has now re-emerged as a vacation spot for lovers of the outdoors. This is good news; previously, you had to know where to look to find the three McCloud falls, but now the Forest Service has created well-marked lookout points and nice walking trails to the falls. McCloud is located at the south base of Mount Shasta. From I-5, turn east on Highway 89 and go straight until you reach town.

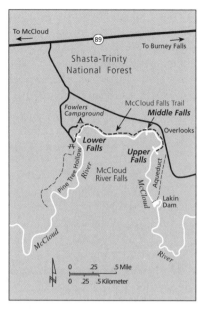

LOWER MCCLOUD FALLS ★★

BEST SEASON: April–July
ELEVATION: 3200 ft
TRAIL LENGTH: 0.25 mile
USGS QUAD: Lake McCloud
CONTACT: Shasta-Trinity
National Forest; 530-964-2184

Lower Falls is probably the least exciting of the three falls along the McCloud River in the vicinity of Fowlers Campground—that is, if you are looking for pure sightseeing. It may be the most fun of the three for other recreational uses. About 15 feet high, Lower

Lower McCloud Falls

Falls is popular with swimmers as a natural waterslide into the swimming hole below, and it is not unusual to find people fishing here either. If you plan to hike along the river to see all three falls, Lower Falls will be the first fall you see along the trail, and it sits very close to the parking area. Entering the Fowlers Campground area from Highway 89 5 miles east of McCloud, follow signs for Lower McCloud Falls and pick up the trail from the parking area.

MIDDLE McCLOUD FALLS ★★★★★

BEST SEASON: April–August
ELEVATION: 3400 ft
TRAIL LENGTH: 2 miles
USGS QUAD: Lake McCloud
CONTACT: Shasta-Trinity National Forest; 530-964-2184

Middle McCloud Falls is a spectacular sight. It is only about 50 feet high, but it is at least 80 feet wide. It is a heavily photographed fall, and it is commonly considered one of the best falls in this region. Middle Falls makes a perfect day trip for

Middle McCloud Falls

families, because the hike to reach it is fairly easy. Park at the Lower McCloud Falls trailhead and hike about a mile up the river to reach Middle Falls. At this point, you can either turn back or continue to Upper Falls. Either way, look for breathtaking views of Mount Shasta on your return trip.

If merely seeing the waterfall is your goal and you do not have time for this lovely hike, there is also a viewpoint of Middle Falls that you can reach by car. After turning into the Fowlers Campground area from Highway 89, look for a road on your left with a sign for Middle McCloud Falls. Follow this road to a parking area with a vista point above the falls.

Upper McCloud Falls ★★★

BEST SEASON: April–August
ELEVATION: 3500 ft
TRAIL LENGTH: 0.2 mile
USGS QUAD: Lake McCloud
CONTACT: Shasta-Trinity
National Forest; 530-964-2184

Upper McCloud Falls

Upper Falls is about 30 feet high, and it is the most obscure of the McCloud River waterfalls. It can be reached in two ways—as a continuation of a roughly 3 mile round-trip hike from the Lower Falls parking area, or as a 0.2 mile round trip from the Upper Falls parking area. For the former, follow the signs to Lower Falls then hike up the river and begin a climb after passing Middle Falls. To reach Upper Falls directly, take the access road on your left before entering the Fowlers Campground from Highway 89 and follow the sign to Upper McCloud Falls. Park your car and then walk a few hundred yards to view the waterfall.

Lower Squaw Valley Creek Falls ★★

BEST SEASON: May–October
ELEVATION: 2600 ft
TRAIL LENGTH: 5 miles

USGS QUAD: Yellowjacket
Mountain (ns)
CONTACT: Shasta-Trinity National
Forest; 530-964-2184

The lower fall on Squaw Creek is about 15 feet high. The waterfall and the upper one along the trail are not the best parts of the hike, but they make nice detours. To reach the waterfall, take Squaw Valley Road south from Highway 89 in McCloud. Continue just over 6 miles until you reach Squaw Valley Creek Road, then turn right and go just over 3 miles more until the parking area and trailhead on the left, which lies just past the bridge. Start hiking at the trailhead. Cross the first bridge, but not the second one. You will reach the first waterfall in 1.5 miles.

UPPER SQUAW VALLEY CREEK FALLS ★

BEST SEASON: May–October
ELEVATION: 2600 ft
TRAIL LENGTH: 7 miles
USGS QUAD: Yellowjacket Mountain (ns)
CONTACT: Shasta-Trinity National Forest; 530-964-2184

Upper Squaw Valley Creek Falls is only about 10 feet, but still is a nice detour for Squaw Creek Trail hikers. Follow the directions to Lower Squaw Valley Creek Falls, and after passing the first waterfall, continue another mile to a spur trail to view the fall.

8 DUNSMUIR

In 1886 a rich Canadian named Alexander Dunsmuir offered the town of Pusher a deal: he would build a water fountain if the town changed its name to "Dunsmuir." The townsfolk agreed, the name stuck, and you can still see the fountain in the town park. Speaking of water, Dunsmuir prides itself on having the cleanest water in the world. The water starts as snow on Mount Shasta and trickles through the layers of lava rocks for over 500 years before it reaches its Dunsmuir outlets, which include both Hedge Creek and Mossbrae Falls. The water is so clean no treatment whatsoever is required. You can give it a taste test of your own on your way down to Hedge Creek Falls; you pass right by the famous fountain. Dunsmuir has several exits right off I-5.

Mossbrae Falls ★★★★★

BEST SEASON: March–August
ELEVATION: 2400 ft
TRAIL LENGTH: 3 miles
USGS QUAD: Dunsmuir
CONTACT: Siskiyou County Visitors' Bureau; 530-926-3850

Mossbrae Falls is one of the most memorable waterfalls you will see in California. The walk to reach it is suitably unusual. The water falls into the Sacramento River, but the water itself seems to come out of the hill alongside the river. Mossbrae Falls is about 50 feet high but well over 100 feet wide—a striking sight impossible to capture in a photograph. In the 1800s, travelers taking the train used to stop at Mossbrae Falls for a rest. Since then and to this day, people living in the region have hiked along the tracks to relax and wade beside the falls.

A small section of Mossbrae Falls

Hedge Creek Falls

To reach Mossbrae Falls, take the Dunsmuir Avenue/Siskiyou Avenue exit off I-5, and then go south on Dunsmuir Avenue for 0.6 mile. Look for Scarlett Way/Shasta Retreat on your right, which will be such a sharp right under the arch that you will practically make a complete U-turn to enter it. Follow the road, which narrows to one lane, until you cross the railroad tracks. Park here, then head south, upstream, along the railroad tracks for about a mile and a half. The waterfall will be on your right, obscured by the trees, but a short trail leads down to it. You will be walking right next to the still-active tracks to reach the falls, so be very careful and watch for trains. The trail may not be suitable for very young children.

HEDGE CREEK FALLS ★★★

BEST SEASON: March–June
ELEVATION: 2700 ft
TRAIL LENGTH: 0.25 mile
USGS QUAD: Dunsmuir (ns)
CONTACT: Siskiyou County Visitors' Bureau; 530-926-3850

Hedge Creek Falls is a roughly 30-foot fall on Hedge Creek in a corner of Dunsmuir. It is easy to reach, and the small park at the trailhead makes a pleasant place to have a picnic before or after the short hike. It is only about a quarter-mile round trip to the fall, but the trail descends down a steep hill. Take the Dunsmuir Avenue/Siskiyou Avenue exit off I-5, then turn under the highway and head north briefly on Dunsmuir Avenue until you reach a small parking area across the street from the picnic area and trailhead.

9 CASTLE CRAGS STATE PARK

This 4350-acre park got its name from the spectacular, jagged edge of glacier-polished crags towering some 6000 feet above sea level. The crags are easily spotted from I-5. In addition to the waterfalls, the crags also offer a chance to dream of more materialistic enrichment. Back in wilder days, bandits hit the jackpot when they robbed a stagecoach carrying a huge gold load. They hid the treasure

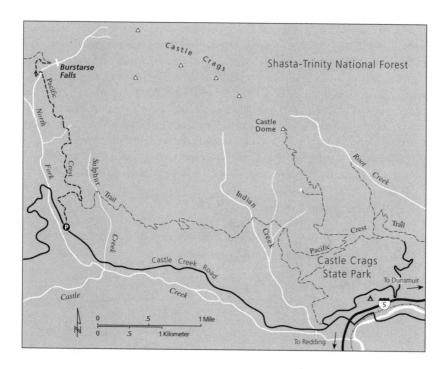

someplace around Castle Crags but were never able to recover it—leaving the bounty up for grabs. Feeling lucky? Grab some digging gear and see if you can outsmart the others who also figured a few drops of sweat was a worthy bet in the gamble for riches.

To get here, look for the Castella exit off I-5 about 6 miles south of Dunsmuir, then head west on Castle Creek Road until you see the park entrance road on your right. These waterfalls technically fall outside park boundaries, but the park is an interesting destination itself.

BURSTARSE FALLS ★★★

BEST SEASON: March–May
ELEVATION: 3400 ft
TRAIL LENGTH: 5 miles
USGS QUAD: Dunsmuir (nl)
CONTACT: Castle Crags State Park; 530-235-2684

A 50-foot plunge on Burstarse Creek, Burstarse Falls has a very short life during the year and regularly dries up in

summer. It is a splendid waterfall if you catch it in season, but the 5-mile round trip to reach it will have you understanding where the waterfall may get its name.

Burstarse Falls does not actually fall within Castle Crags State Park; it lies in the Castle Crags Wilderness. Still, the state park rangers can point you in the right direction if you have trouble locating the trailhead. From I-5, take the Castle Crags/Castella exit and head west on Castle Creek Road for 3.2 miles. Look for a parking area on your right. Find the unmarked trailhead on the west end of the parking area. The trail is less than obvious to the eye. Begin hiking uphill and watch your step since the trail is covered with loose material and pinecones. In just over a half mile, you will reach a junction with the Pacific Crest Trail. At the junction, turn left and hike along a lovely hillside for about 2 miles. Upon reaching the sign for Burstarse Creek, hike upstream a few hundred yards to reach the falls.

SWEETBRIAR FALLS ★★

BEST SEASON: February–May
ELEVATION: 2300 ft
USGS QUAD: Tombstone Mountain (ns)
CONTACT: Siskiyou County Visitors Bureau; 530-926-3850

Sweetbriar Falls is a 20-foot cascade on Sweetbriar Creek that falls right under a road. It is easy to get to, but not worthy of a trip on its own. It does, however, make a nice stop for I-5 travelers who would like some fresh air. Taking the Sweetbriar exit from I-5, go 0.5 mile east and park by the railroad tracks. You can follow the creek to the falls.

10 TRINITY ALPS WILDERNESS

Trinity Alps is the second largest official wilderness area in the state, spanning a majestic 517,000 acres over three national forests. Located in the mountains between Highway 101 and I-5, some 50 miles northwest of Redding, it provides a wide variety of scenery. Elevations range from a relatively flat 1360 feet to peaks at over 9000 feet with enough trails to keep even the most dedicated hikers busy for months.

GRIZZLY LAKE FALLS ★★★★★

BEST SEASON: June–August
ELEVATION: 7200 ft
TRAIL LENGTH: 12 miles
USGS QUAD: Thompson Peak (nl)
CONTACT: Shasta-Trinity National Forest; 530-623-6106.

Grizzly Lake Falls is nothing short of spectacular, pouring over 170 feet into Grizzly Lake from Grizzly Creek. Part of the falls is a free-falling plunge and the lower half is a cascade, making the whole waterfall one of the most beautiful in the

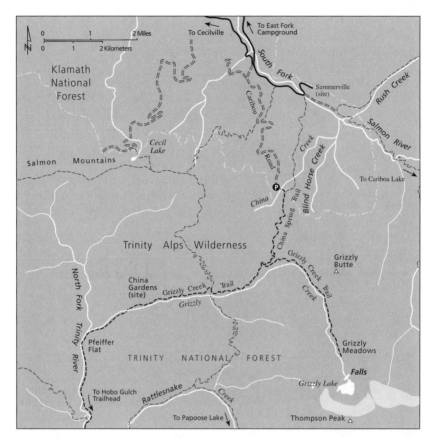

area. Grizzly Lake Falls would likely be a major tourist draw were it not for the strenuous 12-mile round-trip hike. The trail is extremely difficult with close to 5000 feet of elevation gain; so do

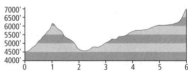

not expect a quick and easy day hike. To reach the trailhead, head west 28 miles on Cecilville Road from Callahan to the East Fork Campground, and then head south on Caribou Road until the pavement ends. Look for a dirt road on the right. Follow this road to a parking area for the China Spring Trail. Hike up the China Spring Trail, then pick up the Grizzly Creek Trail after 2.5 miles and turn left. It's also possible to reach the falls via a 19-mile one-way backpacking trip from Hobo Gulch. Check with a park ranger for more information.

Swift Creek Falls (u) ★★

BEST SEASON: June–August
ELEVATION: 3000 ft

TRAIL LENGTH: 2 miles
USGS QUAD: Trinity Center (ns)
CONTACT: Shasta-Trinity National Forest; 530-623-2121

Unless you feel like scrambling down into the canyon, your view of the Swift Creek waterfall will be distant. Otherwise, you can see this 25-foot cascade from the Swift Creek Trail. From Trinity Center, take Swift Creek Road about 7 miles to the trailhead. Once you are on the trail, hike a mile to get a glimpse of the falls. At this point, if you want to get in closer, look for a good spot to climb down—but use caution since there is no established trail here!

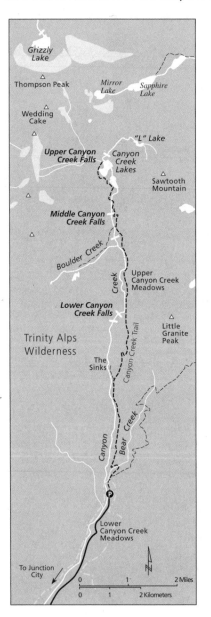

CANYON CREEK FALLS ★★★

BEST SEASON: June–August
ELEVATION: 4300 ft
TRAIL LENGTH: 8 to 15 miles
USGS QUAD: Mount Hilton
CONTACT: Shasta-Trinity National Forest; 530-623-2121

There are actually many waterfalls along Canyon Creek; the upper, lower, and middle falls, and a number of smaller cascades. The upper, lower, and middle falls are 50, 100, and 150 feet tall respectively. Reaching the upper falls requires a 15-mile backpacking journey, but you can reach the lower falls in an 8-mile round-trip hike. The middle falls are about 6 miles in along the trail, but you have to look for a spur trail to find the falls since the main trail does not go alongside them. Or better yet, bring a GPS receiver.

Regardless of how far you decide to go, the Canyon Creek Trail is a popular and highly regarded destination within the Trinity Alps Wilderness, and you are sure to enjoy your journey. Find the trailhead by taking Highway 299 8 miles west of Weaverville to Canyon

Creek Road. Head right and continue 13 miles. For those with GPS receivers, the lower falls is at 40.93108N 123.02341W; the middle falls is at 40.95305N 123.02387W; and the upper falls is at 40.97839N 123.02509W.

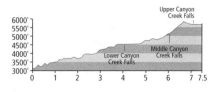

KICKAPOO WATERFALL ★★★

BEST SEASON: April–June
ELEVATION: 3400 ft
USGS QUAD: Ycatapom Peak
CONTACT: Shasta-Trinity National Forest; 530-266-3211

Kickapoo Waterfall is about 30 feet high and 5 to 10 feet wide. It runs near the East Fork of Coffee Creek, flowing year-round but most impressively after snowmelt. Surprisingly, it is accessible by car. From Highway 299 toward Weaverville, take Highway 3 to the town of Trinity Center (29 miles) and continue another 8 miles to Coffee Creek Road. Turn left and drive 7 to 8 miles, and the waterfall is right by the side of the road.

11 SHASTA LAKE

Shasta Lake is man-made, even though the sheer size of it (29,500 acres) makes that sound unlikely at first. Because of its twists and turns and multiple arms, the shoreline is longer than that of the entire San Francisco Bay! The reservoir, which also happens to be the largest of its kind in the state, was created in the late 1930s when Shasta Dam was built by thousands of families who had swarmed to the area in anticipation of employment. Several small boomtowns mushroomed up around the dam. Many of these towns still stand today.

One thing to look for around the lake is its population of bald eagles. As of this writing, there are no fewer than eighteen pairs of resident eagles living here. There are several designated wildlife-viewing spots scattered around the lake, so bring binoculars and keep your eyes on the sky. To get here, go north of Redding on I-5. There will be exits both before and after the bridge crossing the lake.

POTEM FALLS ★★★★

BEST SEASON: May–August
ELEVATION: 1200 ft
TRAIL LENGTH: 0.5 mile
USGS QUAD: Devils Rock
CONTACT: Shasta-Trinity National Forest; 530-226-2500

Redding is not the first place one would expect to find a waterfall like Potem Falls, a surprisingly strong 70-foot year-round free fall on Potem Creek near the intersection with the Pit River. Potem Falls is a common destination for sight-seers in the Redding area and would be more popular except for the 30-mile drive to reach it. Visitors can take Highway 299 east from Redding to Fenders Ferry Road, then turn left and drive 9 miles to a pullout parking area on the left, at which point it is a 0.25-mile hike to the falls. Use caution when visiting the fall and do not attempt to go to the top; two people have died here falling from the cliffs above the falls.

LION SLIDE FALLS ★★★

BEST SEASON: May–August
ELEVATION: 3000 ft
TRAIL LENGTH: 0.5 mile
USGS QUAD: Montgomery Creek; 530-275-1587
CONTACT: Shasta-Trinity National Forest

Lion Slide Falls is a very popular spot for swimmers. The waterfall itself is only about 20 feet high, falling on Hatchet Creek, but it is powerful and has quite a

Lion Slide Falls

roar. Lion Slide is the most commonly visited of the waterfalls on Hatchet Creek and thus is also subject to some name confusion. Recreation brochures and a few hiking books refer to it as Hatchet Creek Falls, but topographic maps call it Lion Slide Falls and give the former name to a different waterfall farther in toward the Pit River Reservoir. Regardless of its true name, Lion Slide Falls is a fun destination and great place to escape the summer heat. To get there, drive 35 miles east of Redding on Highway 299, then turn left on Big Bend Road and go a mile to a parking area on the right just before the bridge. From there, follow the trail a few hundred yards to the falls.

Montgomery Creek Falls ★★

BEST SEASON: April–June
ELEVATION: 2000 ft
USGS QUAD: Montgomery Creek
CONTACT: Shasta-Trinity National Forest; 530-275-1587

In a more picturesque setting, Montgomery Creek Falls might be a tourist attraction. Where it sits, it is barely worthy of a side trip. The fall is about 60 feet tall and it sits in a deep gorge near the town of Montgomery Creek, but there is little

Montgomery Creek Falls

to do or see in the immediate area except look at the fall. From Redding, drive 32 miles east on Highway 299 to Montgomery Creek Falls Road, then turn left and drive a short distance to the bridge. Be careful when looking in; losing your footing here would be dangerous.

SHASTA DAM ★★

BEST SEASON: After very
heavy rains
ELEVATION: 1100 ft
USGS QUAD: Shasta Dam
CONTACT: Bureau of Reclamation; 530-275-1554

Shasta Dam occasionally provides a 400-foot man-made waterfall when the dam overflows, making it the tallest man-made waterfall in the country. Unfortunately, it flows only after very heavy rainy seasons, which are rare in the Redding area. To tour Shasta Dam, waterfall or not, contact the Shasta Lake Bureau of Reclamation for available dates and times.

Shasta Dam (Photo courtesy of U.S. Bureau of Reclamation)

12 WHISKEYTOWN LAKE

With a name like Whiskeytown, you might assume there was a major distillery or at least a number of particularly rowdy bars here. Surely, there was some of that back in the Gold Rush days, but local folklore has another explanation for the name's origin. When an accident-prone miner named Billie Peterson was hauling supplies back to his mine, he lost control of the cart and his precious barrel of whiskey came loose. It rolled down to a nearby creek and smashed open against a rock by the water, pouring its contents into the water. This epic tragedy prompted the creek to henceforth be known as "Whiskey Creek," which eventually led to the offbeat town name.

Today, the old town is covered with water thanks to a 1959 statewide initiative to create dams for the benefit of agriculture. People were relocated and in 1963 the construction was completed. Some pieces of town were preserved and can still be viewed in the park. To get here, go 8 miles west of Redding on Highway 299 and look for the visitor center exit on your left. The park charges an entrance fee.

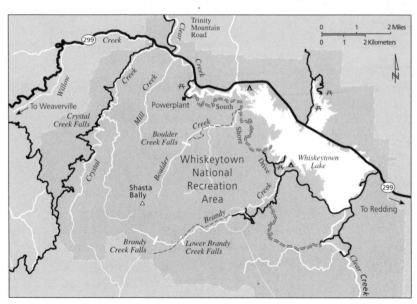

BOULDER CREEK FALLS ★★★★

BEST SEASON: March–June
ELEVATION: 2250 ft
TRAIL LENGTH: 7 miles
USGS QUAD: French Gulch (ns)
CONTACT: Whiskeytown National Recreation Area; 530-242-3400

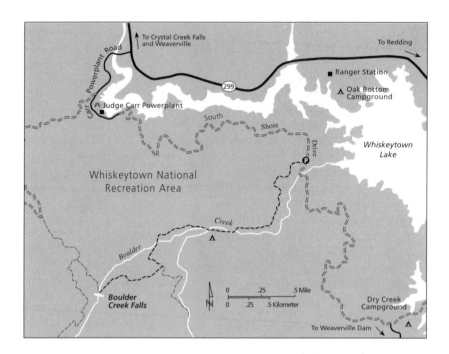

Boulder Creek Falls is a series of three cascades, totaling about 140 feet, falling on Boulder Creek. The area is popular with day hikers, leading visitors on a 7-mile round-trip trek through forests full of native trees and wildlife. From the visitor center off Highway 299, continue 7 miles west and turn south on Carr Powerplant Road, then left on South Shore Drive after 1.1 miles. Drive 2.5 miles on South Shore Drive to the trailhead, which will be on the right. Bring plenty of water for the hike; you face about 1000 feet of elevation gain on the way to the falls, and it can be hot here in the summer.

LOWER BRANDY CREEK FALLS ★★

BEST SEASON: March–June
ELEVATION: 2000 ft
TRAIL LENGTH: 0.5 mile
USGS QUAD: Igo (ns)
CONTACT: Whiskeytown National Recreation Area; 530-242-3400

Lower Brandy Creek Falls is a pretty pair of cascades on Brandy Creek and an easy side trip along the trail to the main Brandy Creek Falls. From Highway 299, turn left at the Whiskeytown Visitor Center and continue 4.7 miles to the sign for Sheep Camp/Shasta Bally Road. Turn left, heading 2.5 miles to the sign for the Brandy Creek Trail, then turn left again and go a mile to the parking area at the end of the road. The trailhead is up the hill. Lower Brandy Creek Falls sits about a quarter mile up the trail, just before you cross the creek.

BRANDY CREEK FALLS ★★★

BEST SEASON: March–June
ELEVATION: 2600 ft
TRAIL LENGTH: 3 miles
USGS QUAD: Igo (ns)
CONTACT: Whiskeytown National Recreation Area; 530-242-3400

Brandy Creek Falls is about 30 feet high and falls on Brandy Creek in Whiskeytown National Recreation Area. It is further upstream from Lower Brandy Creek Falls and requires a 3-mile round-trip hike from the parking area. From Lower Brandy Creek Falls, continue on the Brandy Creek Trail for another mile to reach the main falls.

Crystal Creek Falls

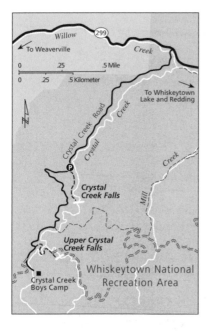

CRYSTAL CREEK FALLS ★★★★

BEST SEASON: December–April
ELEVATION: 1700 ft
TRAIL LENGTH: 0.25 mile
USGS QUAD: French Gulch (ns)
CONTACT: Whiskeytown National
Recreation Area; 530-242-3400

Crystal Creek Falls may be the prettiest waterfall in the Whiskeytown area. This spectacular 50-foot cascade on Crystal Creek will have you marveling over its beauty—if you hit it in the right season. Heading west on Highway 299 from Oak Bottom, turn left on Crystal Creek Road a half mile past Trinity Mountain Road. Go 2 miles on Crystal Creek Road until you reach a round, gravelly area. Turn left and follow the dirt road to a locked gate. Park and hike on the dirt road a few hundred yards to the falls. Follow the roaring creek and resist the temptation to peek down through the bushes; you will come around a corner just past some picnic tables, and Crystal Creek Falls will greet you there in all its glory. The trail is fairly flat and could probably be navigated by a wheelchair.

UPPER CRYSTAL CREEK FALLS ★★★★

BEST SEASON: December–April
ELEVATION: 2800 ft
TRAIL LENGTH: 2.5 miles
USGS QUAD: French Gulch (ns)
CONTACT: Whiskeytown National Recreation Area; 530-242-3400

Even less widely known than the easily accessible lower cascade on Crystal Creek is the upper falls. This is a three-tiered, nearly vertical cascade close to 400 feet in height, but access can be a bit tricky. Continue up Crystal Creek Road past the turnoff for the lower Crystal Creek Falls, and then go about two miles—almost to Crystal Creek Boys Camp. The trailhead is on the left about a quarter mile before a gate; if you reach the gate, turn around.

Starting on the trail, hike about a half mile until you reach the second creek crossing. Just before the creek, there is a forest road on your right. Turn onto it and head up the hill (south), and then hang left in the fork some 150 yards along. Continue to the creek intersection. This is where things get tricky; the last part to the falls requires some rock hopping and making your way across the water, which is not easy. While it is not much more than a mile to the falls from here, you should expect to spend at least an hour getting there. The falls may be difficult to access during the highest flow periods due to several creek crossings; you may want to go later in the season for an easier trip.

Upper Crystal Creek Falls (Photo courtesy of National Park Service; Russ Weatherbee)

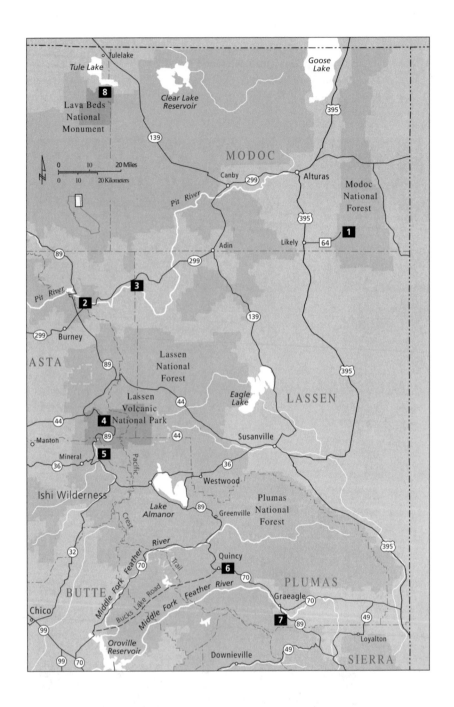

LASSEN REGION

Tired of the crowds in the big-name parks? Fed up with having to park a mile away from the trailhead because the parking lot is full? Finding it hard to enjoy the serenity of a majestic waterfall because some jerk with a boom box insists that gangsta rap on full blast will enhance the experience?

These are the kind of issues you will not have to worry about in most of the Lassen region. With no major cities around, only serious outdoor enthusiasts will make the long drive to reach the extreme northeastern corner of the state. Add the sheer size of the forests up here, and you will always be able to find your own, peaceful refuge from civilization. And if this sounds appealing, wait until you see the waterfalls around here!

The undisputed king among the Lassen falls is Burney Falls. This fall is not the tallest or the biggest in the state, but it packs an enormous visual impact that makes it one of the top three must-see waterfalls in California. You have not truly lived until you have stood at the base of this roaring body of water.

Then, there is Lassen Volcanic National Park. Geology buffs and waterfall enthusiasts alike will love trekking back and forth across this strange but fascinating area to discover one gem after another.

But do not let the big-name attractions fool you into thinking they are the only game in town. Modoc National Forest covers a whopping two million acres of pristine wilderness, including a 100-foot waterfall. The tiny community of Mineral has a lot of nice waterfalls within easy striking distance. And do not discount the many small towns scattered along the roads either.

Finally, let us just clarify that Burney Falls and Lava Beds National Monument are technically in Siskiyou and Shasta Counties. Nonetheless, we have included them in this region based on how the roads are laid out. In other words, if you are in this neck of the woods, you are most likely doing it as part of a Plumas/Lassen/Modoc trip, not a Siskiyou-Trinity trip. Hence, we hope it makes more sense for your travel planning to lay it out like this.

---

1 MODOC NATIONAL FOREST

This sizeable chunk of land contains almost two million acres of peaceful pine forests, lakes, streams, canyons, and high desert plateaus. Due to the low population density in the region and the distance from any major cities, this is one of your best bets for getting away from civilization for a while. To get here from the San Francisco Bay Area and Sacramento, take I-5 north to Redding and turn east onto Highway 299. National Forest offices are located in the towns of Adin, Alturas, and Cedarville along Highway 299, as well as in Tulelake up by the Oregon border. The forest branches out in many directions, but turning north on Highway 139 between Adin and Alturas will take you straight through the bulk of it.

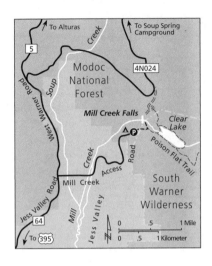

MILL CREEK FALLS ★★★

BEST SEASON: May–September
ELEVATION: 5700 ft
TRAIL LENGTH: 0.5 mile
USGS QUAD: Soup Creek
CONTACT: Modoc National Forest;
530-233-5811

Mill Creek Falls is a 100-foot drop on Mill Creek in the wilderness of the Warner Mountains. Since you are not likely to drive all the way out here just for a waterfall, consider camping at the waterfall's namesake campground. From Highway 395 in Likely, head 9 miles east on County Road 64, then 2.5 miles northeast on West Warner Road. From there, it is another 2 miles east on the Mill Creek Access Road to reach the campground. The trail to Mill Creek Falls is only a short walk from the campground, making less than a half-mile round trip.

---

2 McARTHUR BURNEY FALLS MEMORIAL STATE PARK

With a centerpiece like Burney Falls, it does not matter that this park weighs in with a relatively tiny 910 acres. Even the well-preserved forests, scenic mountains, and minor geological wonders fade in the shadow of Burney Falls. Simply put, a waterfall like this takes your breath away. To get to this must-see waterfall from the south, take I-5 to Redding and turn east on Highway 299. Continue past the town of Burney to Highway 89, where you turn north and continue until you see signs for the park. From the north, take I-5 to the McCloud/Highway 89 exit south of Mount Shasta City and follow Highway 89 until you see signs for the park.

BURNEY FALLS ★★★★★

BEST SEASON: Year–round
ELEVATION: 2900 ft
USGS QUAD: Burney Falls
CONTACT: McArthur Burney Falls Memorial State Park; 530-335-2777

Burney Falls is a misty 129-foot fall on Burney Creek, and like Mossbrae Falls in the Shasta-Trinity Region, it is a wide waterfall that includes water erupting from the side of the cliff as well as falling from the creek above. The waterfall is so neat that it

Burney Falls

has a whole park named after it, and it is probably the best easily accessible five-star waterfall in all of northern California. Barely a hike is required to reach its base, and visitors can get awesome views of the waterfall right from the parking lot.

3 FALL RIVER MILLS

In 1920, a team of daring developers embarked on a publicly ridiculed effort to build a powerhouse in the middle of the Californian wilderness. It took two years and thousands of workers to complete the project. But by the end, the team could triumphantly present a groundbreaking powerhouse with enormous capacity, for the times, that shipped power over 200 miles. As a bonus, the town of Fall River Mills was firmly established. Don't miss the Pit One Powerhouse. Built like a castle, complete with turrets, the powerhouse looks decidedly out of place in the Californian wilderness.

From the south, you get to Fall River Mills by taking I-5 to Redding. Turn east on Highway 299 and go straight for 68 miles. From the north, take I-5 to the McCloud/Highway 89 exit south of Mount Shasta City and stay on Highway 89 until you reach Highway 299. Turn east and go straight until you reach town.

Pit River Falls from the viewpoint

PIT RIVER FALLS ★★

BEST SEASON: April–July
ELEVATION: 3000 ft
USGS QUAD: Hogback Ridge
CONTACT: Bureau of Land Management; 530-233-4666

Pit River Falls is 30 to 40 feet high, falling on the Pit River. It is visible from a pullout along Highway 299 about two miles west of the town of Fall River Mills. The waterfall would be more spectacular were the viewpoint not well over a half mile away from the falls.

4 LASSEN VOLCANIC NATIONAL PARK

As the name implies, Lassen Volcanic National Park is a prime spot for studying the effects of volcanic activity. All four existing types of volcanoes are found within park boundaries, along with a rich assortment of steam vents, boiling pools, painted dunes, mud pots, and of course a multitude of strangely shaped rocks and lava cones. The park is more or less encapsulated within Lassen National Forest.

From the south, take I-5 to Red Bluff and turn east on Highway 36. Continue past the town of Mineral and turn north on Highway 89. From the north, take I-5 to Redding and turn east on Highway 44. Continue until you get to the junction with Highway 89, where you turn south.

HAT CREEK CASCADES ★★

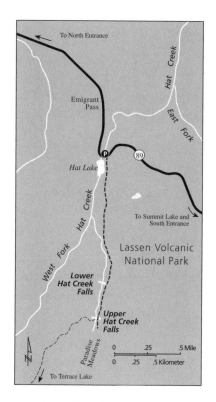

BEST SEASON: mid June–August
ELEVATION: 6500 ft
TRAIL LENGTH: 3 miles
USGS QUAD: Reading Peak (ns)
CONTACT: Lassen Volcanic National Park; 530-595-4444

There are two cascades on the Paradise Meadows Trail, falling 15 and 10 feet respectively on the West Fork of Hat Creek. Both are very nice and make lovely picnic locations. Enter through the north entrance and go 9.5 miles to Hat Lake. Park in the parking lot, cross the road, and look for the trailhead sign across from the lot. Hike 1.5 miles each way to view both falls.

KINGS CREEK CASCADES ★★★

BEST SEASON: late June–August
ELEVATION: 6500 ft
TRAIL LENGTH: 2 miles
USGS QUAD: Reading Peak
CONTACT: Lassen Volcanic National Park; 530-595-4444

The views along Kings Creek are indeed fit for a king. As you descend down the trail to Kings Creek Falls, you will find yourself almost perilously close to a series of cascades falling over 100 feet that are worthy waterfalls in their own right. However, on this trip, they are relegated to a nice appetizer for the main waterfall course to come. The downhill hike is extremely steep, so in tackling the trip to Kings Creek Falls, be sure to remember that you have to make it back up the hill on your return trip. Start the hike from the trailhead along Highway 89 about 17 miles south of the northernmost entrance.

Kings Creek Cascades

KINGS CREEK FALLS ★★★★

BEST SEASON: late June–August
ELEVATION: 6800 ft
TRAIL LENGTH: 3 miles
USGS QUAD: Reading Peak
CONTACT: Lassen Volcanic National Park; 530-595-4444

Kings Creek Falls is a 50-foot plunging cascade, and it is possibly one of the prettiest cascade-style waterfalls in the north state. To reach it, continue downhill past the cascades for about a mile from the start of the trail. As mentioned above, save some energy for the tough hike back up the trail.

MILL CREEK FALLS ★★★★

BEST SEASON: June–August
ELEVATION: 6400 ft
TRAIL LENGTH: 3 miles
USGS QUAD: Lassen Peak
CONTACT: Lassen Volcanic National Park; 530-595-4444

Mill Creek Falls is a 75-foot plunge on Mill Creek. It is a gorgeous sight and easily overwhelms viewers with its beauty. Start the hike near the first campground north of the park's south entrance. It is just over a mile and a half of moderate hiking each way to reach the falls.

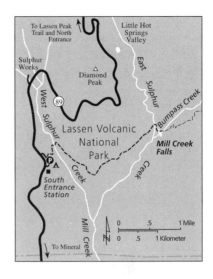

Bluff Falls ★★★

BEST SEASON: June–August
ELEVATION: 6500 ft
USGS QUAD: Lassen Peak
CONTACT: Lassen Volcanic National Park; 530-595-4444

Bluff Falls is a 50-foot plunge on an offshoot of Mill Creek. It is a shimmering sheath that falls over a wide rock face. It does not actually fall within the Lassen Volcanic National Park boundaries, but you can see it from your car about 1.7 miles south of the park's southern entrance. Park in a pullout on the east side of the road. It is possible to hike up closer to the waterfall, but watch your footing.

5 MINERAL

The town of Mineral is a tiny community located about 40 miles east of Red Bluff, just southwest of Lassen Volcanic National Park. While the locals may not have the kind of amenities found in nearby Redding, they enjoy some spectacular natural scenery and waterfalls. To get here, take I-5 to Red Bluff and turn east on Highway 36 until you reach town.

Deer Creek Falls

DEER CREEK FALLS ★★

BEST SEASON: March–
August
ELEVATION: 3630 ft
USGS QUAD: Onion Butte
CONTACT: Lassen National
Forest; 530-258-2141

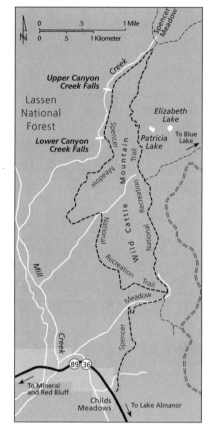

The upper Deer Creek Falls is just
over a dozen feet high, but it is still an
interesting sight to see in its high-flow
period. From the southern border of
Lassen Volcanic National Park, take
Highway 89 south for about 15 miles
to the intersection with Highway 32.
Turn right on Highway 32 and drive
for about 9 miles to a sign for Deer
Creek Falls, from which point it is just
a brief stroll to the waterfall.

LOWER DEER CREEK FALLS ★★★

BEST SEASON: March–
August
ELEVATION: 3000 ft
TRAIL LENGTH: 3.5 miles
USGS QUAD: Onion Butte
CONTACT: Lassen National Forest; 530-258-2141

Lower Deer Creek Falls is a powerful but small waterfall of about 20 feet. It is
somewhat more impressive than its upper counterpart, and it requires a 3.5-mile
round-trip hike to reach it. Heading south on Highway 32, continue just over 3
miles past the turnoff for the upper Deer Creek Falls. There will be a trailhead
on the right just before a bridge.

LOWER CANYON CREEK FALLS ★★★

BEST SEASON: March–August
ELEVATION: 6200 ft

TRAIL LENGTH: 10 miles
USGS QUAD: Reading Peak (nl)
CONTACT: Lassen National Forest; 530-257-2151

Lower Canyon Creek Falls is the first of two waterfalls on Canyon Creek, found near the Spencer Meadow National Recreation Trail. Unfortunately, this first fall is not visible from the trail and you will have to follow your ears to reach the waterfall. Using a GPS receiver will make the task easier; the falls sit at 40.39939N 121.49414W, about 5 miles from the trailhead. To find the trailhead, take Highway 36 5 miles east from its junction with Highway 89. It will be about a quarter mile past Childs Meadows. After starting on the trail, there will be a fork after about a mile and a half. Take the left path.

Upper Canyon Creek Falls ★★★

BEST SEASON: March–August
ELEVATION: 6200 ft
TRAIL LENGTH: 11 miles
USGS QUAD: Reading Peak (nl)
CONTACT: Lassen National Forest; 530-257-2151

The upper fall on Canyon Creek is also somewhat difficult to find since the trail does not pass right by it. After viewing the lower fall, return to the Spencer

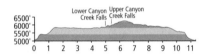

Meadow National Recreation Trail and continue about a half mile farther north. The GPS coordinates to look for are 40.40813N, 121.49267W.

After viewing the falls, return to Childs Meadows or continue farther to reach Spencer Meadow and return on the other leg of the loop.

Battle Creek Falls ★★

BEST SEASON: March–August
ELEVATION: 4600 ft
USGS QUAD: Lyonsville (ns)
CONTACT: Lassen National Forest; 530-258-2141

Battle Creek Falls is about 20 feet high and easily accessible by car. Lassen National Forest rangers say that this fall is on private property, so please enjoy it from the road. From Mineral, head west on Highway 36 for almost two miles to the Battle Creek Campground. Turn left after crossing a bridge over the creek, and then turn left again onto Road 140A. Continue 1.25 miles to reach the falls.

Battle Creek Falls

---

6 QUINCY

Like most other towns in the region, Quincy was born in the rowdy, latter part of the nineteenth century and soon established itself as a viable logging and mining town. It sits at the crossroads of Highway 70, Highway 89, and Bucks Lake Road; anyone driving around up here is likely to end up passing through town at some point. To get there from the south, take Highway 70 from Sacramento until you reach town. From the north, take I-5 to Red Bluff and turn east on Highway 36. Continue until you reach Highway 89, where you turn south and stay straight until you reach town.

INDIAN FALLS ★★★

BEST SEASON: March–August
ELEVATION: 3200 ft
TRAIL LENGTH: 0.5 mile

USGS QUAD: Crescent Mills
CONTACT: Plumas National Forest; 530-283-2050

Indian Falls is only 20 feet high, falling on Indian Creek, but the falls are very powerful and striking to see. The hike is a 0.5-mile round trip and offers some swimming opportunities near the falls. The falls are 2 miles north of the intersection of Highway 70 and Highway 89, 10 miles west of Quincy. Take Highway 89 north and look for a parking area on the east side of the highway after Indian Falls Road.

7 GRAEAGLE

The odd spelling of Graeagle may prompt questions about how the town got that name. While there are some dramatic and romanticized takes on the matter, local historians say it comes from a naming contest where they tried to find a better name than Davies' Mill. A bookkeeper saw a sign for Gray Eagle Creek and simply removed the y. She won twenty-five dollars for her submission, and the town has borne the name since. Graeagle is located along Highway 89, just south of the junction with Highway 70. Being an hour's drive from Reno and just over two hours from Sacramento, it has grown into a secret getaway destination where city-dwellers can escape the hustle for a weekend.

To get here from the south, take I-80 east past Sacramento. In the town of Truckee, turn north on Highway 89. From the north, take I-5 to Red Bluff and turn east on Highway 36, then turn south on Highway 89 and continue until you reach town.

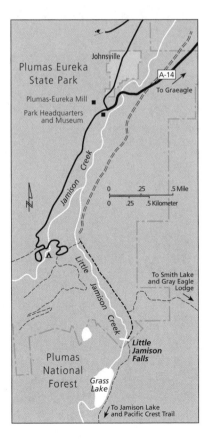

LITTLE JAMISON FALLS ★★★

BEST SEASON: May–July
ELEVATION: 5800 ft
TRAIL LENGTH: 2.5 miles
USGS QUAD: Gold Lake (nl)
CONTACT: Plumas National Forest; 530-836-2575

Little Jamison Falls is a 30-foot drop on Little Jamison Creek. Most people find it while hiking on the trail to Grass

Lake, and it makes a nice sight along that trip. Head west on Road A-14/Graeagle Johnsville Road from Highway 89 in Graeagle, and follow it about 4.5 miles to Jamison Mine Road. Turn left and continue to the trailhead in 1.2 miles. The trail is an uphill climb for a mile before you reach a sign for the fall. After viewing the fall, continue another quarter mile to visit Grass Lake.

HAWSLEY FALLS ★★

BEST SEASON: May–July
ELEVATION: 6100 ft
TRAIL LENGTH: 2.5 miles
USGS QUAD: Gold Lake (nl)
CONTACT: Plumas National Forest; 530-836-2575

Hawsley Falls is a 20-foot cascade on Gray Eagle Creek. It is sometimes spelled Halsey Falls. About a mile south of Graeagle, take the Gold Lake Highway exit southwest from Highway 89. Continue 5 miles to the Gray Eagle Lodge sign.

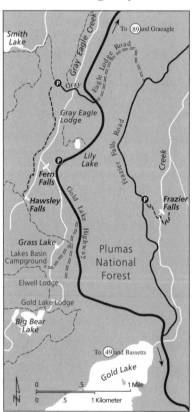

Turn right and go 0.3 mile, then take another right and proceed a short distance farther to a parking area for the Hawsley Falls Trail and Smith Lake Trail. Look for the trailhead on the left side of the parking lot, and follow it along the creek, heading upstream for about a mile. Take a short trail to the left to view the falls.

FRAZIER FALLS ★★★★

BEST SEASON: May–June
ELEVATION: 6100 ft
TRAIL LENGTH: 1 mile
USGS QUAD: Gold Lake
CONTACT: Plumas National Forest; 530-836-2575

Frazier Falls is one of the most popular waterfalls in the region, falling about 250 feet on Frazier Creek. The main waterfall is 176 feet high, but with the lower cascade included, it is even higher. The waterfall is best viewed in midspring as

Frazier Falls at low flow

the snow melts, although the fall will still have water into late summer.

From Highway 89 about a mile south of Graeagle, take the Gold Lake Highway exit, drive southwest about 2 miles, and look for a Frazier Falls sign. Turn left and continue 4.5 miles to the parking area. It is about a half-mile hike to the falls on a paved, wheelchair-accessible trail. There are a few semisteep sections, but it's mostly level.

FERN FALLS ★★

BEST SEASON: May–July
ELEVATION: 6000 ft
TRAIL LENGTH: 0.25 mile
USGS QUAD: Gold Lake
CONTACT: Plumas National Forest; 530-836-2575

Fern Falls is a series of cascades of varying heights. It has its own picnic area, and a nearby trail loops around Lily Lake and connects with the Gray Eagle Trail toward Hawsley Falls. From the junction of Highway 89 and the Gold Lake Highway a mile south of Graeagle, head southwest on the Gold Lake Highway for about 6 miles to a picnic area. The falls are visible from the picnic area, but a short vista trail leads in closer to the falls.

8 LAVA BEDS NATIONAL MONUMENT

This area may seem downright unearthly at times. Strangely shaped cones, twisted rock, and solidified lava bring to mind sci-fi movies rather than northern California. Indeed, geology buffs and laypeople alike will appreciate the insight this national monument provides into California's geologically violent past—and perhaps pause for a minute of quiet contemplation about the subterranean forces still at work today.

During the Modoc War of 1872-73, this was a key region. The natives used the rugged terrain to their advantage in their long holdout against a superior foe. The most prominent example of this is Captain Jacks Stronghold, a lava fortress created by a whim of nature, which enabled about sixty Modoc warriors to hold out for five months against more than 500 U.S. Army soldiers.

To get here from the south, exit I-5 in the town of Weed and take Highway 97 north. Turn east on Highway 161 and continue to Hill Road and turn south; from there on there will be signs pointing to the visitor center.

Crystal Cave Falls ★★★★

BEST SEASON: December–March
ELEVATION: 4700 ft
TRAIL LENGTH: Less than 1 mile
USGS QUAD: Captain Jacks Stronghold (ns)
CONTACT: Lava Beds National Monument; 530-667-8104

What could be more striking for the waterfall lover than a frozen fall inside an ethereal cave? The frozen waterfall in Crystal Cave is about 15 feet tall and requires a strenuous hike, but viewing it is an experience to remember. The inside of the cave looks like something out of a fairy tale. To visit the falls, you have to book a guided tour between December and March since warm air could damage the cave. In addition, your group is limited to six people. Because the trip is physically demanding, park regulations prohibit children under twelve from hiking in Crystal Cave. Contact the park for more information.

Crystal Cave Falls (Photo courtesy of Andrew Sawadisavi; www.andeys.com)

SAN FRANCISCO BAY AREA

Most visitors to San Francisco tend to focus on Golden Gate, Fisherman's Wharf, and all the other mainstream attractions. Indeed, looking at the sprawling and bustling Bay Area it is hard to believe there would be room for any natural

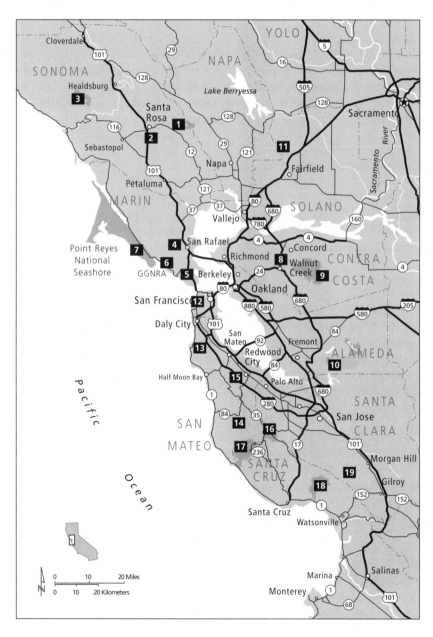

waterfalls among the industrial parks, overlapping highways, and densely packed residential zones.

In reality, there are dozens of great waterfalls within easy driving distance of civilization in this metropolis. Even locals may be surprised to know that there are great opportunities available within an hour's drive, making them easy day trips for the whole family.

One of the area's greatest recreational resources is the Santa Cruz Mountains hugging the western half of the peninsula. Among the numerous redwood trees you find gems such as Berry Creek Falls, Sempervirens Falls, and Maple Falls. Looking to the north, you have Alamere Falls pouring straight from a cliff into the ocean—a spectacular panoramic picture. Even the East Bay, with its hotter and drier climate, features nice falls such as Diablo and Abrigo Falls.

As a rule, all waterfalls in the Bay Area are best seen in the winter, preferably within a few days of rainfall. Unlike the mountainous areas to the north and east, snow and ice is never a problem—but summer heat is, making the falls shrink or dry up altogether. In other words, go waterfall hunting in the winter here, and then hit the mountains in the summer.

---

1 SUGARLOAF RIDGE STATE PARK

This 2700-acre park is home to the headwaters of Sonoma Creek as well as numerous redwoods and, in springtime, an impressive amount of colorful wildflowers. Another noteworthy feature of this park is Ferguson Observatory. This observatory, equipped with a 40-inch telescope, is one of the largest in the western United States dedicated to public viewing and education. Call (707) 883-6979 for schedules and fees for the observatory. For general information or to speak to park staff, call (707) 833-5712.

The park is located 11 miles east of Santa Rosa. Take Highway 12 from Highway 101 (between Santa Rosa and Sonoma) to Adobe Canyon Road just north of the town of Kenwood, and follow the signs. The park campground is open all year for those wishing to make an overnight trip.

SONOMA CREEK FALLS ★★★

BEST SEASON: December–May
ELEVATION: 800 ft
TRAIL LENGTH: 1 mile
USGS QUAD: Kenwood (ns)
CONTACT: Sugarloaf Ridge State Park; 707-833-5712

Sonoma Creek Falls is about 25 feet high, and it is a pretty oasis in a relatively dry region. Naturally, the waterfall is most interesting immediately after rain. Continue to a parking area for the Pony Gate Trail about 100 yards before the

Sonoma Creek Falls at high flow

entrance. You will need to pay an entrance fee to park, so if you do not possess a California State Parks pass, continue to the park entrance to pay the fee before you visit the falls. Once on the trail, it is a half-mile descent to the waterfall.

2 SANTA ROSA

Santa Rosa is a central hub of the famous northern California wine country. Located some 55 miles north of San Francisco and 30 miles inland from the Pacific Ocean, you are within striking distance of several hundred local wineries. Highway 101 passes right through town so you will probably have a chance to get a closer look as you drive toward any of the north coast waterfalls.

MAYACAMA RETREAT FALLS ★★★

BEST SEASON: January–April
ELEVATION: 1700 ft
TRAIL LENGTH: 0.25 mile
USGS QUAD: Kenwood (ns)
CONTACT: Mayacama Mountaintop Retreat; 707-538-8461

This waterfall is on private property, but the owners have a cabin available for rental that has access to the 30-foot waterfall. Access is restricted to guests, but it is a very nice retreat for anyone seeking a getaway in the area. There is a suspension bridge near the waterfall, which makes for a relaxing stroll. Call for a reservation. Be sure to visit in the winter or spring, as the waterfall may dry up by summer.

3 ARMSTRONG REDWOODS STATE RESERVE

At just 805 acres, Armstrong Redwoods State Reserve is more of a grove than a forest or full-size park. Still, it is a nice but little-known refuge from civilization where you can enjoy ancient 300-foot trees and several easy-to-strenuous hikes without driving too far. Get here by taking Highway 101 to Santa Rosa, where you exit at River Road and drive west until you reach the town of Guerneville. Watch for Armstrong Woods Road as you drive through town, and take it north for about 2 miles.

ARMSTRONG FALLS (U) ★★

BEST SEASON: December–April (after heavy rains)
ELEVATION: 200 ft
USGS QUAD: Guerneville (ns)
CONTACT: Armstrong Redwoods State Reserve; 707-869-2015

This unnamed cascade is about 15 feet long, falling right off the road into the Armstrong Redwoods State Reserve. Take Highway 101 to Santa Rosa and take the River Road exit and continue 17 miles to Guerneville. Turn right at the second light onto Armstrong Woods Road and drive 2.5 miles to the state reserve. Continue 1.25 miles into Austin Creek State Recreation Area and watch for the waterfall alongside the road.

4 SAN RAFAEL AND FAIRFAX

The North Bay has plenty of nice waterfalls, and the area around San Rafael and Fairfax is no exception. The proximity to the ocean makes for comfortable hiking even on hot days. To get here, head north on either Highway 580 or 101. Start looking for your specific exit soon after the 580/101 merge.

Opposite: The falls at Mayacama Mountaintop Retreat (Photo courtesy of Michael Lockert, Tranquility Arts)

Stairstep Falls at high flow

STAIRSTEP FALLS ★★

BEST SEASON: December–March
ELEVATION: 600 ft
TRAIL LENGTH: 2.5 miles
USGS QUAD: San Geronimo (ns)
CONTACT: Samuel P. Taylor State Park; 415-488-9897

Stairstep Falls is a three-part series of cascades, stretching about 40 feet in height. It falls on Devils Gulch Creek, and its impressiveness varies considerably throughout the year. Visit during rainy season immediately after rain to get the best view.

Take the Sir Francis Drake Boulevard exit off Highway 101 toward San Anselmo, and then drive 15 miles to Samuel P. Taylor State Park. Look for the Devil's Gulch Horse Camp parking area on the left about one mile past Camp Taylor. Cross Sir Francis Drake Boulevard; the trail starts a little way up the service road. Follow this trail to a bridge; cross it and turn left at the sign for Bill's Trail. After 0.6 mile, turn left on the Stairstep Falls Trail. The total round-trip distance is about 2.5 miles. You will hear a few other waterfalls

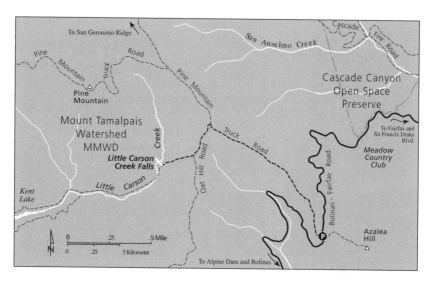

along the way, but there is too much brush to get a good view and nowhere safe to scramble down.

LITTLE CARSON CREEK FALLS ★★★

BEST SEASON: December–March
ELEVATION: 1100 ft
TRAIL LENGTH: 3 miles
USGS QUAD: Bolinas (ns)
CONTACT: Marin Municipal Water District; 415-945-1455

Little Carson Creek Falls is sometimes just called Carson Falls. It consists of more than 100 feet of cascades, dropping in five tiers—the largest being 40 feet tall. Like most other waterfalls in the region, it is most impressive in the rainy season and barely worth a visit in the summer.

Little Carson Creek Falls can be stunning at the right time, although it is a little difficult to find. Take the Sir Francis Drake Boulevard exit off Highway 101 in San Rafael and head 6 miles to Fairfax, where you turn left on Pastori Avenue, then right on Center Boulevard, which becomes Broadway. Watch for Bolinas Road and turn left. From there, it is just under 4 miles to Pine Mountain Road, which will be gated on your right with a parking area on the left. Hike a mile up Pine Mountain Road, then at the top of the mountain, turn left on Oat Hill Road. Hike a quarter mile downhill to an offshoot trail on your right. It is a steep quarter mile downhill from here to where you can view the falls. Swimming and wading in watershed streams is prohibited. Avoid stepping in the water at all costs since rare frogs breed in these pools created by the falls.

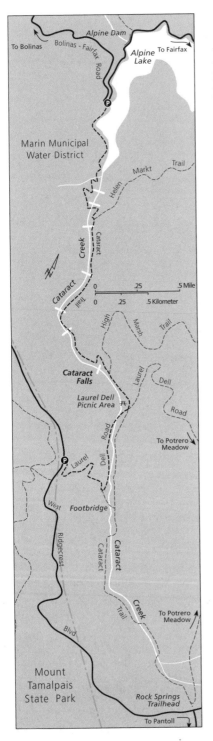

CASCADE FALLS ★★

BEST SEASON: December–April
ELEVATION: 320 ft
TRAIL LENGTH: 1.5 miles
USGS QUAD: San Rafael (nl)
CONTACT: Marin County Open
Space District; 415-499-6387

Cascade Falls is a 30-foot cascade on Cascade Creek. It is very pretty in the rainy season but not so much in the summer. Follow the same directions as to Little Carson Creek Falls up to Bolinas Road, but instead of continuing to Pine Mountain Road, drive just under a half mile to Cascade Drive. Turn right, and then drive 1.5 miles to the trailhead. Available parking is minimal. Upon the trail, bear right and head along San Anselmo Creek a half mile to a bridge. Turn right, then continue a quarter mile around the bend to the falls.

PLUNGE POOL ★★

BEST SEASON: December–April
ELEVATION: 500 ft
TRAIL LENGTH: 1 mile
USGS QUAD: San Rafael (ns)
CONTACT: Marin Municipal Water District; 415-945-1455

Plunge Pool is a series of cascades on San Anselmo Creek, the tallest of which is about 8 feet tall. The area is ecologically fragile, so tread very lightly if you choose to make the trip. After viewing Cascade Falls, return to the bridge and hike in the opposite direction without crossing back over the bridge, then look

Cascade Falls near Fairfax

for a trail on the left that leads to these additional waterfalls. The hike is another half mile from the bridge.

CATARACT FALLS ★★★

BEST SEASON: December–March
ELEVATION: 1800 ft
TRAIL LENGTH: 3 miles
USGS QUAD: San Rafael (ns)
CONTACT: Marin Municipal Water District; 415-945-1455

Cataract Falls is a series of seven cascades along Cataract Creek. The cascades vary between 30 and 60 feet in height, and they can be spectacular during rainy season but dull and uninteresting in dry months. The hike stretches through some beautiful redwood country and offers a nice three-mile round trip for waterfall lovers. Follow the directions for Cascade and Little Carson Creek Falls up to Bolinas Road. After turning on Bolinas Road, drive around 8 miles across the Alpine Lake Dam. Park in a pullout near a sharp turn. The trail will be on the left. Follow the trail 1.5 miles to the Laurel Dell Picnic Area, then turn around and hike back. The waterfalls are along the way; listen for the sound of rushing water along the trail.

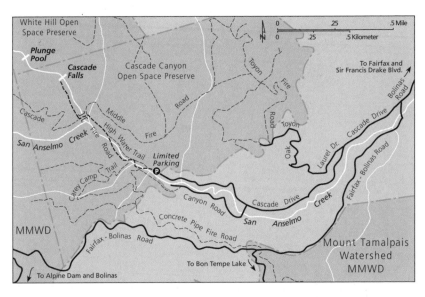

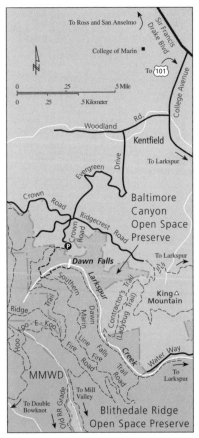

DAWN FALLS ★★

BEST SEASON: December–March
ELEVATION: 250 ft
TRAIL LENGTH: 0.75 mile
USGS QUAD: San Rafael (ns)
CONTACT: Marin County Open
Space District; 415-499-6387

Dawn Falls is a 20-foot fall over a
hillside. It never flows too strongly
and usually flows at more of a trickle
than a downpour, but it can be pretty
immediately after rain. Take the Sir
Francis Drake Boulevard exit from
Highway 101 in Larkspur, and then
go 2 miles to College Avenue and turn
left. After about a quarter mile, turn
right on Woodland Road, then go
another quarter mile before turning
left on Evergreen Drive, which is the
second possible right turn. Continue
a mile, being sure to stay on Evergreen
Drive, and then turn left on Crown
Road. Follow Crown Road less than a
quarter mile to the parking area. Start

Dawn Falls at high flow

on the South Marin Line road and watch for a sign to the Dawn Falls trail after about 0.25 miles.

5 MILL VALLEY

Mill Valley is south of the San Rafael region, a few miles south of the Highway 580/101 merge and some ways inland. Cascade Canyon Open Space Preserve, where Cascade Falls is located, has an abundance of really colorful and beautiful butterflies. Keep your eyes open for them when you go to Cascade Falls.

CASCADE FALLS ★★

BEST SEASON: December–April
ELEVATION: 250 ft
TRAIL LENGTH: 0.25 mile
USGS QUAD: San Rafael (ns)
CONTACT: Marin Municipal Water District; 415-945-1455

Cascade Falls near Mill Valley

This is one of two waterfalls in the Marin region bearing the name Cascade Falls. It is about 20 feet high, and like the other Cascade Falls, it falls on Cascade Creek. It requires only a very brief walk upon reaching the trailhead. Take the Mill Valley/Stinson Beach exit off Highway 101, then turn right on Almonte Boulevard and drive just under 3 miles to Throckmorton Avenue. After turning left, continue 1.1 miles to a turnout that bears a sign for Cascade Falls. Swimming and wading in watershed streams is prohibited.

6 STINSON BEACH

Stinson Beach is a small community with one of those "perfect spots" that are hard to beat. Turn west, and you have a magnificent ocean view. Turn east, and you have redwoods and relative solitude on the Mount Tamalpais State Park trails. And this is all within a short drive of San Francisco. To get here from the

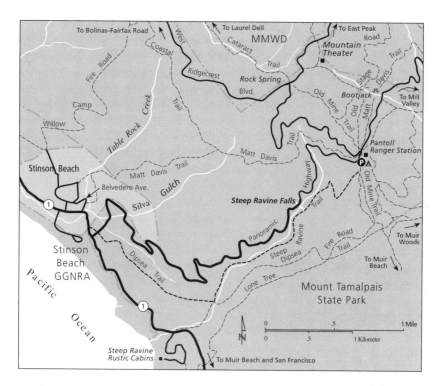

south, cross Golden Gate Bridge on Highway 101 from San Francisco, then take the Highway 1/Stinson Beach exit and keep going until you reach town. If you come from the north or the east, take Highway 580 across the Bay to San Rafael and turn south on Highway 101 toward San Francisco; use the same Highway 1/Stinson Beach exit as those coming from the south.

Morses Gulch Falls ★★★

BEST SEASON: December–May
ELEVATION: 0 ft
TRAIL LENGTH: 1 mile
USGS QUAD: Bolinas (ns)
CONTACT: Golden Gate National Recreation Area; 415-561-4700

Morses Gulch Falls is one of the least known waterfalls on California's northern coastline. It is a 50-foot plunge along Highway 1 just north of Stinson Beach, and it is rarely crowded. The only bad things about this trail are that it is not well maintained and can be tough to find. Head north on Highway 1 exactly 2.6 miles from the junction with the Panoramic Highway near Stinson Beach. There will be a pullout on the right. Expect a creek crossing and plenty of overgrown plants along the trail.

Steep Ravine Falls ★★

BEST SEASON: December–May
ELEVATION: 1000 ft
TRAIL LENGTH: 4 miles
USGS QUAD: San Rafael (ns)
CONTACT: Mount Tamalpais State Park; 415-388-2070

Do not be fooled by the two-star rating on this waterfall; the hike to the falls is spectacular, taking you through picturesque scenery, with plentiful ocean views. There are two waterfalls along Webb Creek in the Steep Ravine Canyon; the first is a 30-foot cascade, and the second is 20 feet and sends hikers up a ladder to continue past it on the trail. Turn right at the junction of Highway 1 with the Panoramic Highway near Stinson Beach, and then park at the Pantoll Ranger Station on the left. The Steep Ravine Trail begins in the lower parking lot of the ranger station. Taking the Steep Ravine Trail to the falls and back is a 4-mile round trip.

Hikers interested in enjoying this area further have the option of a loop of six or more miles by taking the Matt Davis Trail from Pantoll Ranger Station to Stinson Beach and returning on the Dipsea Trail before taking the Steep Ravine Trail 2 miles back to the ranger station. Another scenic option is to take the Old Mine Trail from the Pantoll area, turn right on the Dipsea Trail, and then right again on the Steep Ravine Trail for a 4-mile loop.

7 Point Reyes National Seashore

Point Reyes illustrates California's violent geological history as well as the richness of its fauna. Literally balancing on the edge of the San Andreas Fault, you can stand atop a hill and see the scars of seismic activity underneath with your naked eye. At the same time, the peninsula is home to thirty-seven land species and dozens of marine species, along with almost 20 percent of California's flowering plant species. To get here from San Francisco, head north across Golden Gate Bridge and stay on Highway 1 until you reach the park. From Highway 101, take Sir Francis Drake Boulevard west through Samuel P. Taylor State Park to the connection with Highway 1 in Olema. Then head south to the exit for Olema Bolinas Road.

Alamere Falls ★★★★★

BEST SEASON: December–May
ELEVATION: 200 ft
TRAIL LENGTH: 11 miles
USGS QUAD: Double Point
CONTACT: Point Reyes National Seashore; 415-464-5100

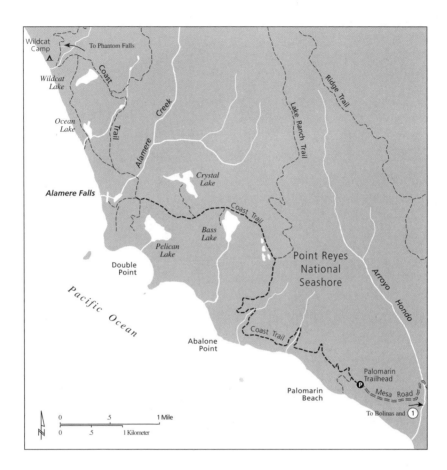

Alamere Falls, a 50-foot plunge into the Pacific Ocean, is the end point of a popular 8-mile round-trip hike along California's Coastal Trail. There are a few different routes by which to reach it, but the shortest route is by way of the Palomarin Trailhead. Take Highway 1 to the turnoff for Olema Bolinas Road just north of Bolinas Lagoon. Turn west and head south 2 miles to the junction with Mesa Road. Turn right and continue 4 miles to the Palomarin Trailhead, at the end of the road.

Follow the Coast Trail north for a winding trek of over 5 miles. Stay on it past the Crystal Lake Trail and follow signs to reach Wildcat Campground. From the campground, hike back along the beach to find the falls. If you wish to camp at Wildcat Beach, you will need a permit. The park service suggests reservations because of high demand.

Alamere Falls is one of two famous coastal waterfalls in California; the other is McWay Falls on the Big Sur coast much farther south. Both pour magnificently over cliffs into the ocean. McWay Falls tends to get more glory due to its easy accessibility right off Highway 1 with a quarter-mile hike. Alamere Falls, however, is equally spectacular and worthy of waterfall lovers' attention. It is just a little harder to get to.

Alamere Falls (Photo courtesy of Andrew Sawadisavi; www.andeys.com)

PHANTOM FALLS ★★★

BEST SEASON: January–May
ELEVATION: 200 ft
TRAIL LENGTH: 13 miles
USGS QUAD: Double Point (ns)
CONTACT: Point Reyes National Seashore; 415-464-5100

Phantom Falls is a little known 150-foot plunge, sitting about a mile north of Wildcat Campground. The waterfall is seasonal and dries up by summer. Follow the Coast Trail from the Palomarin Trailhead about 5.5 miles to the campground, and then continue a mile north to find the falls. It is also possible to reach Wildcat Campground by way of the Stewart Trail from the east or the Bear Valley Trail from the northeast. Before attempting to reach Phantom Falls, stop by a visitor center to discuss your plans and only attempt the hike during low tide. Hikers have been stuck here before.

Horsetail Falls ★★

BEST SEASON: January–May
ELEVATION: 200 ft
TRAIL LENGTH: 14 miles
USGS QUAD: Double Point (ns)
CONTACT: Point Reyes National Seashore; 415-464-5100

Horsetail Falls is a 30-foot drop sitting about 450 yards north of Phantom Falls. As with Phantom Falls, it is important to check with a ranger before visiting and to only attempt the hike during low-tide periods. Horsetail Falls is also seasonal and dries up by summer.

8 WALNUT CREEK

Briones Regional Park in Walnut Creek on the northeastern part of the San Francisco Bay Area is home to Abrigo Falls. Despite the proximity to nearby towns like Walnut Creek, Concord, Martinez, and Pleasant Hill, the hills in this 5756-acre park offer some rather spectacular wilderness views. Please note that there are cattle in some areas of the park; be sure to close any gates you pass through. From Highway 680, turn west on Highway 24 in Walnut Creek and go about 5 miles to Upper Happy Valley Road. Drive north for 1.5 miles until you turn left on Bear Creek Road.

Abrigo Falls ★

BEST SEASON: December–March
ELEVATION: 1000 ft
TRAIL LENGTH: 3 miles
USGS QUAD: Briones Valley
CONTACT: East Bay Regional Park District; 510-562-PARK

Abrigo Falls barely qualifies as a waterfall, being only a tiny trickle of about a dozen feet. Even after a rainstorm, it will barely have any flow and will certainly not be anything to impress you. Visit this waterfall only if you have an inclination to hike in the area anyway. Look for the trailhead on the left immediately upon entering the park. The hike is just over 1.5 miles each way, and you will need to stay on the Abrigo Valley Trail the entire way. Do not turn at any of the junctions. The park does charge an entrance fee.

9 MOUNT DIABLO STATE PARK

For a nice bonus, try to go to Mount Diablo the day after a storm, when the skies have just cleared up and the smog and haze have not yet returned—the view from the summit of the Sierra Crestline is something else. To the west, you see Golden Gate Bridge and the ocean; all around you, mountains, from the Santa Cruz area in the south to Mount Saint Helens to the north.

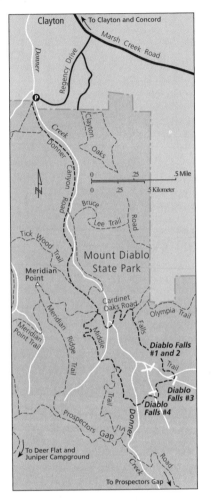

MOUNT DIABLO FALLS ★★★

BEST SEASON: December–April
ELEVATION: 1600 ft
TRAIL LENGTH: 6 miles
USGS QUAD: Clayton (ns)
CONTACT: Mount Diablo State Park; 925-837-2525

The waterfalls on Mount Diablo are a series of four cascades and plunges on Donner Creek. The falls are seasonal and usually dry up by late spring or early summer, but they can be very pretty after winter rains. From Highway 680 heading north, take the Ygnacio Valley Road exit near Walnut Creek and head east for 7 miles to Clayton Road. (From Highway 680 heading south, take the North Main Street exit and go south to Ygnacio Valley Road.) Turn right and go 3 miles to Regency Drive, then follow Regency Drive to

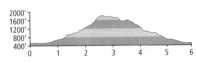

the right about a half mile to the trailhead. Park and begin hiking on the gated fire road (Donner Canyon Road) 1.5 miles to the junction with Cardinet Oaks Road. Turn left, and after 0.5 mile of difficult switchbacks, look for the Falls Trail on the right. Hike it past the falls, and bear right when it comes back down to the Middle Trail. Follow the Middle Trail to its junction with Meridian Ridge Road and turn right to merge shortly onto Donner Canyon Road for the return trip. The total trip is about 6 miles.

10 SUNOL-OHLONE REGIONAL WILDERNESS

The Sunol-Ohlone Regional Wilderness is only accessible via the Ohlone Wilderness Trail, a tough 28-mile hike for those who enjoy a challenge. The good news is that you only have to go a small part of that distance to reach Murietta Falls.

MURIETTA FALLS ★★

BEST SEASON: January–March
ELEVATION: 3000 ft
TRAIL LENGTH: 16 miles
USGS QUAD: Mendenhall Springs (ns)
CONTACT: Sunol–Ohlone Regional Wilderness; 925-862-2244

Murietta Falls is between 50 and 80 feet tall. Unfortunately, the fall is still only worth seeing shortly after rainstorms, and it does not have a very powerful flow even then. Nevertheless, for those waterfall lovers who are fond of backpacking and who would like to see a rarely visited yet tall waterfall, Murietta Falls could be worth a look. The surrounding area is certainly scenic, particularly in spring.

To reach the fall, take the North Livermore Avenue exit off 580; turn south and stay on it through town. Its name changes to Tesla Road but just keep going until you see Mines Road on your right. Turn right and continue 6 miles to the fork. Hang right onto Del Valle Road and you are soon in Del Valle Regional Park.

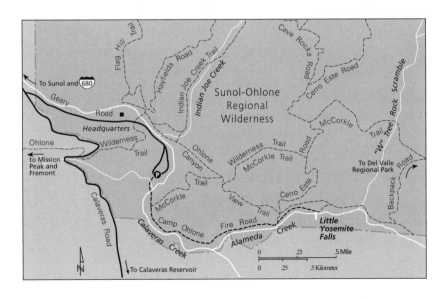

Continue straight until you cross a bridge, where you turn right and park in the second parking lot. The gates are locked at the posted time, so arrive early for a day hike. From the trailhead, take the Ohlone Trail toward Stewart's Camp (a backpacking site; the fall is half a mile or so before the actual camp). The waterfall is on the right hand side and requires a short detour off Ohlone near trail post 35. Look at the map and have a ranger point out exactly where to find it. (Park visitors are required to pay a two dollar map fee in addition to the parking fee.) The hike is about 8 miles each way and is very steep and challenging. Beware of poison oak and rattlesnakes.

LITTLE YOSEMITE FALLS ★★

BEST SEASON: January–March
ELEVATION: 500 ft
TRAIL LENGTH: 3 miles
USGS QUAD: La Costa Valley (ns)
CONTACT: Sunol–Ohlone Regional Wilderness; 925-862-2244

Little Yosemite Falls sits in the Sunol–Ohlone Regional Wilderness. Take the Calaveras Road exit off 680 in Sunol (not the one in Milpitas; the two are frequently confused). Turn south on Calaveras Road leading away from the town of Sunol. Stay on Calaveras for 4 miles, and then turn left on Geary Road, which dead-ends in Sunol–Ohlone Regional Wilderness. There is a paved 1-mile loop, and at the far end is a fire road. Either park early and make it a hike, or drive all the way to the beginning of the fire road. Hike the easy gravel fire road for 1.5 miles next to the creek and you pass right by the falls. Strollers are okay, and even wheelchairs can make the trip if they have suitable tires. Beware of poison oak all year and rattlesnakes in the summer and spring, especially.

---

11 VACAVILLE

Vacaville is hot and dry. With an average summer temperature of 94 degrees and less than 18 inches of annual precipitation, it is impossible to sugarcoat that. But that only makes it a more pleasant surprise to find a gem like Creek Walk Falls hidden away in this unlikely place. Vacaville is located right off Highway I-80 about midway between San Francisco and Sacramento.

CREEK WALK FALLS ★★

BEST SEASON: March–July
ELEVATION: 200 ft

Opposite: Murietta Falls at high flow (Photo courtesy of Kevin Gong; kevingong.com)

TRAIL LENGTH: 0.5 mile
USGS QUAD: Elmira (ns)
CONTACT: City of Vacaville Public Works; 707-449-5170

Creek Walk Falls is about 20 feet tall and 5 feet wide. It is in Andrews Park on the corner of Main Street and Davis Street. (Take the Davis exit off the highway.) The waterfall is easy to find within the park, and it is wheelchair and stroller accessible.

---

12 SAN FRANCISCO

Looking at the densely populated City by the Bay, it is hard to imagine there being any space for any waterfalls. Fortunately, there is. Most San Francisco waterfalls are easily accessible by bus or trolley, allowing nondrivers an opportunity to enjoy the calming effect of a trickling fall. Three of the four falls are found in Golden Gate Park, which stretches across northwestern San Francisco.

MARTIN LUTHER KING JR. MEMORIAL FALLS ★★★

BEST SEASON: Year–round
ELEVATION: 280 ft
USGS QUAD: San Francisco North (ns)
CONTACT: Yerba Buena Gardens; 415-541-0312

The waterfall in Yerba Buena Gardens is man-made, but it is still interesting nonetheless, particularly given that it sits in the middle of a beautiful memorial to Martin Luther King, Jr. About 20 feet high and 50 feet wide, it is also larger than many other northern California waterfalls. Yerba Buena Gardens sits atop the Moscone Center, a well-known San Francisco building. To reach it, follow signs for I-80 East from Highway 101 North. Take the Fourth Street exit to Bryant, and then turn left on Third Street and left on Howard Street. Look for parking in any of the facilities near the Moscone Center, which is in the 700 block on Howard.

RAINBOW FALLS ★★★

BEST SEASON: Year–round
ELEVATION: 275 ft
USGS QUAD: San Francisco North
CONTACT: San Francisco Recreation & Park Department; 415-831-2700

Rainbow Falls is a 40-foot drop in Golden Gate Park in northern San Francisco. From looking at it, it is hard to tell that this is an artificially created waterfall. The waterfall is also the starting point for an annual 5K run, held every March in the park. To visit the waterfall, take Highway 1 (Crossover Drive) to John F.

Kennedy (JFK) Drive and go east for a few hundred feet. The fall is clearly visible from the road and even has a sign.

HUNTINGTON FALLS ★★★

BEST SEASON: Year–round
ELEVATION: 260 ft
USGS QUAD: San Francisco North
CONTACT: San Francisco Recreation & Park Department; 415-831-2700

Huntington Falls is another very pretty artificial waterfall in Golden Gate Park. Totaling about 30 feet in height, the falls are located on the east side of Stow Lake Island. If coming from 19th Avenue from the south, take Martin Luther King, Jr. (MLK) Drive and make a right, then left onto Stow Lake Drive. From the north, taking 25th or 14th Avenue, turn left onto JFK Drive, then right onto Stow Lake Drive. Stow Lake Drive goes all around the island; you can park by either bridge and walk across to the falls.

Huntington Falls

TEA GARDEN FALLS ★★★

BEST SEASON: Year–round
ELEVATION: 250 ft
USGS QUAD: San Francisco North
CONTACT: San Francisco Recreation & Park Department; 415-831-2700

This waterfall is about 15 feet tall, but it adds a pleasing atmosphere to the already lovely Japanese Tea Garden in Golden Gate Park. This is also an artificial waterfall, but that does not detract from its appeal. To find it, park on MLK Drive across from the arboretum. Enter the tea garden (entrance fee required) and look for the waterfall about 20 paces straight ahead.

---

13 SAN PEDRO VALLEY COUNTY PARK

At 1150 acres, San Pedro Valley is not a big park, but in the winter and spring it somehow manages to remain fairly uncrowded despite the proximity to San Francisco and the peninsula's dense population. While the park features three freshwater creeks that flow year-round, Brooks Falls is unfortunately seasonal. San Pedro Valley is located south of Pacifica; take Highway 1 to Linda Mar Boulevard and go east until you reach Oddstad Boulevard. Turn right and look for the entrance on your left.

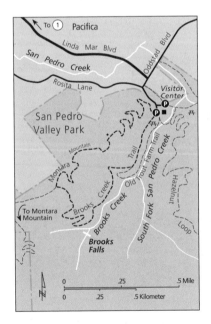

BROOKS FALLS ★★★

BEST SEASON: December–May
ELEVATION: 600 ft
TRAIL LENGTH: 1.6 miles
USGS QUAD: Montara Mountain (ns)
CONTACT: San Pedro Valley
County Park; 650-355-8289

Brooks Falls is a three-tiered drop on Brooks Creek totaling about 175 feet. It would be nice if it were possible to get closer to it; unfortunately, all you get are views of it from a distance. It looks like a thread cascading down the mountain off in the distance. Still, this is a lovely park with numerous hiking possibilities.

The trail begins near the restrooms in the upper parking lot to your right.

Start hiking on the Montara Mountain Trail, and then take the Brooks Creek Trail when it forks off. Upon reaching the viewpoint for the falls, you can turn around and head back for a 1.6-mile round trip or continue hiking to make a 3.5-mile loop when the Brooks Creek Trail meets the Montara Mountain Trail.

14 LA HONDA

La Honda is located smack in the middle of the Santa Cruz Mountains, between the bustle of Silicon Valley in the east and the scenic ocean views in the west. Both waterfalls are a bit south of the town, off Pescadero and Alpine Roads. Coming from the coast, take either Pescadero Road or Highway 84/La Honda Road. From the north Bay Area, take Highway 84/La Honda Road, and from the east or south Bay Area, take Alpine. All these roads more or less intersect within striking distance of both waterfalls.

TIPTOE FALLS ★★

BEST SEASON: January–May
ELEVATION: 500 ft
TRAIL LENGTH: 2 miles
USGS QUAD: Mindego Hill (ns)
CONTACT: Portola Redwoods State Park; 650-948-9098

Tiptoe Falls is very small, measuring only about 6 feet as it falls on Fall Creek. However, it is still a nice waterfall and draws numerous Bay Area hikers every year. The Iverson Trail will lead you past it along its 2-mile route; start at the trailhead near the visitor center or pick up the trail elsewhere in the park. Look for a side trail at Fall Creek to lead you to the falls. If you are visiting in the winter, check with the ranger station since the rangers remove the bridges over the creeks during the winter; this could leave you unable to access the falls without crossing a creek or taking an alternate 2-mile route.

To find the park, take the Alpine Road exit west from Highway 35, then drive 3 miles to turn left on Portola State Park Road, which will lead you straight into the park after another 3 miles. Do not attempt to take Alpine Road off Highway 280 since it dead-ends before reaching the park.

POMPONIO FALLS ★★

BEST SEASON: January–April
ELEVATION: 250 ft
TRAIL LENGTH: 0.25 mile
USGS QUAD: La Honda (ns)
CONTACT: Memorial County Park; 650-879-0238

Pomponio Falls (Photo courtesy of Tim Burkhart, San Mateo County Parks)

Pomponio Falls is a 20-foot drop from an unnamed creek onto Pescadero Creek in one of the lesser-known redwood-laden parks of the Santa Cruz Mountains. It is not the most memorable of waterfalls, but it is set in a nice area with campgrounds and multiple possibilities for family activities. Go up Highway 1 and turn right on Pescadero Road; stay on Pescadero for 9.5 miles. Enter the park and go to the Azalea Flat Campground. From here, the fall is less than 100 yards away on a flat trail that is stroller-friendly and handicap accessible. The park requires an entrance fee.

UPPER POMPONIO FALLS ★

BEST SEASON: January–April
ELEVATION: 250 ft
USGS QUAD: La Honda (ns)
CONTACT: Memorial County Park; 650-879-0238

If you will be visiting Pomponio Falls, the 8-foot upper cascade makes a nice little bonus side trip. This fall is located just off the highway 200 yards west of the park entrance. Look for a gate with a No Parking sign but park elsewhere if you intend to leave your car.

---

15 EDGEWOOD COUNTY PARK

Edgewood Park is a small park in Redwood City on the San Francisco peninsula. It covers just 467 acres but provides a welcome sanctuary for locals and passers-through. The biggest draw aside from easy access is spectacular wildflowers that cover these hillsides in spring. The park is just off Highway 280; take the Edgewood Road exit and drive a mile north to the park entrance. You can also access the park from Highway 101 by taking the Whipple Avenue exit. Go southwest on Whipple for 1.5 miles, then turn right on Alameda de las Pulgas for a short distance before turning left onto Edgewood Road. Continue 2 miles to the park entrance on your left.

Sylvan Trail Falls ★

BEST SEASON: January–April
ELEVATION: 300 ft
TRAIL LENGTH: 1 mile
USGS QUAD: Woodside (ns)
CONTACT: Edgewood County Park; 650-368-6283

Sylvan Trail Falls is only about 5 feet high and runs seasonally, but it is a pleasant and easy family-friendly walk. Start at Old Stage Camp in the northernmost part of the park (parking just off Edgewood Road; go through the picnic area and hang left). Go down 0.35 mile on the Sylvan Trail. There is one fork in the trail, hang left on the "south wing" of Sylvan. From there the trail continues pretty much straight until a sudden switchback, which is where the waterfall is visible from the trail.

16 Castle Rock State Park

Expect to encounter rock climbers here. Castle Rock State Park is full of steep surfaces just begging to have someone climb up or rappel down, and plenty of people from San Francisco and the peninsula are ready to step up to the challenge. If you decide to continue past the waterfall to the actual Castle Rock, you will have opportunities to study some very odd-looking stone formations and caves along the way.

Castle Rock Falls at high flow

From the south, take Highway 9 to Highway 35 and turn south. Look for the park entrance on your right after about 2.5 miles. From the north and east, take Highway 92 west from Highway 280. Then turn onto Highway 35, also known as Skyline Boulevard, for 28 miles (2.5 miles past the Highway 9–Highway 35 junction).

CASTLE ROCK FALLS ★★

BEST SEASON: December–March
ELEVATION: 2500 ft
TRAIL LENGTH: 1.6 miles
USGS QUAD: Castle Rock Ridge
CONTACT: Castle Rock State Park; 408-867-2952

Castle Rock Falls is about 50 feet tall, falling on Kings Creek in Castle Rock State Park. The waterfall's flow is very low throughout most of the year, so visit during rainy season in order to see it as a true waterfall. It is a 1.6-mile round-trip hike to the falls from the parking lot. From the parking lot, look for a sign pointing toward Castle Rock Falls or ask the ranger at the entrance kiosk if in doubt.

17 BIG BASIN REDWOODS STATE PARK

If you have not visited Big Basin before, you are in for a treat! This park is home to some of the most impressive redwood trees in the world. Almost every tree here is huge, making for a humbling experience as you walk through the forest. If you hit the trails early in the morning, when the fog still blankets the forest, the experience gets downright surreal! Big Basin also holds the distinction of being the state's oldest state park, established in 1902, covering over 18,000 acres.

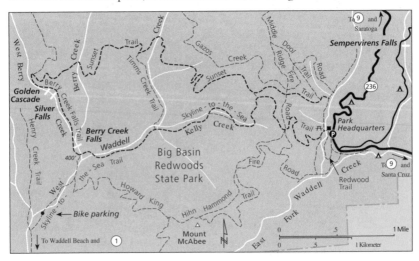

To get here from Highway 1, take Highway 9 in Santa Cruz and go 15 miles to Boulder Creek. Turn left at the town's only stop sign onto Big Basin Way and go 9 miles to the park entrance.

From the South and East Bay Area, take Highway 880 south until it becomes Highway 17. Watch for the sign for Big Basin (Mt. Hernon Road) where you turn right. Continue through Scotts Valley until you reach the crossing with Graham Hill Road, where you turn right. The next light allows you to enter Highway 9—turn right and drive to Boulder Creek. Turn onto Big Basin Way/Highway 236 at the town's only stop sign.

From San Francisco and the peninsula, take Highway 280 or 101 to 85 South. Exit at Saratoga Road and stay on it westward for a few miles until you see the sign for Highway 9. Follow the directions for the south and east Bay Area from here. There are day-use fees required to enter the park.

BERRY CREEK FALLS ★★★★

BEST SEASON: December–May
ELEVATION: 400 ft
TRAIL LENGTH: 11 miles
USGS QUAD: Franklin Point
CONTACT: Big Basin Redwoods State Park; 831-338-8860

Berry Creek Falls is one of the most photographed and popular of all waterfalls in the San Francisco Bay Area, tumbling more than 60 feet on Berry Creek over a moss-covered rock base.

The falls (and creek) were named for lumberjack Tilford George Berry, who had a cabin at the foot of the falls in the 1860s and mysteriously died after disappearing into the woods.

It takes an 11-mile round-trip hike to reach the falls—and while it is not an easy hike, it sure is a pretty one. You will pass through some of the most interesting ecosystems of the whole Big Basin forest, including wildflowers, huge fallen trees, and giant ferns. Once you reach the falls, you can enjoy it from a bench at the base. There are two options for starting the hike. One is to begin the waterfall trail from the parking lot at the park headquarters, which is more difficult but about a mile shorter. Since a few options exist for the route, ask a ranger to recommend the best trail for the time of your hike. The other option is to hike or bike in from another trailhead near Waddell Beach off Highway 1. To reach the Waddell Beach trailhead, follow Highway 1 north for 18 miles from Santa Cruz, and then start hiking or biking from the trailhead on the east side of the highway. If you are biking, you can only go the first 5.25 miles; you will have to lock your bike at the rack and hike the last three quarters of a mile to the falls.

Berry Creek Falls at low flow

SILVER FALLS ★★★

BEST SEASON: December–May
ELEVATION: 740 ft
TRAIL LENGTH: 11 miles
USGS QUAD: Franklin Point (nl)
CONTACT: Big Basin Redwoods State Park; 831-338-8860

Silver Falls is a 60-foot cascade upstream from Berry Creek Falls on the west fork of Berry Creek. After viewing Berry Creek Falls, follow the trail upstream for a half mile to reach Silver Falls. If you started your hike from the park headquarters, you can return via the Sunset Trail for a loop or head back to Berry Creek Falls to take the Skyline-to-the-Sea Trail back to the park headquarters or to Waddell Beach.

GOLDEN CASCADE ★★★

BEST SEASON: December–May
ELEVATION: 740 ft
TRAIL LENGTH: 11.5 miles
USGS QUAD: Franklin Point (nl)
CONTACT: Big Basin Redwoods State Park; 831-338-8860

The Golden Cascade is a two-tiered cascade of about 60 feet, falling on Berry Creek upstream from Silver Falls. This waterfall is unique because the creek flows as a thin sheath over an interesting golden-colored formation. Reach it by continuing up the trail from Silver Falls, then return to the Skyline-to-the-Sea Trail or follow the Sunset Trail back to the park headquarters.

Sempervirens Falls ★★★

BEST SEASON: December–May
ELEVATION: 1150 ft
USGS QUAD: Big Basin (ns)
CONTACT: Big Basin Redwoods State Park; 831-338-8860

In the park's earliest years, Sempervirens Club members used to camp near Sempervirens Falls, and a club member once claimed to have caught ninety-three fish in a single fishing trip there. This pleasant 25-foot fall is the easiest to see of all the Big Basin Park falls. You can access it by foot or by car. If you take the Sequoia Trail from the park headquarters, it is about a 2.5-mile round-trip hike to get there. You will follow a trail that runs alongside the road. When you reach the road, cross and continue down the hill to get a good look at the falls. You can either return the way you came or climb up and over to the Skyline-to-the-Sea trail for a return loop. To drive to the falls, turn right toward the Wastahi Campground from Highway 236 just before the park headquarters and watch for the Sempervirens Falls side trail on the right.

---

18 Forest of Nisene Marks

From 1883 until 1923, extremely heavy logging ravaged this area. Leaving barely a single tree standing, the loggers eventually moved on to new forests and the land was later donated to the state in 1963. Fortunately, the forest has proven remarkably resilient and park management now calls it a "monument to forest regeneration." Indeed, you can still see the ugly scars of overzealous logging, but it is also reassuring to see how well the forest has rebounded. To reach the park, take the State Park Drive exit off Highway 1 in the town of Aptos. Go east on State Park Drive until you reach Soquel Drive, where you turn right and continue about a mile to Aptos Creek Road. Turn left and enter the park.

Five Finger Falls ★★

BEST SEASON: December–May
ELEVATION: 800 ft
TRAIL LENGTH: 12 miles
USGS QUAD: Loma Prieta
CONTACT: Forest of Nisene Marks State Park; 831-763-7062

Five Finger Falls is a 20-foot spout falling on Aptos Creek. It is named for the multitude of five-finger ferns growing nearby, and it is also oc-

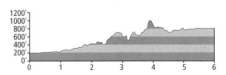

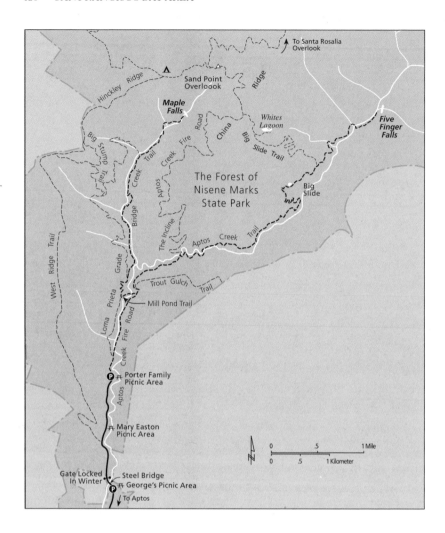

casionally called Aptos Creek Falls and Monte Vista Falls, depending on the source. The waterfall is relatively unspectacular, but for history buffs, the trail does meander past a sign labeling the epicenter of the horrific Loma Prieta earthquake of 1989.

To reach the fall, you face a 12-mile round-trip hike that can be strenuous in spots. Pass through the park entrance, and then park at Porter Picnic Area, or George's Picnic Area. During some parts of the year, you can continue to Porter Picnic Area for a 10-mile round-trip hike. Start by hiking 2.5 miles on the Aptos Creek Road to the Loma Prieta earthquake sign, and then cross Aptos Creek to find the Aptos Creek Trail. Follow it for 2 miles; at the intersection with the Big Slide Trail, continue to follow along the creekside for another 1.5 miles to find the falls.

MAPLE FALLS ★★★

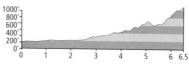

BEST SEASON: December–May
ELEVATION: 900 ft
TRAIL LENGTH: 13 miles
USGS QUAD: Laurel (ns)
CONTACT: Forest of Nisene Marks State Park; 831-763-7062

Maple Falls is a 40-foot rushing splash falling on Bridge Creek. It is the more impressive of the two waterfalls in the Forest of Nisene Marks. It erupts from a rocky canyon, creating quite a picture amid the diverse greenery and peaceful atmosphere of the forest. Start the hike in the same place as for Five Finger Falls, either George's Picnic Area or Porter Picnic Area. Follow the Aptos Creek Road to the intersection at which Mill Pond Trail heads off to the left. Take the Mill Pond Trail, then turn right on the Loma Prieta Grade Trail, and then bear right on the Bridge Creek Trail. From here, it is about another 2 miles to the falls, following along Bridge Creek. Past the Bridge Creek Historic Site, the trail disappears, so you will have to follow the creek to reach the falls.

19 UVAS CANYON COUNTY PARK

Uvas Canyon is a nice little 1133-acre park tucked away in the mountains just south of the greater Bay Area. From the north, take Highway 101 to Bernal in South San Jose and head west. Turn left on Santa Teresa Boulevard and go south about 3 miles. Turn right on Bailey Road. Continue just over 2 miles to McKean Road, where you turn left. Continue 6 miles to Croy Road, where you turn right and go straight for 4.4 miles. From the south, take Highway 101 north to Morgan Hill and exit at Tennant where you head west. Turn left on Monterey Road and turn right shortly thereafter on Watsonville Road. Keep going on Watsonville until you see Uvas Road; turn right and go for a couple of miles until you see Croy Road on your left. Croy ends in the park, but right before that you will pass through a private resort called Sveadal. Respect the speed limit. The road is very narrow and there may be playing children around, so be very careful!

GRANUJA FALLS ★★

BEST SEASON: December–May
ELEVATION: 1100 ft
TRAIL LENGTH: 0.5 mile
USGS QUAD: Loma Prieta (ns)
CONTACT: Uvas Canyon County Park; 408-779-9232

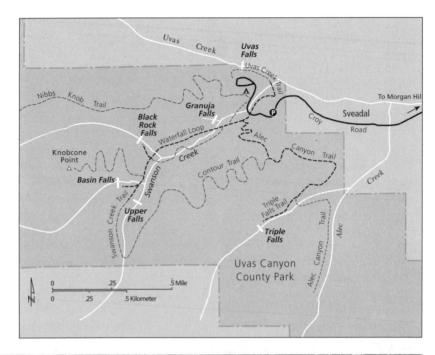

Granuja Falls

Granuja Falls is the first and smallest of the waterfalls on the popular waterfall loop in Uvas Canyon. It is only about 5 feet tall, falling on lower Swanson Creek. Look for a sign for Granuja Falls past the campground as you begin around the waterfall loop.

BLACK ROCK FALLS ★★★

· BEST SEASON: December–May
ELEVATION: 1400 ft
TRAIL LENGTH: 2 miles
USGS QUAD: Loma Prieta (nl)
CONTACT: Uvas Canyon County Park; 408-779-9232

Black Rock Falls is usually the most impressive waterfall in Uvas Canyon, boasting 35 feet in height as it falls on an offshoot of Swanson Creek. Continue along the main waterfall loop trail until you reach a sign for Black Rock Falls, which leads up a hill to the point with the best view.

UPPER FALLS ★★

BEST SEASON: December–May
ELEVATION: 1500 ft
TRAIL LENGTH: 1.5 miles
USGS QUAD: Loma Prieta (nl)
CONTACT: Uvas Canyon County Park; 408-779-9232

Upper Falls in Uvas Canyon

Upper Falls is 20 to 25 feet high, falling on Swanson Creek less than a quarter mile past the spur trail to Black Rock Falls. It is on the left side of the trail, falling in a little nook on the opposite side of the path that leads to Basin Falls.

BASIN FALLS ★★

BEST SEASON: December–May
ELEVATION: 1800 ft
TRAIL LENGTH: 2 miles
USGS QUAD: Loma Prieta (nl)
CONTACT: Uvas Canyon County Park; 408-779-9232

Basin Falls is a tiered 20-foot cascade on Swanson Creek. It is the farthest waterfall along the waterfall loop trail. Follow the offshoot trail 0.2 mile past Upper Falls to reach it. Return to Upper Falls afterward to complete the loop.

Basin Falls

Uvas Falls ★★

BEST SEASON: December–May
ELEVATION: 1000 ft
TRAIL LENGTH: 0.5 mile
USGS QUAD: Loma Prieta (ns)
CONTACT: Uvas Canyon County Park; 408-779-9232

Uvas Falls is not actually on the waterfall loop, but it is a worthy waterfall of about 20 feet falling near the intersection of Swanson and Uvas Creeks. You will find a trail near the campground leading down to Swanson Creek; if you take this trail down to Uvas Creek and then make your way back to the intersection of the two, it should be under a quarter mile of walking each way.

Triple Falls ★★

BEST SEASON: December–May
ELEVATION: 1000 ft
TRAIL LENGTH: 2.5 miles
USGS QUAD: Loma Prieta (nl)
CONTACT: Uvas Canyon County Park; 408-779-9232

Triple Falls rarely flows with any kind of strength, but in heavy rain years it can be a pleasant cascade of about 35 feet. It falls about a mile in on the Alec Canyon Trail, which is an almost steady uphill climb until it reaches an offshoot trail to Triple Falls, which is still another climb. There are some great views along the Alec Canyon Trail, so even if the waterfall is barely flowing, the hike is worth the trouble.

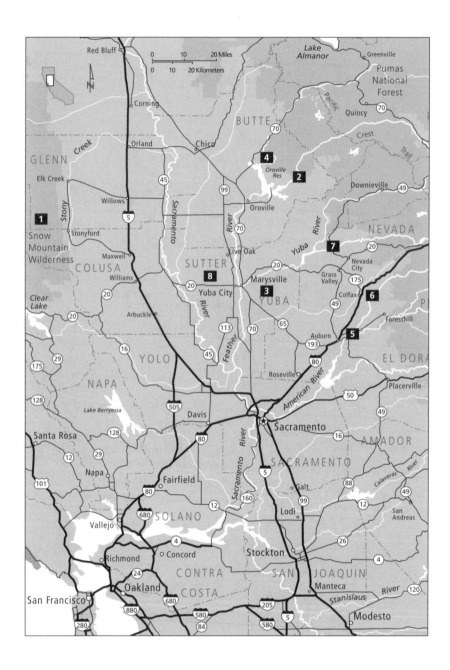

SACRAMENTO AND SAN JOAQUIN VALLEY

Driving through San Joaquin Valley, it is hard to believe there could be any water worth mentioning here, let alone anything remotely resembling a waterfall. True enough, the opportunities are tightly rationed. There are, however, hidden gems sprinkled about this hot, dry, and flat landscape. And that makes finding one of these little surprises all the sweeter.

The Willows area is a prime example. Finding even a drop of water around here seems improbable. And yet, drive west for a while and suddenly you are within striking distance of Stony Creek Falls.

Once you reach the Sierra Foothills, such as Spenceville Wildlife and Recreation Area, you find the kind of gently rolling hills and streams coming down from the Sierras that make for ample waterfall opportunities.

Then you have the oddly shaped Sutter Buttes, soon to become one of California's newest state parks. They may look perfectly nondescript as you drive by in the distance, but once you get closer you will notice that there's more to the story. This mountain range forms an almost perfect circle, 10 miles in diameter, which is actually the very tip of a huge, dormant volcano!

Those of you who like to test your whitewater skills will definitely like Auburn State Recreation Area east of Sacramento. This area offers a bunch of exciting rapids between the falls—a perfect vacation spot to enjoy every angle of the water rushing by. The bottom line: do not discount the Sacramento/San Joaquin area based on what you see from your car window. There is much more to this charming area than heat and dust—it's just a matter of knowing where to look.

1 SNOW MOUNTAIN WILDERNESS

The Snow Mountain Wilderness had a brush with fire in fall 2001. The area is steadily recovering, but the charred trunks along the hike serve as a somber warning to take the fire-hazard signs seriously. This area can be quite a tinderbox by the end of the season.

STONY CREEK FALLS ★★★

BEST SEASON: June–October
ELEVATION: 5000 ft
TRAIL LENGTH: 5 miles
USGS QUAD: Crockett Peak (ns)
CONTACT: Mendocino National Forest; 530-833-5544

Stony Creek Falls is a lively 35- to 40-foot waterfall in an unlikely place. It is also called "Middle Fork Stony Creek Falls of the Snow Mountain Wilderness."

Driving through the central valley, the town of Willows won't be the first place in which you might expect to find a waterfall hike nearby. However, Stony Creek Falls is a pleasant year-round waterfall that remains accessible all the way into November via either a 5-mile round-trip hike or a 13-mile backpacking expedition.

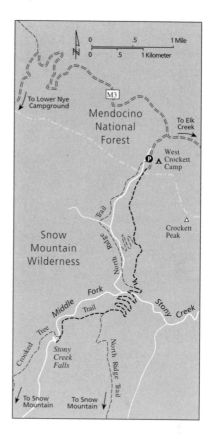

From I-5, take the Elk Creek exit, which is the second exit from the south and first from the north when passing through Willows. Go west on Highway 162 about 21 miles until there's a bridge and a junction. Turn left at the junction, passing through the town of Elk Creek, which has food and gas. Turn right on County Road 308 in Elk Creek and follow it 5.2 miles. Turn right on Road 20N0 (Ivory Mill Road) and continue 9.5 miles to Road M-3/24N02. Turn left on M-3 and go 15 miles to Road 18N66 (signed West Crockett Camp/North Ridge). Turn left and follow it 0.4 mile to the trailhead. The trailhead is found in the campground by the signboard. The hike is 2.5 miles each way. At the first junction, hang right onto Crooked Tree Trail. Follow the signs. For hikers interested in the backpacking loop, check with the ranger station for a Snow Mountain Wilderness map.

---

2 OROVILLE

Oroville is 70 miles north of Sacramento. Though hot and dry in the summer, spring offers some excellent opportunities to view some spectacular waterfalls. To get here, take I-80 to Sacramento, then head due north on Highway 70 until you reach town. If you come from the north, take I-5 south to Red Bluff. Exit at Highway 99 and head southeast. Take the left road, Highway 149, in the fork about 10 miles south of Chico. This brings you to Highway 70, where you head south to the town of Oroville.

Opposite: Stony Creek Falls (Photo courtesy of Annemarie Fiorella)

FEATHER FALLS ★★★★★

BEST SEASON: April–July
ELEVATION: 2200 ft
TRAIL LENGTH: 8 miles
USGS QUAD: Brush Creek
CONTACT: Plumas National Forest; 530-534-6500

Feather Falls is a magnificent 640-foot drop on the Fall River that is nationally renowned and has a whole scenic area devoted to it. The waterfall would

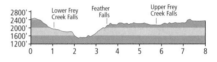

likely be an even bigger attraction were it not for the very long hike required to reach it. Viewing Feather Falls takes a minimum of an 8-mile round trip, but it can be as long as an 11-mile trip depending on which segment of the trail you take. The bonus for the short side is that you reach the waterfall faster, but the downside

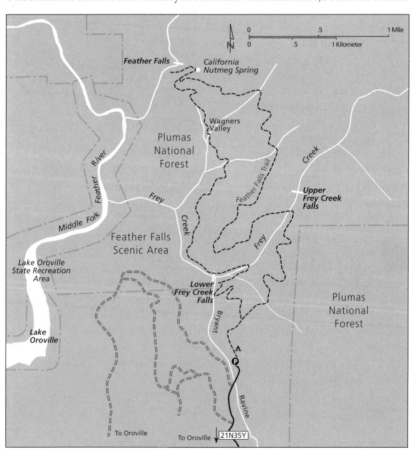

is that the trail is more strenuous. The longer trail is gentler on your body but obviously requires a few miles more hiking. If you are not in hurry, an appealing possibility is to make it a loop. The whole trail is bicycle-friendly, but more so on the longer side of the loop.

Starting from Oroville, go 6.7 miles east on Highway 162 to Forbestown Road. Turn right and drive 6 miles farther to Lumpkin Road, where you turn left and continue 11.4 miles to a sign for Feather Falls. At the sign, turn left and you will reach the trailhead after another 1.5 miles. Bring plenty of water and pack energy-rich snacks to last through this hike. Bug spray is a good idea too if you will be hiking in mosquito season.

Feather Falls at low flow

Upper Frey Creek Falls (u) ★

BEST SEASON: March–June
ELEVATION: 2150 ft
TRAIL LENGTH: 4 miles
USGS QUAD: Brush Creek (ns)
CONTACT: Plumas National Forest; 530-534-6500

On the longer side of the Feather Falls Trail loop, you will see a 25- to 30-foot cascade on Frey Creek. In most seasons, this cascade is no more than a trickle, but in spring and early summer during snowmelt, it can be a rushing appetizer or dessert on the way to or from Feather Falls. Look for it at the bridge over Frey Creek.

Lower Frey Creek Falls (u) ★

BEST SEASON: March–June
ELEVATION: 2000 ft
TRAIL LENGTH: 4 miles
USGS QUAD: Brush Creek (ns)
CONTACT: Plumas National Forest; 530-534-6500

Frey Creek Falls

Like the upper fall on Frey Creek, this 15-foot cascade does not stand on its own as an interesting attraction but more as something nice to look at while hiking to Feather Falls. Look for it on the bridge over Frey Creek on the short side of the Feather Falls Trail.

SEVEN FALLS ★★★★★

BEST SEASON: March–July
ELEVATION: 2700 ft
TRAIL LENGTH: 0.75 mile
USGS QUAD: Cascade (ns)
CONTACT: Plumas National Forest; 530-534-6500

This seven-tiered waterfall is on the South Branch Middle Fork of the Feather River, and although it often

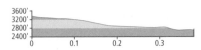

gets overlooked in the hoopla over Feather Falls, it is nearly equal to Feather Falls in beauty and overall impressiveness. Unfortunately, the trail is not maintained and it is extremely difficult to find. Once you locate the trail, the trek involves a scrambling 800-foot descent into a canyon in the span of 0.4 mile. This trip is not for the faint of heart. We strongly encourage anyone planning to hit these falls to consult with a local ranger station prior to the trip.

From Highway 70, take Highway 162/Oroville Dam Boulevard East. Turn right (south) to stay on Highway 162 on what is first Olive Highway and then becomes Forest Service Road 119. Continue to Brush Creek, and then look for the second Bald Rock Road exit and turn (it should have a sign to Milsap Bar Campground). Drive 0.5 mile; turn on Milsap Road (22N62) and go about 8 miles to the campground. Continue 3.5 to 4 miles uphill, and watch for a wide spot in the road. Note that there are multiple wide spots, so it may require some trial and error to find the right one. The trail is only three quarters of a mile, and while you cannot see all seven tiers at once, together they are over 500 feet.

MILSAP BAR FALLS (U) ★★

BEST SEASON: March–July
ELEVATION: 1600 ft
TRAIL LENGTH: 0.25 mile
USGS QUAD: Brush Creek (ns)
CONTACT: Plumas National Forest; 530-534-6500

Milsap Bar Campground has two small waterfalls, one of 15 feet and and one of 20 feet. Both are cascades and make pleasant sights for campers. But the drive to reach Milsap Bar Campground is very slow and the road is not in good shape. Follow the directions to Seven Falls, but instead of continuing, stop at the campground to find the falls.

CURTAIN FALLS ★★★

BEST SEASON: April–August
ELEVATION: 1200 ft
TRAIL LENGTH: 5 miles
USGS QUAD: Brush Creek
CONTACT: Plumas National Forest; 530-534-6500

Curtain Falls is a 40-foot fall on the Feather River. The hike to reach it is strenuous but rewarding, and the waterfall itself even provides some swimming opportunities. 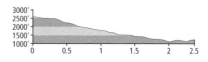 A true waterfall lover could make a memorable weekend trip by hiking to Curtain Falls, Seven Falls, and Feather Falls over three days. To reach the falls, take Highway 162 east from Oroville for 17 miles. At Bald Rock Road, go right for 9 miles to an intersection. Continue straight on Road 21N51Y for 3 miles, then turn left and go a quarter mile farther to the trailhead. Start hiking on the Dome Trail, which leads you down to the river. You will have to scramble upstream and cross the river to get closer to the falls. The trip is not suitable for families with small children.

CHAMBERS CREEK FALLS ★★★★

BEST SEASON: April–June
ELEVATION: 3700 ft
TRAIL LENGTH: 3.5 miles
USGS QUAD: Storrie (ns)
CONTACT: Plumas National Forest; 530-534-6500

Chambers Creek Falls is lovely, falling close to 200 feet in a series of cascades. To reach the trail from Oroville, go north on Highway 70 for 42.5 miles to the trailhead parking area on the right. The trail has nearly 2000 feet of elevation gain along 3 miles, and even more if you decide to ascend the whole trail to the Chambers

Chambers Creek Falls (Photo courtesy of U.S. Forest Service)

Peak summit at 5500 feet (an 8-mile round trip), but the trail is a winding one and inclines gradually. Expect a stream crossing. The hike can be very

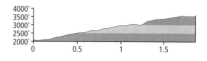

difficult in summer since there is little shade along the trail. In spring, watch for wildflowers—numerous species grow here.

3 SPENCEVILLE WILDLIFE AND RECREATION AREA

This scenic 11,213-acre Wildlife and Recreation Area is located in the Sierra foothills, offering rolling hills, splendid mountain views, and lots of rushing water in the spring.

LOWER FAIRY FALLS ★★

BEST SEASON: December–May
ELEVATION: 590 ft
TRAIL LENGTH: 5 miles
USGS QUAD: Camp Far West (ns)
CONTACT: California Department of Fish and Game; 530-538-2236

The lower fall on Dry Creek is much less impressive than its neighbor, but it offers an appetizer for waterfall seekers hiking the trail through the Spenceville Wildlife and Recreation Area to reach the main falls.

From Highway 20 in Smartville, turn south on Smartville Road near the sign for Beale Air Force Base (AFB). Continue on Smartville Road at the left fork in 0.9 mile, and drive another 3.8 miles to Waldo Road. Turn left on Waldo Road (a gravel road) and continue for 1.8 miles to the Waldo Bridge. Cross the bridge, then head left on Spenceville Road for 2.3 miles. You will reach a pullout parking area near an old bridge. Park here and begin hiking on the dirt trail across the bridge. Follow the main road along Dry Creek about 2.5 miles to the first waterfall, which your ears will detect before your eyes will. You will have to scramble to get a decent view; use caution.

UPPER FAIRY FALLS ★★★

BEST SEASON: December–May
ELEVATION: 590 ft
TRAIL LENGTH: 5 miles
USGS QUAD: Camp Far West
CONTACT: California Department of Fish and Game; 530-538-2236

UpperFairy Falls is actually called Shingle Falls on the topographical maps, but nearly everyone else seems to call it Fairy Falls. It is a 60-foot plunge on Dry Creek in the Spenceville Wildlife and Recreation Area near Marysville in Yuba County. The hike to reach it is a 5-mile round trip suitable for bikes and children, but the trip is best taken in the spring before the summer heat rolls in. From the lower fall, continue another hundred yards to find the larger fall.

4 NORTH TABLE MOUNTAIN ECOLOGICAL PRESERVE

As you approach North Table Mountain, you will understand how it earned its name. Towering almost 1000 feet above the surrounding landscape, this peculiar mountain has very steep sides, which inspires thoughts of the famous mesas of Arizona. The area is mostly undeveloped as of this writing, but plans are in place to create real trails and facilities in the future.

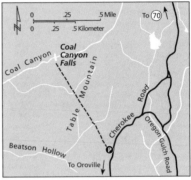

COAL CANYON FALLS ★★★★

BEST SEASON: December–April
ELEVATION: 1300 ft
TRAIL LENGTH: 5 miles
USGS QUAD: Cherokee (ns)
CONTACT: California Department of Fish and Game; 530-538-2222

Coal Canyon Falls (Photo courtesy of Henry Lomeli)

Coal Canyon Falls is a 150-foot drop in Coal Canyon near North Table Mountain. It is popular with locals but not commonly known among visitors. To reach the park, take the Nelson Avenue/Grand Avenue exit off Highway 70 in Oroville. Follow Grand Avenue east to Table Mountain Boulevard and turn north, then east onto Cherokee Road. Follow Cherokee Road for 6 miles to the state parking area on the north end. Be watchful of private property and respect private landowners' rights. Look for State Wildlife Area signs to mark the park boundaries. From the parking area, head northwest for about 2 miles to find the fall. There is no established trail and no reliable landmarks, so asking a local for advice may be advisable on your first trip. If you possess a GPS receiver, go to N39.60386 W121.5529 and continue another 0.5 mile northwest.

5 AUBURN

Auburn State Recreation Area (SRA) sits east of I-80 just northeast of Sacramento. Do not expect solitude—Auburn SRA receives more than half a million visitors each year. The good news is that this 35,000-acre park covers 40 miles of the North and Middle Forks of the American River. Expect to see a lot of whitewater enthusiasts here, as more than thirty whitewater outfitters are licensed to operate on the class II, III, and IV runs in the park. To get here, take Highway 80 to the Highway 49 exit toward Placerville in the town of Auburn and go east. You will reach the park boundaries within a mile.

AMERICAN CANYON FALLS ★★★

BEST SEASON: March–June
ELEVATION: 1750 ft
TRAIL LENGTH: 4 miles
USGS QUAD: Greenwood
CONTACT: Auburn State Recreation Area; 530-885-4527

American Canyon Falls is a 30-foot plunge falling through a thin rock gorge on American Canyon Creek near the Middle Fork of the American River. To reach it, start in the town of Cool near Auburn. From the junction with Highway 49, head 6 miles east on Highway 193 to Pilgrim Court. Turn left, and then continue a short distance to the trailhead. You will reach the waterfall after 2 miles of hiking south on the American Canyon Trail.

KNICKERBOCKER FALLS ★★

BEST SEASON: March–June
ELEVATION: 600 ft
TRAIL LENGTH: 2 miles

USGS QUAD: Pilot Hill (ns)
CONTACT: Auburn State Recreation Area; 530-885-4527

Knickerbocker Falls is a 30- to 40-foot drop into a steep canyon near the American River. The trip to reach it involves a trek on the interestingly named Cardiac Bypass Trail. Start at the Auburn Staging Area, which is off Pacific Avenue (take Auburn-Folsom Road to Pacific Avenue). Hike southwest on the Pioneer Express Trail (part of Cardiac Bypass Trail). The hike is just over a mile and takes about half an hour to get to the falls. There are lots of forks, but there should be signs. We recommend picking up a map as you enter the park. Knickerbocker Falls is actually across the river so you have to view it from afar, but you cannot miss it.

LAKE CLEMENTINE FALLS ★★★

BEST SEASON: year–round
ELEVATION: 700 ft
USGS QUAD: Auburn (ns)
CONTACT: Auburn State Recreation Area; 530-885-4527

Lake Clementine Falls is man-made and consists of a 100-foot plunge over the North Fork Dam. It is quite striking when in full flow and is as interesting as most

Lake Clementine Falls

natural waterfalls. Take Foresthill Road 3.4 miles east from I-80 in Auburn, and then turn left on Lake Clementine Road and go 2.5 miles farther.

PARADISE CANYON FALLS ★★

BEST SEASON: March–June
ELEVATION: 800 ft
USGS QUAD: Greenwood (ns)
CONTACT: Auburn State Recreation Area; 530-885-4527

This is a roughly 100-foot splash into the Middle Fork of the American River. It may not be a mighty or powerful waterfall, but it is worth a look nonetheless. Take Foresthill Road 8 miles east from Auburn, and then turn right on Drivers Flat Road. Follow it about 3.25 miles to the canyon, and do not be fooled by the name. Drivers Flat Road is anything but flat and can be a tough trip for a car without high ground clearance.

CODFISH FALLS ★★★

BEST SEASON: March–August
ELEVATION: 900 ft
TRAIL LENGTH: 3 miles
USGS QUAD: Greenwood
CONTACT: Auburn State Recreation Area; 530-885-4527

Codfish Falls is a 50-foot cascade on Codfish Creek. It is strikingly pretty and involves a relaxing hike along the Codfish Falls Trail and the North Fork of the American River. Take the Weimer/Cross Road exit off I-80 in Weimar. Turn west immediately on Ponderosa Way and follow it for almost 6 miles until you reach a bridge crossing the American River. The road will turn to dirt part of the way along the trip. Park near the bridge at the American River, and then begin hiking downstream on the trail. Follow the river for about 1.25 miles, then turn right to follow Codfish Creek about a quarter mile to find the falls. The round trip is just shy of 3 miles.

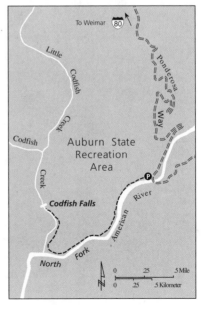

6 COLFAX

Colfax is a genuine railroad town. It was the western end of the transcontinental railroad, making it the Gateway to the High Sierras. It remains a key stop for Amtrak to this day, and the Chamber of Commerce suitably resides in a vintage Southern Pacific railcar just across from the train station. Colfax is located just off I-80 about halfway between Sacramento and Truckee.

DEVILS FALLS ★★★

BEST SEASON: April–June
ELEVATION: 1250 ft
USGS QUAD: Colfax (ns)
CONTACT: Auburn State Recreation Area; 530-885-4527

Devils Falls is an 80- to 100-foot series of drops and cascades from Devils Canyon into Shirttail Creek. The height depends on where you start measuring it. The

Devils Falls at low flow

waterfall is almost despicably easy to reach, sitting right next to the road, but the road can sometimes be tough depending on the time of year. From I-80 in Colfax, take the Colfax/Grass Valley exit and turn immediately west on Canyon Way. Follow it about 2 miles to Yankee Jims Road. Turn left and take the road about 5 miles (crossing the bridge) to the falls, which will be easily visible on your right. To see the entire waterfall, try scrambling down to the base. Only a small portion is visible from your car.

Mexican Gulch Falls ★★

BEST SEASON: April–June
ELEVATION: 1500 ft
USGS QUAD: Colfax (ns)
CONTACT: Auburn State Recreation Area; 530-885-4527

Mexican Gulch Falls is a series of cascades totaling about 40-50 feet, falling from Mexican Gulch into Shirttail Creek. To view it, continue just under a mile past Devils Falls and you will pass right by it.

Indian Creek Falls ★★

BEST SEASON: May–June
ELEVATION: 1100 ft
TRAIL LENGTH: 3 miles
USGS QUAD: Colfax (ns)
CONTACT: Auburn State Recreation Area; 530-885-4527

Indian Creek Falls is a two-tiered drop of 30 to 40 feet on Indian Creek near its intersection with the American River. The hike is about 3 miles round trip and involves a tricky creek crossing; during the waterfall's peak season, the creek often flows too strongly to get safely across. Park at the bridge on Yankee Jims Road, about a half mile before Devils Falls. On the south side of the bridge, find a set of stairs down into the canyon and turn upstream. Cross over Shirttail Creek, if you can, and then follow the trail along the river until you reach Indian Creek after about a mile (it is the fifth creek along the trail). Then, look for a way to scramble upstream to view the falls.

Stevens Creek Falls ★★

BEST SEASON: March–June
ELEVATION: 2200 ft
TRAIL LENGTH: 3 miles

Indian Creek Falls

USGS QUAD: Colfax (ns)
CONTACT: Bureau of Land Management (Folsom); 916-985-4474

Stevens Creek Falls is a very tall series of cascades totaling well over 100 feet, falling on Stevens Creek. Take the Colfax exit off I-80 and turn east at the stop sign for Canyon Way. Find the trailhead parking area after 0.7 mile. It is 1.5 miles of downhill hiking to reach the waterfall, but there are a few intersections to watch out for. At the first intersection, turn right. At the second, continue straight and take the narrow trail on the left. When you reach the waterfall, you will have to scramble to get a full view of the lower cascades, but a spur trail will take you to the upper cascade.

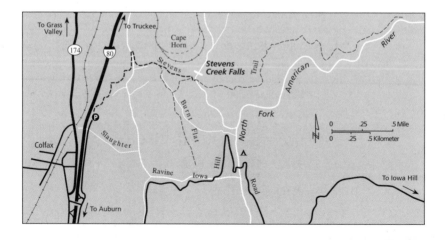

7 NEVADA CITY

Fire was a constant threat to early Nevada City, burning large parts of the town on several occasions. With this in mind, look for something of a Darwinian evolution in the prevalence of brick buildings with metal shutters among the older houses in town. Fortunately, this goes well with the 1800s-style streetlights and other heritage restoration efforts, creating a genuinely pleasant atmosphere for a lunch break on the way to the many waterfalls in the region. To get to Nevada City, take I-80 to the Highway 49 exit in Auburn. Go north, toward Grass Valley, for 27 miles until you reach town.

HUMBUG CREEK FALLS ★★

BEST SEASON: March–June
ELEVATION: 2200 ft
TRAIL LENGTH: 3 miles
USGS QUAD: North Bloomfield (ns)
CONTACT: Malakoff Diggins State Historic Park; 530-265-2740

Humbug Creek Falls is an interesting 40-foot fall on Humbug Creek near Malakoff Diggins State Historic Park. It is best viewed in spring and involves an approximately 1.5-mile hike from the trailhead on North Bloomfield Road. To access the waterfall, turn onto Highway 49 toward Downieville from the intersection with Highway 20 in Nevada City. After a quarter mile, head north on North Bloomfield Road and take it for 13 miles to the park (part of the way will be dirt road). The Humbug Creek Trailhead will be on the right side of the road. Interested hikers should continue along the trail after passing the fall for some very lovely views.

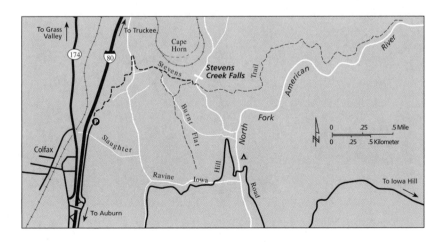

RUSH CREEK FALLS ★★

BEST SEASON: April–June
ELEVATION: 1100 ft
TRAIL LENGTH: 2 miles
USGS QUAD: Nevada City (ns)
CONTACT: South Yuba River State
Park; 530-432-2546

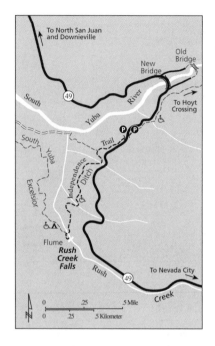

Rush Creek Falls is a series of three
cascades totaling about 50 to 60 feet.
The trail is very easy and flat, making it accessible even to wheelchairs.
The Independence Trail is the first
wheelchair-accessible wilderness trail
in the country that offers folks with
physical disabilities a way to enjoy the
wilderness without pavement. The
trail is best hiked in spring, since it will
still be green and not too hot—not to
mention the waterfall will most likely be flowing at its peak. It tends to dry to a
mere trickle by summer.

To reach the trailhead, head north on Highway 49 from Nevada City. After
8 miles, look for a parking area near the bridge for the South Yuba Independence

Yuba River Falls

Trail. Head to the right on the trail to reach the falls; it will be an easy 2-mile round trip. Unfortunately, you can catch only a glimpse of the upper falls from the trail; to view the entire waterfall, take the wheelchair-accessible wooden walkway to the base of the falls.

YUBA RIVER FALLS ★★

BEST SEASON: April–August
ELEVATION: 1950 ft
TRAIL LENGTH: 1 mile
USGS QUAD: Nevada City (ns)
CONTACT: South Yuba River State Park; 530-432-2546

Yuba River Falls is a 20-foot plunge on the South Yuba River near its intersection with Spring Creek. It is a very pleasant and easy 1-mile round-trip hike. Take Highway 49 north from Nevada City to North Bloomfield Road (the first traffic light, which you will reach after about a half mile). Turn right and follow North Bloomfield Road to Edwards Crossing Bridge. Cross the bridge and pick up the trail downstream.

8 SUTTER BUTTES

This peculiar mountain range forms a circle about 10 miles in diameter, with peaks reaching well over 2000 feet above the sea. Experts believe this is the top of a huge volcano that has lain dormant for over a million years. All of the area is privately owned but guided tours are available. Access is limited to tours only, so it is imperative to call the property owners in advance to check availability and book a tour. To get here, take the Williams exit off I-5 and head east on Highway 20 toward Colusa. After 9.5 miles, turn left on Bridge Street and then, after crossing the bridge, turn right to head east on Butte Slough Road and continue 6 miles. Turn left on Pass Road and go 2.5 miles, then turn left on West Butte Road.

THE FALLS ★★★

BEST SEASON: January–March
ELEVATION: 530 ft
TRAIL LENGTH: Up to 7 miles
USGS QUAD: Sutter Buttes
CONTACT: Sutter Buttes Tours; 530-696-2646

The Falls is a series of cascades falling in Braggs Canyon. The total height is about 80 feet, with most of the waterfall being 3 to 4 feet wide. The waterfall is on private property, and the only way to access it is by taking one of the tours operated by the property owners. The tours cover about 7 miles total hiking distance, but the waterfall is early on in the tour and is very easily accessible. A portion of tour fees goes to a Catholic school in Colusa. Call well in advance to make an appointment. The waterfall is best in the winter after rains.

The Falls at Sutter Buttes (Photo courtesy of Sonja Steidlmayer, Sutter Buttes Tours)

LAKE TAHOE REGION

Lake Tahoe, America's largest alpine lake, has an unreal shade of blue that distinguishes it among Sierra Nevada lakes. Then there's the depth—it's the third deepest lake in America and the tenth deepest in the world.

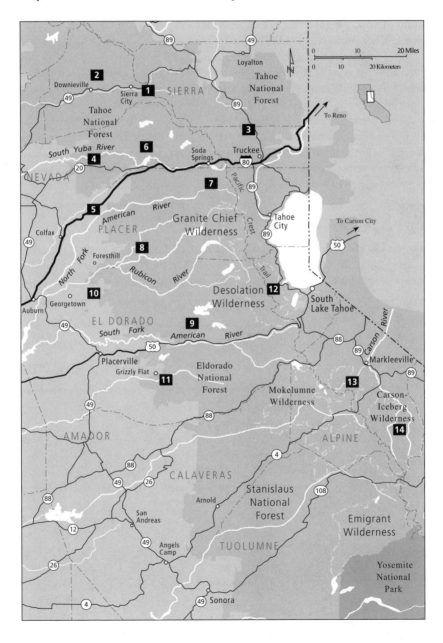

Another quirk of Lake Tahoe is that it straddles the California-Nevada border. One third of the lake is in Nevada, and the town of South Lake Tahoe has a neat but obvious dividing line running straight through it. You recognize it by the many casinos mushrooming up within a few feet on the Nevada side of the border.

The surrounding towns and communities date back to the gold rush and lumber days. In many cases, they have pasts as colorful as Lake Tahoe is blue. Placerville's official name used to be Hangtown for the local brand of swift justice in days of yore. The infamous Hangman's Tree, a mighty oak that has since been cut down, was notorious enough to earn an official State Landmark designation.

Other towns, like Gold Run, earned fame by the fabulous amounts of wealth produced during the rush days. Downieville deserves a special mention, as it was once a strong contender for the seat as state capital, despite the somewhat isolated location. As is the case elsewhere in the Sierras, the Tahoe region gets a lot of snow in the winter. This means plenty of water to feed the waterfalls, but spring and early summer trips can be problematic. Be sure to check the weather forecast before embarking on a trip here, and always bring warm clothes and snow chains since bad weather can blow in at any time. Local ranger stations can answer questions about the accessibility of specific trails.

---

1 SIERRA CITY

History buffs know that fire played a key role in wiping out some otherwise prospering gold rush towns. Sierra City evaded this fate, only to be almost completely destroyed by another force of nature—a spring avalanche. This catastrophic event

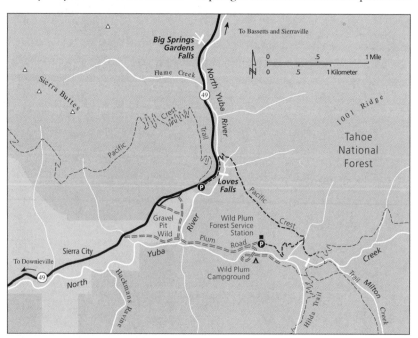

took place in 1853, effectively shutting down the gold mining business for years until a bunch of adventurous souls with a taste for gold braved Mother Nature again by setting up another settlement in 1858. Those interested in this part of California history will enjoy the many historic mines, buildings, and constructions that still stand today.

To find this semi-isolated community, take I-80 to the Highway 49 exit northeast of Sacramento and drive until you reach town. If you come from the east, go to the town of Truckee and turn north on Highway 89. Soon Highway 49 joins Highway 89—keep going until they split and follow Highway 49 west until you reach town. From the north, take I-5 to Red Bluff and turn south on Highway 99. Keep going as it becomes Highway 149 and Highway 70. Turn east on Highway 20 in the town of Marysville and follow it until you pick up Highway 49 North.

LOVES FALLS ★★★

BEST SEASON: May–July
ELEVATION: 4550 ft
TRAIL LENGTH: 0.5 mile
USGS QUAD: Haypress Valley
CONTACT: Tahoe National Forest; 530-288-3231

Loves Falls, sometimes spelled Love's Falls, is actually a series of drops on the North Yuba River. Most carry the characteristic block shape of river waterfalls. Loves Falls has a strong flow in its peak seasons and is popular with whitewater kayakers. It makes a pleasant hike, as well, with a short and a long way to reach it.

For a short and quick view, take Highway 49 west from its intersection with Highway 89. The falls are near the highway between the town of Bassetts and Sierra City; look for them about a mile and a half before Sierra City. Park in a

Loves Falls

pullout near a Pacific Crest Trail sign; it is about a quarter mile to the falls from here. You should be able to hear it on the south side of the highway. If you desire a longer hike, start from the Wild Plum Campground about a half mile past Sierra City and find the trailhead off Wild Plum Road.

BIG SPRINGS GARDEN FALLS ★★★

BEST SEASON: April–July
ELEVATION: 5000 ft
USGS QUAD: Haypress Valley (nl)
CONTACT: Big Springs Garden; 530-862-1333

This waterfall is easy to miss despite being along Highway 49 on the way to or from the Loves Falls pullout. Look for a large pullout area on the north side of the road about 3 miles east of Sierra City. There you will find a wide waterfall originating from Big Springs. Its outlet creek cascades down about 100 feet total, although not in a continuous drop, eventually meeting the North Yuba River. The part visible from Highway 49 is only 15 to 20 feet. The rest can be viewed from the garden, but the garden is privately owned and requires an entrance fee, so call the number above for more information.

Big Springs Garden Falls from Highway 49

2 DOWNIEVILLE

Take a good look around as you enter Downieville. Now imagine the State Capitol building looming tall on Main Street. An impossible thought? Hardly. Downieville was once in the running for the state capital seat, back in the heady gold rush days when the town was bustling with over 5000 people and a seemingly endless stream of gold was pouring out of the hillsides. As it turned out, Sacramento beat Downieville to the punch, but it makes an interesting "what if" topic to discuss if you decide to stop for lunch on your way through.

For those interested in the less happy aspects of gold rush history, Downieville was one of the few places in the west—possibly the only one in California—where a woman was tried and executed for her crimes. The gallows, not used since 1885, still stand outside the courthouse.

To get here, take I-80 to the Highway 49 exit northeast of Sacramento and drive until you reach town. From the north, take I-5 to Red Bluff and turn south on Highway 99. Keep going as it becomes Highway 149 and Highway 70. Turn east on Highway 20 in the town of Marysville and follow it until you pick up Highway 49 heading north.

PAULEY CREEK FALLS ★★★

BEST SEASON: March–June
ELEVATION: 3000 ft
TRAIL LENGTH: 0.5 mile
USGS QUAD: Downieville (ns)
CONTACT: Tahoe National Forest; 530-288-3231

Pauley Creek Falls is a common attraction for residents of Downieville, falling about 20 feet on Pauley Creek. It is technically on private property, according to the Forest Service, but it is open to public usage at the time of this writing. Should this change and No Trespassing signs appear, respect the property owner's rights. To get there, park at the PG&E maintenance station off Main Street and walk south along the fence for a couple hundred feet.

3 SIERRAVILLE

Sierraville is a rustic gold rush town tucked away at the south edge of Sierra Valley, the largest alpine valley in the continental United States. While mostly known for its hot springs, Sierraville has plenty more water to offer—there are more than 130 lakes within a 25-mile radius of town.

The quickest way to get here is to take I-80 to Truckee, turn north on Highway 89 and go until you reach town at the junction of Highway 49 and Highway 89. From the north, take I-5 to Red Bluff, turn east on Highway 36 and continue to the

Webber Falls at low flow

Highway 89 junction. Turn on Highway 89 south and go until you reach town.

WEBBER FALLS ★★★★

BEST SEASON: May–August
ELEVATION: 6700 ft
USGS QUAD: Webber Peak (nl)
CONTACT: Tahoe National Forest; 530-994-3401

Webber Falls is a 60- to 80-foot tiered drop on the Little Truckee River. The land is owned by Louisiana Pacific Lumber Company, but the company allows the public to access the waterfall. Camping and building fires are forbidden. Take Highway 89 north from Truckee or south from Sierraville to Road 07 (Jackson Meadows Road), where you should see a sign for Independence and Webber Lakes. Turn west and go about 7 miles (past a turnoff on the right for Lake of the Woods). You will see a very rough dirt road on the left. Turn on this road and follow it to a junction, then turn left again to reach a parking lot for the waterfall.

4 WASHINGTON

Even though the business ended well over a hundred years ago, the tiny town of Washington still shows the scars of hydraulic mining. It may be tempting to take a closer look at the old shafts and perhaps even venture in for a look at the miner's life of days past. Resist the urge—these old shafts are unsafe and should not be entered under any circumstances. The easiest way to get here is to take I-80 northeast of Sacramento to the Highway 20 exit by Lake Spaulding. Go west on Highway 20 until you turn north on Washington Road and continue the last few miles to town. Another option is to take I-5 to the town of Williams and turn on Highway 20 east; then go straight until you reach Washington Road, where you turn north.

KILLER FANG FALLS★★

BEST SEASON: March–July
ELEVATION: 3200 ft
TRAIL LENGTH: 1 mile
USGS QUAD: Blue Canyon (ns)
CONTACT: Tahoe National Forest; 530-265-4531

Killer Fang Falls is a 15-foot plunge on the South Yuba River, so named by kayakers. It is difficult to reach, but it is a great destination for those who like to swim. From the town of Washington, take Washington Road over the South Yuba River Bridge. Turn right onto Maybert Road and follow it as far as your car will allow you. Maybert Road is best navigated by those with an off-road vehicle. If you make it to the end of the road 5.5 miles from the turnoff, it is a half-mile hike along the river to reach the falls.

5 GOLD RUN

How Gold Run earned its name is fairly obvious. In fact, the town earned an official State Landmark designation (#405) for its highly efficient hydraulic mines. Between 1865 and 1878, Gold Run's mines shipped a whopping $6,125,000 in gold. While this may seem like a modest monthly salary for a modern-day CEO, it was a truly mind-boggling number at the time. Hydraulic mining was outlawed in 1882, effectively putting an end to Gold Run's streak of fortune, but the upside is that the ban helped preserve the natural beauty of the area for the benefit of generations of hikers and outdoor enthusiasts since. Gold Run is located just off I-80, right between Sacramento and Truckee.

SOUTH FORK DEER CREEK FALLS ★★★

BEST SEASON: April–June
ELEVATION: 3500 ft
USGS QUAD: Washington (nl)
CONTACT: Tahoe National Forest; 530-587-3558

South Fork Deer Creek Falls is a nice waterfall, but a little remote for most waterfall seekers. It is about 60 feet high and falls on South Fork Deer Creek a short drive away from Nevada City. The road to reach it is a little rough, but is probably navigable by most cars. Take the Broad Street exit off Highway 20 in Nevada City, and turn right on Boulder Street at the stop sign, and then after another 0.5 mile, turn right again onto Red Dog Road. Follow that road about 4 miles to Banner Quaker Hill Road, and then turn left. Turn right at a stop sign in 0.5 mile to stay on Banner Quaker Hill Road. Go just over 6 miles to a junction and continue straight on Powerhouse Road. Look for the waterfall after 0.75 mile. It can be difficult to view from the road, so consider making the drive with your window rolled down and listen for it. The fall is probably on private property, according to the Forest Service, so please view from the road only.

6 EMIGRANT GAP

Emigrant Gap is a tiny community right off I-80 between Sacramento and Truckee, about two-thirds of the way from Sacramento. Once you leave the highway, it won't take more than five minutes until pristine forests and rugged mountains surround you.

BEAR RIVER FALLS ★★

BEST SEASON: April–June
ELEVATION: 4600 ft
TRAIL LENGTH: 0.75 mile
USGS QUAD: Blue Canyon (ns)
CONTACT: Pacific Gas & Electric; 916-386-5164

Bear River Falls

Bear River Falls is a 12-foot plunge on the Bear River in a recreation area maintained by PG&E. The trail is a short and easy loop hike of about 0.75 mile, accessible to wheelchairs with assistance. It is also possible to bypass most of the loop to view the waterfall as a hit and run, but the trail is short enough that it is worth taking the full loop even if you are busy. Take Highway 20 west from its intersection with I-80 for 4.25 miles to Bowman Lake Road. Turn right, and drive just over a half mile to the parking lot for the Sierra Discovery Trail. For the loop, head right on the trail. For a quick shortcut to the waterfall, take the trail to the left.

BOWMAN LAKE FALLS (U)★★★

BEST SEASON: June–August
ELEVATION: 5700 ft
TRAIL LENGTH: 0.75 mile
USGS QUAD: Graniteville (ns)
CONTACT: Tahoe National Forest; 530-288-3231

Bowman Lake Falls is another waterfall with many names. Some call it Sawmill Falls, and still others call it Canyon Creek Falls since it falls on Canyon Creek. The total cascade is 70 to 80 feet in length, and it involves a short but tricky hike that includes crossing Jackson Creek. Follow the same directions as Bear River Falls, but after turning on Bowman Lake Road, continue for 15 miles to reach the lake. The last portion will be rough, dirt road. Upon reaching

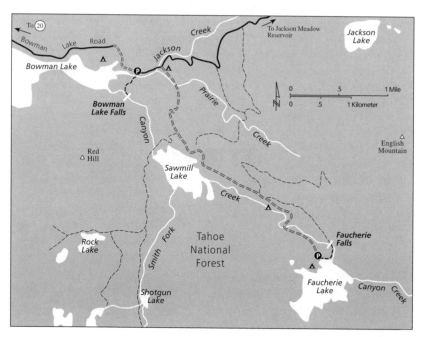

the lake, follow another rough, dirt road to the east for 3 miles to the Jackson Creek crossing. Watch along the way for a far-off glimpse of the fall. To get to the base, carefully cross over Jackson Creek by foot and hike south on a faded trail, following the sound of the fall.

FAUCHERIE LAKE FALLS (U)★★★

BEST SEASON: June–August
ELEVATION: 6100 ft
TRAIL LENGTH: 0.5 mile
USGS QUAD: English Mountain (ns)
CONTACT: Tahoe National Forest; 530-288-3231

The waterfall at Faucherie Lake is a wide downpour of about 25-30 feet, falling from Canyon Creek into the lake. The hike is short and easy, but the trip to reach the trail is slow and rough. Follow the directions to Bowman Lake, and at the end of Bowman Lake Road where it meets the lake, continue following the dirt road 3.5 miles until it meets a junction. Turn right at the junction and drive another 3.5 miles to Faucherie Lake. Walk toward Canyon Creek's junction with the lake to view the fall.

---

7 SODA SPRINGS

Skiing and snowboarding are huge in Soda Springs, and for good reason. The area is blessed with generous amounts of powder most winters, providing a great environment for the ski resorts. That is good news for waterfall enthusiasts too, as lots of winter snow equals lots of melt water in the spring.

Getting here is easy—take I-80 almost all the way to Truckee, exiting at Soda Springs/Norden. Go south on Donner Pass/Soda Springs Road until you reach Soda Springs.

HEATH FALLS ★★★

BEST SEASON: May–June
ELEVATION: 4900 ft
TRAIL LENGTH: 10 miles
USGS QUAD: Royal Gorge (ns)
CONTACT: Tahoe National Forest; 530-587-3558

Heath Falls is a tall, impressive drop on the North Fork of the American River. Unfortunately, the fall itself sits on private property, so it is only possible to get

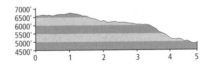

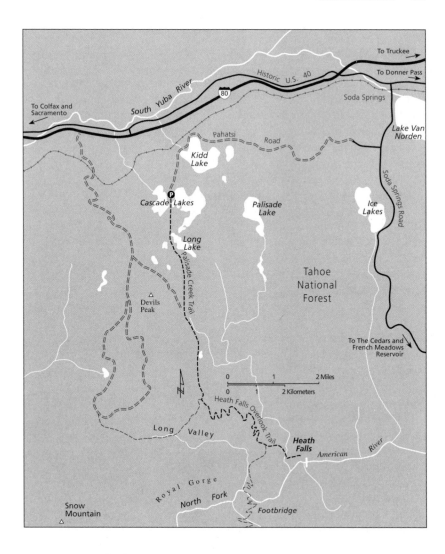

a distant view of it from the Heath Falls Overlook Trail that branches off from the Palisade Creek Trail, making a 10-mile round-trip hike that is all downhill on the way there and uphill on the way back.

From I-80, take the Soda Springs/Norden exit in the town of Kingvale and pick up Old Highway 40 heading east. Follow it 0.8 mile to Soda Springs Road and turn south, crossing I-80. Turn right on Pahatsi Road after almost a mile, and then follow that road 4.3 miles as it turns to a dirt road and becomes Kidd Lake Road. The road passes Kidd Lake and ends at Cascade Lakes. Park at Cascade Lakes and look for the trailhead for the Palisade Creek Trail. Hike south for 4.5 miles. About a quarter mile after crossing the Palisade Creek Bridge, look for the Heath Falls Overlook Trail branching off to the east. From there, it is another 0.5 mile to the overlook for the falls.

8 FORESTHILL

Foresthill is nice, but the rough 17-mile drive to town used to be a ding against going there for day hikes. Fortunately, that is no longer the case as the road was improved in the 1990s. To get here, take I-80 past Sacramento and exit on Auburn Ravine Road. Continue east through Auburn State Recreation Area on Foresthill Road until you reach town.

GROUSE FALLS ★★★★★

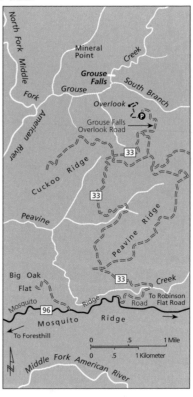

BEST SEASON: April–June
ELEVATION: 4000 ft
TRAIL LENGTH: 1 mile
USGS QUAD: Michigan Bluff (nl)
CONTACT: Tahoe National Forest; 530-367-2224

Grouse Falls is one of the tallest California waterfalls outside of Yosemite. It is 700 feet tall, falling on Grouse Creek in a picturesque area of Tahoe National Forest. The hike to reach the viewpoint is relatively easy, only a mile round trip, but the drive takes you a bit away from civilization. From Foresthill, take Mosquito Ridge Road (also called Forest Road 96) for 19 miles to Forest Road 33 (which may not be signed) and turn left. Continue 5 miles to a sign for the Grouse Falls Overlook and turn left again. The parking area is 0.5 mile from the overlook, which is at the end of the trail identified by a wooden observation deck. Forest Road 33 is often closed for snow well into April, so it is wise to call the ranger station to check the road status before making the trip here.

9 POLLOCK PINES

Pollock Pines may seem secluded today, but it sits right on the Wagon Trail and the Mormon Emigrant Trail along a key passage into California. In addition, the legendary Pony Express service had its only overnight stop here, allowing riders

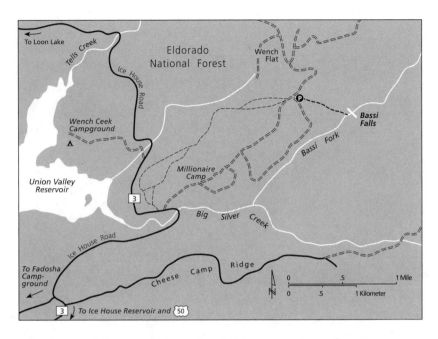

to catch some well-deserved sleep after pitching in to get letters from Sacramento to New York City in a mere nine days—quite a feat in the days before paved roads and motorized vehicles. The town has gone to great lengths to preserve this heritage. Be sure to catch the annual historical reenactments if you have an interest in California history. The scenic drive starts in Sacramento, where you take Highway 50 east toward Placerville/Fresno. Continue for about 53 miles until you reach town.

BASSI FALLS ★★★★★

BEST SEASON: April–June
ELEVATION: 5500 ft
TRAIL LENGTH: 1 mile
USGS QUAD: Loon Lake
CONTACT: Eldorado National Forest; 916-644-2349

Bassi Falls is a magnificent 150-foot drop on Bassi Creek near the Union Valley Reservoir. The hike is reasonably easy and suitable even for children. From Placerville, head east on Highway 50 for about 20 miles. Watch for a sign for the Crystal Basin Recreation Area, and then turn left on Ice House Road after crossing a bridge. Follow Ice House Road for 16.5 miles to the Union Valley Reservoir, and then watch for a dirt road across from the parking area for Big Silver Campground. Turn right on this road and follow it 0.2 mile. Upon reaching the forest gate, turn left on Forest Road 12N32A. Follow this road about 1.2 miles to

Bassi Falls

a small parking area. Fallen logs may occasionally block the road and force you to take a longer hike. When you reach the parking area, find the trail and follow your ears to the fall.

Bridal Veil Falls ★★

BEST SEASON: April–June
ELEVATION: 3400 ft
USGS QUAD: Riverton (ns)
CONTACT: Eldorado National Forest; 530-644-2324

Do not confuse Bridal Veil Falls with the famous Bridalveil Falls of Yosemite National Park. The two are not quite in the same league. Still, for springtime visitors to the Lake Tahoe area, this is a pleasant drive-by waterfall. Watch for a sign when heading east on Highway 50, about 5.5 miles past Pollock Pines. The fall is about 150 feet tall, falling on Esmerelda Creek.

Bridal Veil Falls

SLY PARK FALLS ★★★

BEST SEASON: December–June
ELEVATION: 3500 ft
TRAIL LENGTH: 2 miles
USGS QUAD: Sly Park (ns)
CONTACT: El Dorado Irrigation District; 530-622-4513

Sly Park Falls is a roughly 50-foot plunge off a partially man-made diversion on Camp Creek near Jenkinson Lake. To get here, take Sly Park Road east of Jenkinson Reservoir almost all the way down to Mormon Trail Road and enter Sly Park Recreation Area on the left. Turn in and go to the back of the park to Hazel Creek, where there is a parking lot. The trailhead is right there, and it should have a big sign making it easy to see. Cross the first bridge, go right, and turn east (left) just before the second bridge. From here, there are only a few hundred feet to the fall. It is very noisy so you will hear it. The hike from the parking lot to the fall is about a mile one-way.

10 PLACERVILLE

Like many other Gold Rush towns, Placerville had its fair share of rowdy and eccentric characters in the wilder days of yore. But it seems Placerville dealt with the issue in true Clint Eastwood style, which explains the town's original, more colorful name: Hangtown. The original Hangman's Tree that was put into service in 1849 has been cut down, but its notoriety earned it an official State Landmark designation (#141). A bar called Hangman's Tree Bar has been built over the stump. Finding it is easy—just drive down Main Street and watch for the building with a life-size mannequin dangling from a noose out front. It is not advisable to pick a fight with the bartender. To get to Placerville, take Highway 50 east from Sacramento and go straight for 42 miles until you reach town.

PILOT CREEK FALLS ★★

BEST SEASON: April–August
ELEVATION: 3500 ft
TRAIL LENGTH: 6 miles
USGS QUAD: Tunnel Hill (ns)
CONTACT: Eldorado National Forest; 530-333-4312

Pilot Creek Falls is also called University Falls. It is a 70-foot series of cascades on Pilot Creek near Quintette and Georgetown. Take I-80 to the Highway 49 exit in Auburn and pass through the Auburn State Recreation Area (SRA). As you exit Auburn SRA on Highway 49, turn left onto Highway 193 near the town of Cool. Stay on Highway 193 to the town of Georgetown, where you make a left onto Main Street. After a mile it becomes Wentworth Springs Road. Watch for the gate on your left about 7.5 miles from town. Park away from the gate, as emergency vehicles may need to access it. The trailhead is right near the gate. Stay on the main trail for about 3 miles until you reach the falls. Be careful and avoid climbing down beyond the third fall. There have been serious incidents here. Also, note that you will be crossing private property on your way to the falls. As always, show proper respect and pack out anything you pack in.

---

11 GRIZZLY FLAT

The remote community of Grizzly Flat is not so much a town as a loose cluster of houses scattered about in the pristine pine forest. In other words, those who get uncomfortable being more than five minutes away from a Starbucks will not like this place, but outdoor enthusiasts with a taste for peace and quiet will be overjoyed. As you may guess, this place was named after a particularly large grizzly bear who attacked, and was then killed by, a group of early pioneers. Don't worry about such an encounter today; grizzlies have been extinct in California for a long time.

Grizzly Flat can be accessed by taking Highway 50 east from Sacramento for 32 miles, then take the ramp toward Mother Lode Drive, go a few miles and then hang right onto Pleasant Valley Road when you reach the fork. Drive 8 miles, then turn right on Bucks Bar Road and go 5 miles to Happy Valley Road, where you turn right and continue a short distance to Rooster Lane, where you make another right. Rooster Lane will make a sharp U-shaped curve; keep going until you reach the Grizzly Flat Road junction. Turn left and drive 10 miles.

BUTTERMILK FALLS ★★

BEST SEASON: May–July
ELEVATION: 3800 ft

USGS QUAD: Caldor (ns)
CONTACT: Eldorado National Forest; 530-644-2324

Buttermilk Falls, also called Middle Dry Creek Falls, is a 20-foot plunge at the intersection of Middle Dry Creek and Dogtown Creek. It is visible by car from about the middle of May, but determined off-trail hikers can journey about a third of a mile to the fall's base to get a better view. From Grizzly Flat, take Grizzly Flat Road about 7 miles to Caldor. Look for an intersection that is a junction with another paved road, along with some dirt roads. Make a hard right onto dirt road 9N45. The waterfall is visible from the road 3.5 miles down the road, but you may not spot it at first; if you have not seen it by the time you pass the 4-mile marker, make a U-turn and head back and you will see it.

12 SOUTH LAKE TAHOE

Lake Tahoe has been a popular vacationing spot for well over a hundred years. America's largest alpine lake, Lake Tahoe has an unreal indigo blue color, making it the subject of postcard-perfect vacation pictures with snowcapped mountains in the background. It is not just shallow beauty either. In fact, the lake's depth may surprise you: Tahoe is the third deepest lake in North America and the tenth deepest in the world. The eastern third of the lake is in Nevada, and the border cuts right through the town of South Lake Tahoe; you will know it by the towering casinos appearing literally within a few feet of the borderline.

The shortest way to reach South Lake Tahoe is by taking Highway 50 from Sacramento, but be sure to check traffic reports during tourist season. On Friday afternoons, the congestion sometimes starts hundreds of miles west in the Bay Area, and accidents on these mountain roads can be very disruptive. Some people take I-80 to Truckee and make their way down Highway 89 to avoid the worst jam. Others take the Highway 88 route by way of Stockton. Bottom line: if you must go during rush hours, taking a few minutes to evaluate your options before you leave can save hours of travel time.

HORSETAIL FALLS ★★★★

BEST SEASON: April–August
ELEVATION: 7300 ft
TRAIL LENGTH: 2.5 miles
USGS QUAD: Echo Lake
CONTACT: Eldorado National Forest; 530-647-5437

Horsetail Falls is a spectacular waterfall of around 500 feet falling on Pyramid Creek in the Desolation Wilderness. It is at its most powerful during snowmelt but continues to flow impressively well into summer. The hike is about 2.5 miles round trip and of medium difficulty. Start at the trailhead along Highway 50. Find the parking area in Twin Bridges, 2 miles east of the town of Strawberry, and pay the parking fee. Take the Wilderness Boundary Trail and fill out the wilderness permit at the station (no fee for day use). From here, stick to a trail that follows along the creek and heads toward the waterfall; the trails are not always clearly marked. Upon reaching the cliffs at the base, proceed with extreme caution. Many hikers like to scramble up the rocks to get a better look, but the rocks are slippery and people have been seriously injured or killed here.

CASCADE FALLS ★★★★

BEST SEASON: April–July
ELEVATION: 6800 ft
TRAIL LENGTH: 2 miles
USGS QUAD: Emerald Bay (nl)
CONTACT: Lake Tahoe Basin Management Unit; 530-573-2600

This billowing waterfall has also been Snow Falls or White Cloud. A majestic 200 feet, it pours down Cascade Creek into Cascade Lake. During the season of

Cascade Falls

snowmelt, it is a roaring force of nature not soon forgotten. Unfortunately, the trail does not offer any truly great views of the falls, so you may have to be creative (and careful) to get a good look. Park at the Bayview Campground along Highway 89 about 7.5 miles north of South Lake Tahoe. Start on the Bayview Trail and bear left at the trailhead to the Cascade Falls Trail. The trip is 2 miles there and back.

UPPER EAGLE FALLS ★★★

BEST SEASON: April–July
ELEVATION: 6700 ft
TRAIL LENGTH: 0.5 mile
USGS QUAD: Emerald Bay (ns)
CONTACT: Lake Tahoe Basin Management Unit; 530-573-2600

Upper Eagle Falls is the easiest to reach of the two Eagle Falls. It is a roughly 45-foot cascade on Eagle Creek. To reach it, head north on Highway 89 from South Lake Tahoe for about 8 miles. Park at the Eagle Falls Parking Area, but beware that this area is extremely popular and parking can be difficult. Start hiking on the west side of the highway toward Eagle Lake and you will reach the bridge and a delightful view of the upper fall in about a quarter mile.

Upper Eagle Falls

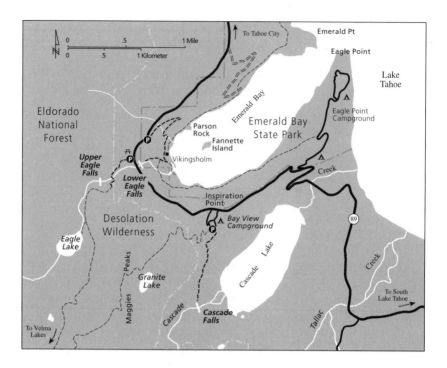

LOWER EAGLE FALLS ★★★★

BEST SEASON: April–July
ELEVATION: 6500 ft
TRAIL LENGTH: 2 miles
USGS QUAD: Emerald Bay
CONTACT: Lake Tahoe Basin Management Unit; 530-573-2600

Lower Eagle Falls is the fall marked as Eagle Falls on the topographic maps. It is a grand 175-foot cascade pouring down a mountainside. You can see it from the highway, but the best view of it requires a 2-mile round-trip hike. Continue about a half mile north of the Eagle Falls Parking Area to the lot for Emerald Bay State Park/Vikingsholm. The trail begins in the parking lot and passes Vikingsholm, which is a fascinating replica of a Scandinavian castle.

UPPER GLEN ALPINE FALLS ★★★

BEST SEASON: April–August
ELEVATION: 6700 ft
TRAIL LENGTH: 1 mile

USGS QUAD: Emerald Bay (nl)
CONTACT: Lake Tahoe Basin Management Unit; 530-573-2600

The hike to reach the upper falls on Glen Alpine Creek is pleasant and easy. Once known as Modjeska Falls, the waterfall is a 30-foot thunderous plunge during snowmelt. From Highway 89 about 2 miles north of South Lake Tahoe, turn left on Fallen Leaf Road. Drive about 5 miles to Road 1216 and turn left. You will pass the lower fall; continue about 0.5 mile farther to a parking area and trailhead.

Lower Eagle Falls from the trail

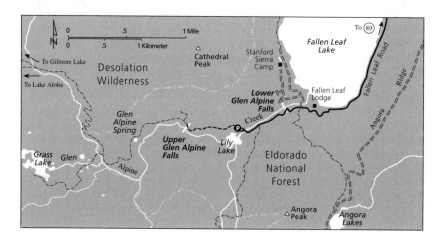

From here a gravel road continues toward the west past a closed gate. It is a short and easy 1-mile round-trip hike. The falls will come into view to the south as you hike toward Glen Alpine Springs.

LOWER GLEN ALPINE FALLS ★★★★

BEST SEASON: May–August
ELEVATION: 6500 ft
USGS QUAD: Emerald Bay (nl)
CONTACT: Lake Tahoe Basin Management Unit; 530-573-2600

The lower fall on Glen Alpine Creek is the more impressive of the two, and it is even accessible by car in the summer. Also known as Fallen Leaf Falls, this is a roughly 80-foot wide cascade that, like the upper fall, is most impressive during snowmelt. It is a popular location for weddings due to its easy access and picturesque scenery. Follow the directions to the upper fall, but instead of continuing to the trailhead, stop to get a closer look as you drive past them. The road may be closed in snowy seasons.

Lower Glen Alpine Falls

13 MARKLEEVILLE

Markleeville is named after an unfortunate entrepreneur, Jacob Marklee, who laid claim to a strategic position along a tributary of the Carson River and built a toll bridge in 1861. With the silver boom in full swing, he figured he would make a nice profit on the travelers and supply wagons going back and forth across the river. It can be speculated that this business idea did not go over well with his intended customers, as records show he was shot shortly thereafter. It appears local authorities did not vigorously pursue the matter either, given that they let the killer walk out the door on a self-defense plea.

You get here by taking Highway 50 from Sacramento toward South Lake Tahoe. Turn south on Highway 89 just before you enter South Lake Tahoe and continue down 12 miles.

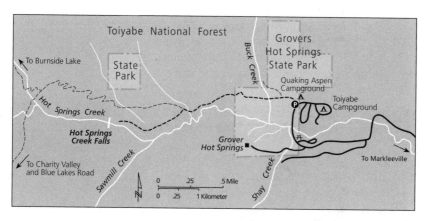

HOT SPRINGS CREEK FALLS ★★★

BEST SEASON: April–July
ELEVATION: 6400 ft
TRAIL LENGTH: 3 miles
USGS QUAD: Markleeville (ns)
CONTACT: Grover Hot Springs State Park; 530-694-2248

Hot Springs Creek Falls is a 50-foot cascade on Hot Springs Creek, which is sometimes called Markleeville Creek. It looks like an exploded waterfall at its highest flow. Large rocks in the middle of the waterfall give it a neat appearance. The hike to reach it is a 3-mile round trip that is fairly level except for the last section, making the trip easy for most hikers.

Turn west on Hot Springs Road from Highway 89 in Markleeville, and go 3.5 miles to the entrance for Grover Hot Springs State Park. The trailhead is just past the campground on the left. It will be marked as the Burnside Lake Trail.

Veer left onto a narrow trail at the first junction. Hike another mile, then turn left. Follow the creek for a while, then continue up over a pile of rocks along the trail, which will lead you to the waterfall.

CAPLES CREEK FALLS ★★

BEST SEASON: June–August
ELEVATION: 7500 ft
TRAIL LENGTH: 1 mile
USGS QUAD: Caples Lake (ns)
CONTACT: Eldorado National Forest; 209-295-4251

The waterfall on Caples Creek is a 15-foot plunge, and the creek cascades in other sections along the trip; it makes a nice side trip for those planning to camp in the area. From the intersection of Highway 88 and 89 north of Markleeville, take Highway 88 west for 15 miles to the sign for Kirkwood Lake, then turn right and continue roughly 0.5 mile to the campground. Look for a trail on the west end of the campground that descends; you will reach the waterfall in about 0.5 mile of downhill hiking.

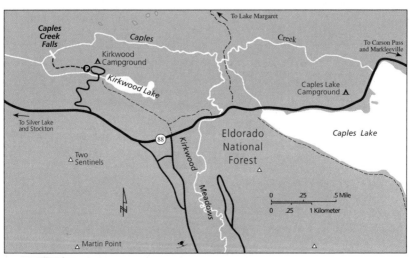

HAWLEY GRADE TRAIL FALLS ★★

BEST SEASON: May–July
ELEVATION: 6500 ft
TRAIL LENGTH: 0.5 mile
USGS QUAD: Echo Lake (ns)
CONTACT: Eldorado National Forest; 209-295-4251

This waterfall is a relatively small 20-foot segmented drop on the Upper Truckee River, but you can reach it with a short, half-mile hike on the Hawley Grade National Recreation Trail. From Meyers, take Upper Truckee Road south about 4 miles to a sign for the trail. Turn right and drive another quarter mile. Upon the trail, look for an offshoot trail heading to the left after less than a quarter mile of hiking. The round trip is only about 0.5 mile.

14 CARSON-ICEBERG WILDERNESS

The Carson-Iceberg Wilderness covers about 160,000 acres within Humboldt-Toiyabe and Stanislaus National Forests. The wilderness borders both Highways 4 and 108 some distance northwest of Yosemite National Park.

LLEWELLYN FALLS ★★

BEST SEASON: June–July
ELEVATION: 8000 ft
TRAIL LENGTH: 12 miles
USGS QUAD: Lost Cannon Peak
CONTACT: Humboldt-Toiyabe National Forest; 775-882-2766

Llewellyn Falls is a nice 20-foot cascade on Silver King Creek. Take Highway 395 to Little Antelope Valley between the towns of Walker and Coleville. Turn west

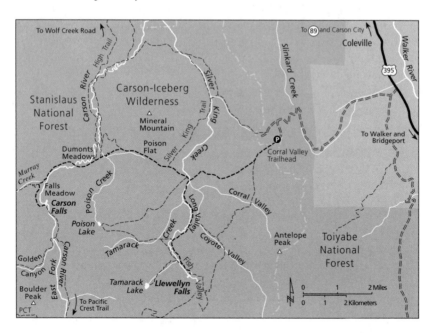

Llewellyn Falls (Photo courtesy of U.S. Fish and Wildlife Service)

on the road signed for Mill Creek/Little Antelope Valley Wildlife Refuge and hang right in the Y-split. Keep going to the Rodriguez Flat pack station at the end of the road. Park and begin hiking on one of the two southbound trailheads (they join up after a few hundred feet). Do not take the larger Snodgrass Trail heading northwest along the creek. Hang right at the first junction after a mile, then left at Silver King Creek 2 miles after that. Follow the creek to the falls. Snow may cover the trail until early June.

CARSON FALLS ★★

BEST SEASON: June–July
ELEVATION: 7000 ft
TRAIL LENGTH: 18 miles
USGS QUAD: Disaster Peak
CONTACT: Humboldt-Toiyabe National Forest; 775-882-2766

For this 50-foot cascade on East Fork Carson River, start with the same directions as for Llewellyn Falls, but at the Silver King Creek junction continue straight for about 5 miles, then turn south and follow the East Fork Carson River to the falls. Carson Falls is between Murray Creek and Golden Canyon Creek. The trek is about 9 miles each way.

YOSEMITE REGION

The Yosemite region is a must-see destination for any resident of or visitor to California. American natives are believed to have lived in Yosemite for over 8000 years, leaving a rich cultural heritage to go with the breathtaking waterfalls, giant

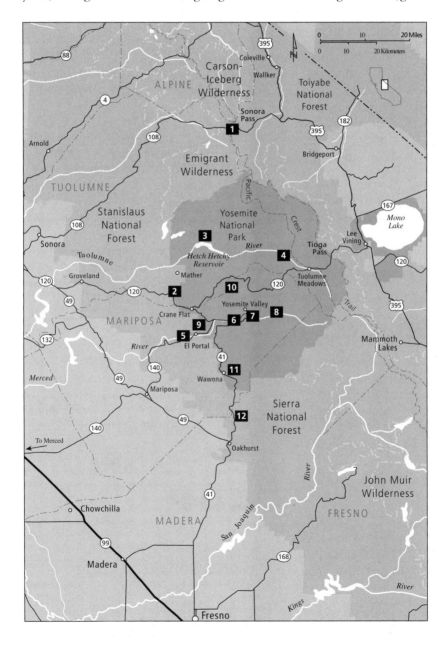

sequoias, unique rock formations, and nearly 2000 varieties of plants and animals. It is no mystery why Yosemite National Park is one of the most popular parks in the nation with three to four million visitors annually.

Fur trappers first discovered the Yosemite Valley in 1833, but it was not until twenty years later that the California gold rush brought westerners farther into the area. After some unfortunate attempts at agriculture, President Abraham Lincoln protected the area from further damage in 1864. This was the first time in United States history that the government enacted this sort of land protection. In 1980 the park became an officially designated national park.

Areas of Yosemite have been forever immortalized in the black and white photography of Ansel Adams and the writings of John Muir. The park's attractions—with majestic sounding names like El Capitan and Glacier Point—are easily some of the most memorable sights found anywhere. Yosemite's waterfalls are one of its major high points—literally. Yosemite Falls, with a total combined drop of 2425 feet, is the fifth tallest waterfall in the world and the tallest in North America. Several other falls follow behind, such as Snow Creek Falls—with a drop greater than 2000 feet. You will also find Ribbon Falls, another famous free fall with a 1612 feet drop. If you prefer raw power to height in waterfalls, hike up the relatively short but challenging Mist Trail for spectacular views of Vernal Falls and Nevada Falls.

While Yosemite National Park's most famous waterfalls reside in Yosemite Valley, many others in the region hold their own as attractions. Wapama and Tueeulala Falls, north of the tourist hustle, offer an interesting hike alongside the Hetch Hetchy Reservoir. If you are not up for a hike, take a road trip through Yosemite Valley or up to Sonora Pass for a number of nice and easily accessible waterfalls. For information on all falls within the Yosemite National Park boundaries, call 209-372-0200.

1 SONORA PASS

Winding through the mountains north of Yosemite, Sonora Pass on Highway 108 has the steepest percentage grade of any passage in California. However, if you make the trip, you will find stunning scenery all around you, including the famous Column of the Giants, a geological wonder with 2 miles of basalt columns on either side of the road. You will also find several waterfalls that you can reach with surprisingly little effort.

LEAVITT FALLS ★★★

BEST SEASON: June–August
ELEVATION: 7800 ft
USGS QUAD: Pickel Meadow (nl)
CONTACT: Humboldt-Toiyabe National Forest; 760-932-7070

Leavitt Falls sits along Highway 108 just shy of 9 miles west of the intersection with Highway 395. At 400 feet, the waterfall is well worth the trip, offering a neat view from the overlook (although trees block the lower portion and its cascades). Bring your binoculars. A trail to the falls originates in the Leavitt Meadows Campground, and a signed turnoff indicates the falls' overlook.

CASCADE FALLS ★★

BEST SEASON: June–October
ELEVATION: 8300 ft
TRAIL LENGTH: 13 miles
USGS QUAD: Tower Peak
CONTACT: Humboldt-Toiyabe National Forest; 760-932-7070

Cascade Falls is a 10-foot cascade on Cascade Creek near the West Walker River. The trip to reach it is a moderate hike of about 6.5 miles each way. The 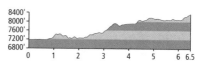 trailhead is in Leavitt Meadows Campground right off Highway 108 (Sonora Pass). Follow the signs to the trailhead in the north part of the camp, then head south along the river, going right at the fork near the end to follow Cascade Creek to the falls. Expect some stream crossings, which may be more difficult after snowy winters.

SARDINE FALLS ★★★★

BEST SEASON: June–August
ELEVATION: 9200 ft
TRAIL LENGTH: 2 miles
USGS QUAD: Pickel Meadow
CONTACT: Humboldt-Toiyabe National Forest; 760-932-7070

Hit Sardine Falls in the right season and you will see a breathtaking rush of multiple water streams cascading down a roughly 70-foot drop on McKay Creek. Visit shortly after snowmelt to view the falls at its most powerful. But unlike some others in the area, this waterfall is still worth a visit even in the summer. Drive 12.4 miles from the intersection of Highway 108 and Highway 395 to Sardine Meadow. You will be able to see the waterfall from the road, and this view may be sufficient with good binoculars. You can also walk across the meadow to get a closer look, making a 2-mile round trip that involves a few stream crossings.

SARDINE CREEK FALLS ★★

BEST SEASON: May–July
ELEVATION: 9700 ft

USGS QUAD: Pickel Meadow (nl)
CONTACT: Humboldt-Toiyabe National Forest; 760-932-7070

Sardine Creek Falls is sometimes called Sonora Pass Falls. It has a relatively short viewing season, but at the right time you can see it from the road. At the junction of Highway 108 and 395, drive 2.3 miles west on Highway 108 from Sardine Meadow to reach the Sonora Pass Summit. You can take a short trail down to the base of the fall if you so desire. It falls about 40 feet on Sardine Creek.

BLUE CANYON FALLS ★★

BEST SEASON: June–August
ELEVATION: 8800 ft
USGS QUAD: Sonora Pass
CONTACT: Stanislaus National Forest; 209-965-3434

From the intersection of Highways 108 and 395, drive just shy of 3 miles past the Sonora Pass summit and park beside the road. There, you will see this pretty, relatively unknown waterfall that drops about 25 feet from Blue Canyon Creek.

DEADMAN CREEK FALLS ★★

BEST SEASON: June–August
ELEVATION: 8400 ft
USGS QUAD: Sonora Pass (nl)
CONTACT: Stanislaus National Forest; 209-965-3434

Deadman Creek Falls is another small waterfall of a mere 30 feet. Its best season is early spring just after snowmelt, when you can see it shooting out from a rushing creek. As the summer progresses, it gets weaker and changes form to a segmented fall. Watch carefully for the fall, taking Highway 108 roughly 5 miles west of the Sonora Pass summit.

KENNEDY MEADOW FALLS (U) ★★★★

BEST SEASON: April–June
ELEVATION: 6300 ft
TRAIL LENGTH: 2 miles
USGS QUAD: Sonora Pass (ns)
CONTACT: Stanislaus National Forest; 209-965-3434

Deadman Creek Falls (Photo courtesy of Rick Nieves of San Jose, CA)

Kennedy Meadow Falls is a huge, seasonal cascade near Kennedy Meadow Resort off Sonora Pass. It is important to hit this one at peak snowmelt for the best effect; the waterfall quickly loses its power after the height of the season. If you time it just right, it is breathtaking. As an interesting bit of trivia, the bridge from which you view the fall appeared in the 1943 movie *For Whom the Bell Tolls* with Gary Cooper and Ingrid Bergman, based on Ernest Hemingway's classic.

Take Highway 108 to Pinecrest and continue 26 to 27 miles to Kennedy Meadow Resort. Turn in and go down 0.5 mile, then park in the public parking area before the resort. Walk through the resort and pick up the Huckleberry Trail. It is about a 1-mile hike to the second bridge, which is where you will catch the most majestic view. The first part of the hike is very easy, but the last bit up to the second bridge is steep. Respect the privacy of the resort.

NIAGARA CREEK FALLS ★★★

BEST SEASON: April–June
ELEVATION: 5200 ft
TRAIL LENGTH: 0.5 mile
USGS QUAD: Donnell Lake (ns)
CONTACT: Stanislaus National Forest; 209-965-3434

As far as fame, California's Niagara Creek Falls holds no candle to the Niagara Falls in New York. Yet, this nearly 1000-foot drop on Niagara Creek is easy to reach and well worth a visit. The fall is the highest in Sierra National Forest and falls in three segments on an interesting "hanging valley" formation into Niagara Valley near Donnell Lake. The first is a 500-foot free fall, followed by a 300-foot cascade, then a lower fall.

Driving west on Highway 108, go about a quarter mile past the Donnells Overlook turnoff. You will see a pulloff area. Stop and park here, then take the unmarked trail into the forest. In about 150 feet, turn left and head west parallel to the highway. You will reach a viewpoint for the falls in about five minutes.

2 WEST HIGHWAY 120

You can visit nice waterfalls before you even reach Yosemite National Park. Highway 120 on the western border of the park is a curvy but well-maintained mountain road that leads through the area west of the famed national park.

DIANA FALLS ★★

BEST SEASON: March–July
ELEVATION: 2300 ft
TRAIL LENGTH: 1 mile
USGS QUAD: Coulterville (ns)
CONTACT: Stanislaus National Forest; 209-962-7825

Diana Falls at low flow

Diana Falls tumbles about 20 feet on Bean Creek. Go early in the season to see the fall at its peak flow, but even then it is not the most impressive around. To get there, take Greeley Hill Road (also known as Road J-20) from Coulterville and head east staying right when Road J-20 splits off after about 10 miles. Continue another 4 miles to a one-lane bridge and park. Cross the road and hike about 0.5 mile to the waterfall on your left.

RAINBOW POOL FALLS ★★

BEST SEASON: Year–round
ELEVATION: 3000 ft
USGS QUAD: Jawbone Ridge (ns)
CONTACT: Stanislaus National Forest; 209-962-7825

Like Diana Falls, Rainbow Pool Falls is better for a family picnic than a sightseeing trip. The waterfall is about 20 feet high and falls on the South Fork of the Tuolumne River. Water flows here year-round, and Rainbow Pool Falls can be a side trip for when the waterfalls of Yosemite are too crowded. To get here, take Highway 120 about 13 miles past Groveland. Heading east, watch for an unsigned turnoff near the bridge over the South Fork of the Tuolumne. Be sure to check your trip meter near Groveland, because there are multiple bridges and few other distinguishing landmarks to indicate the fall's location.

LITTLE NELLIE FALLS ★★

BEST SEASON: March–July
ELEVATION: 4600 ft
USGS QUAD: El Portal
CONTACT: Stanislaus National Forest; 209-962-7825

Little Nellie Falls is a 20-foot trickle on Little Crane Creek. It flows strongest in spring after snowmelt. You can reach it by car, but the roads are bad, so budget time for slow driving. Take Highway 120 to Haraden Flat Road. Turn right, then continue a quarter mile to Road 2S30, where you turn left. Drive 8 miles to Road 1S12 and turn left toward Trumbull Peak. Go 15 miles and make a left turn on an unnamed road. From this point, stay on the main road and do not turn on the many side roads.

JAWBONE FALLS ★★

BEST SEASON: April–May
ELEVATION: 5600 ft

TRAIL LENGTH: 0.25 mile
USGS QUAD: Cherry Lake North
CONTACT: Stanislaus National Forest; 209-962-7825

Jawbone Falls is a small cascade on Jawbone Creek, emptying into a pool. It is a popular stopping point for mountain bikers. To get there, take the Cherry Lake turnoff from Highway 120 about 12 miles east of Groveland. Turn onto Cherry Lake Road (Road 1N07). Go north 25 miles to the intersection with Cottonwood (Road 1N04). At the stop sign, turn left and go 5 miles to the intersection with road 2N22, where you turn right and go about 2 miles to the intersection with 2N78. Turn right, and within a mile you will encounter a road washout. Park the car safely away from the damaged area and walk the last few hundred feet to the fall next to the road.

PRESTON FALLS ★★

BEST SEASON: April–June
ELEVATION: 2800 ft
TRAIL LENGTH: 8 miles
USGS QUAD: Cherry Lake South
CONTACT: Stanislaus National Forest; 209-962-7825

Preston Falls is a 25-foot plunge on the Tuolumne River. The hike is moderate, but it is a nice, relatively crowd-free day hike in the springtime. Take Cherry Lake Road about 10 miles north of Highway 120 until you see a power station compound and a pool on your right. Make a hard right and cross the bridge, then continue until you see the Kirkwood Powerhouse. The trailhead is less than half a mile after the powerhouse, next to a paved parking area with toilets nearby. Turn right across the bridge and continue to the end of the road for 2 miles, where there is a turnout and a trailhead. Hike 4 miles one way.

---

3 HETCH HETCHY RESERVOIR

The Hetch Hetchy Reservoir holds enough water to supply a good part of the San Francisco Bay Area. However, the main attraction is its relative seclusion. Located some 40 miles north of the tourist-dense Yosemite Valley, Hetch Hetchy offers impressive waterfalls without the crowds—perfect for when you are in the mood for some peace and quiet. To get to the reservoir, proceed on Highway 120 about a mile west of the Big Oak Flat Entrance Station and watch for the Hetch Hetchy turnoff. Get on Evergreen Road, continue on Hetch Hetchy Road, and stay straight to the end of the road. Park the car and proceed across the dam and through the tunnel to get to the trailheads. Be sure to study the informative plaques on the way to appreciate the sheer dimensions of the 8-mile reservoir.

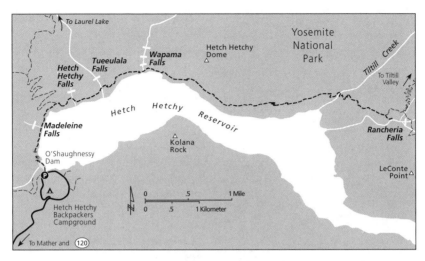

CARLON FALLS ★★

BEST SEASON: Year–round
ELEVATION: 4500 ft
TRAIL LENGTH: 3 miles
USGS QUAD: Ackerson Mountain (ns)
CONTACT: Stanislaus National Forest; 209-962-7825

Carlon Falls is not one of the most visited falls in Yosemite, but it sure is a pretty one. At 35-feet, it falls over a ledge on the South Fork of the Tuolumne River in a lush, green forested setting. To get there, take Highway 120 west to the turnoff for Hetch Hetchy Reservoir, which is 1 mile before the Big Oak Flat Entrance Station. Drive a mile north to the Carlon Day Use Area. Hike on the road north of the bridge, following the river upstream, and you will reach the falls in about 1.5 miles.

MADELEINE FALLS (U) ★★

BEST SEASON: February–April
ELEVATION: 4500 ft
TRAIL LENGTH: 1 mile
USGS QUAD: Lake Eleanor (ns)
CONTACT: Yosemite National Park; 209-372-0200

This is a very seasonal cascading waterfall along the Hetch Hetchy trail toward Tueeulala and Wapama Falls, and it has no official name or recognition. During snowmelt and early in the season after a rainy winter, you will find this and another bonus unnamed waterfall pouring down the mountainsides into the Hetch

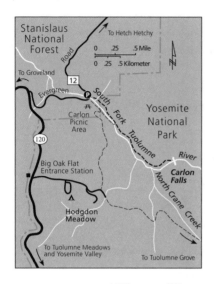

Hetchy Reservoir before you reach Tueeulala Falls, which is also seasonal but more established and consistent in its presence. Look for it about 0.5 mile in from beginning the hike toward Wapama Falls. It appears as an unimpressive thin cascade if you look at it from the O'Shaughnessy Dam parking lot, but it is actually very pretty to look at up close. However, do not call any Yosemite ranger to ask questions about Madeleine Falls; since it had no name and does not fall on a marked creek, we named it after our daughter who found the falls particularly fascinating as we crossed the creek beside it.

HETCH HETCHY FALLS (U) ★★

BEST SEASON: February–April
ELEVATION: 4500 ft
TRAIL LENGTH: 2 miles
USGS QUAD: Lake Eleanor (ns)
CONTACT: Yosemite National Park; 209-372-0200

Hetch Hetchy Falls is a second, slightly larger unnamed waterfall, falling along the Hetch Hetchy trail toward Tueeulala and Wapama Falls. Like Madeleine Falls, its presence depends heavily on seasons, and it does not fall on an established creek or run with a predictable regularity. It is quite striking to view up close from the trail, however. So if you have plans to hike along Hetch Hetchy, it could be neat to plan a trip early in the season to maximize the chances of viewing this fall and Madeleine Falls on the way.

TUEEULALA FALLS ★★★

BEST SEASON: March–June
ELEVATION: 4500 ft
TRAIL LENGTH: 3 miles
USGS QUAD: Lake Eleanor
CONTACT: Yosemite National Park; 209-372-0200

According to noted environmentalist John Muir, Tueeulala Falls "descends like thistledown" as it pours 600 feet over the Hetch Hetchy Reservoir. If you want to see this fall in the height of its glory, visit as early in the season as possible. The fall usually dries up by the end of June.

To view it, you can drive to the Hetch Hetchy Reservoir and park at the O'Shaughnessy Dam. There, you will see it pouring into the reservoir alongside its more energetic sibling, Wapama Falls. You can also hike to Tueeulala Falls' base by crossing the bridge and passing through the tunnel, then following the trail that heads alongside the reservoir to the right. When you come to a fork, follow the one toward Wapama Falls; you will pass Tueeulala Falls first after about 1.5 miles.

WAPAMA FALLS ★★★★★

BEST SEASON: March–July
ELEVATION: 4500 ft
TRAIL LENGTH: 4.5 miles
USGS QUAD: Lake Eleanor
CONTACT: Yosemite National Park; 209-372-0200

Wapama Falls may be the most underrated waterfall in all of Yosemite National Park. It has a magnificent flow best experienced up close, but watch out for the mist. Like Tueeulala Falls, you can see Wapama Falls from the parking lot at O'Shaughnessy Dam, but that view does not do this waterfall justice. The whole fall is a series of cascades that pour down about 1300 feet; you can see only a small

Wapama Falls at low flow in the summer

portion of the lower cascade from the parking lot view. To experience Wapama Falls in all its glory, follow the path alongside the reservoir and through the tunnel, then hike the trail to Wapama Falls' base for a roughly 4.5 mile round trip. It will be hot outside as the summer progresses, so try hitting this trail in the spring for an ideal trip.

RANCHERIA FALLS ★★★

BEST SEASON: May–June
ELEVATION: 4600 ft
TRAIL LENGTH: 13 miles
USGS QUAD: Hetch Hetchy Reservoir
CONTACT: Yosemite National Park; 209-372-0200

It takes some dedication to see Rancheria Falls; you face a 13-mile backpacking trip with an 800-foot elevation gain.  Once you get there though, you will not be disappointed with this series of cascades tumbling 30 feet on Rancheria Creek. Start the hike from O'Shaughnessy Dam and follow the Rancheria Falls Trail. As of the time of this writing, a family of bears live near the Rancheria Falls campground, so be sure to bring any food in bear-resistant containers and use appropriate precautions.

4 GRAND CANYON OF THE TUOLUMNE RIVER

This magnificent canyon begins just below Tuolumne Meadows and stretches all the way up past the Hetch Hetchy Reservoir. Tuolumne River snakes through the canyon from east to west through a series of waterfalls of varying height and scope. For avid hikers, there is a challenging trail running mostly alongside Tuolumne River. It originates at the Tuolumne Meadows and continues down to Pate Valley, a broad plain a few miles from Hetch Hetchy. The hike has often been called "the mother of all waterfall hikes," thanks to the huge number of spectacular falls found along it.

To get to the trailhead, take Highway 120 (Tioga Pass Road) from Yosemite Valley and continue roughly 50 miles heading east to a sign for Dog Lake/Lembert Dome/Soda Springs. Turn left, then park near the gate to find the trailhead.

TUOLUMNE FALLS ★★★★

BEST SEASON: March–July
ELEVATION: 8200 ft

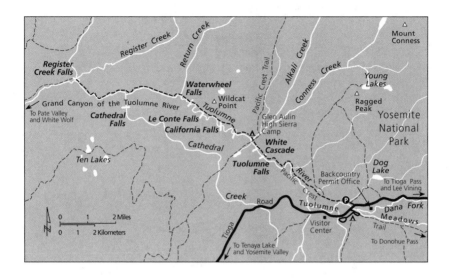

TRAIL LENGTH: 10 miles
USGS QUAD: Falls Ridge
CONTACT: Yosemite National Park; 209-372-0200

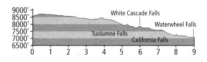

Tuolumne Falls is the first major waterfall on the Grand Canyon of the Tuolumne River Trail, dropping more than 50 feet on the Tuolumne River. The falls rush powerfully, but may not seem so impressive compared to those in Yosemite Valley. Start the hike to Tuolumne Falls (and the rest of the Grand Canyon of the Tuolumne falls) in Tuolumne Meadows. The trail stays fairly level for the first 4 miles or so before it begins to descend. Depending on the season, you may pass two unnamed cascades before you reach Tuolumne Falls, making a total of just under 5 miles on the trail, one-way.

White Cascade ★★★

BEST SEASON: March–July
ELEVATION: 7900 ft
TRAIL LENGTH: 12 miles
USGS QUAD: Falls Ridge
CONTACT: Yosemite National Park; 209-372-0200

The White Cascade is also called Glen Aulin Falls. It falls about 75 feet on the Tuolumne River. Continue for just under a mile past Tuolumne Falls, and you will see it tumbling down.

California Falls ★★★

BEST SEASON: March–July
ELEVATION: 7600 ft
TRAIL LENGTH: 15 miles
USGS QUAD: Falls Ridge
CONTACT: Yosemite National Park; 209-372-0200

California Falls is a neat-looking series of cascades at the western edge of the Glen Aulin Valley. As you pass through Glen Aulin from the White Cascade, you will find California Falls after about another 1.5 miles after leaving the valley.

Le Conte Falls ★★★

BEST SEASON: March–July
ELEVATION: 7000 ft
TRAIL LENGTH: 17 miles
USGS QUAD: Falls Ridge
CONTACT: Yosemite National Park; 209-372-0200

Le Conte is a long, rushing cascade as the Tuolumne River plunges along. To reach it, continue another mile past California Falls, following the trail alongside the Tuolumne.

Waterwheel Falls ★★★★

BEST SEASON: March–July
ELEVATION: 6800 ft
TRAIL LENGTH: 19 miles
USGS QUAD: Falls Ridge
CONTACT: Yosemite National Park; 209-372-0200

Waterwheel Falls, if you can hang in there on the Grand Canyon Trail long enough to reach it, is one of the most interesting waterfalls anywhere. Like the others on the trail, it is a cascade, but its angle and force is unusual in that it sends water spinning into a backwards waterwheel. The fall is on the Tuolumne River and about 360 feet high. See this fall in spring and you will never forget it. However, you have another nearly 1000-foot drop in elevation and another mile past Le Conte Falls before you reach it—bringing you to a total of 9 miles and nearly 2500 feet in elevation loss since leaving Tuolumne Meadows. Needless to say, the trip is not for the faint of heart.

Cathedral Falls ★★

BEST SEASON: March–July
ELEVATION: 5700 ft
TRAIL LENGTH: 22 miles
USGS QUAD: Falls Ridge (ns)
CONTACT: Yosemite National Park; 209-372-0200

Cathedral Falls is a cascade on Cathedral Creek. You can see it from a few different locations, but if you are hiking on the trail in Grand Canyon of the Tuolumne River, find it from the trail between Waterwheel Falls and Register Creek Falls.

Register Creek Falls ★★★

BEST SEASON: March–July
ELEVATION: 5300 ft
TRAIL LENGTH: 25 miles
USGS QUAD: Falls Ridge (ns)
CONTACT: Yosemite National Park; 209-372-0200

The waterfall on Register Creek is not as widely known as the others in the Grand Canyon of the Tuolumne, but it is pretty nonetheless. Roughly 40 feet tall, it plunges between granite rocks along the Grand Canyon Trail. Continue about 3.5 miles past Waterwheel Falls to reach it, or stop to take it in on a long backpacking trip from the other direction.

5 El Portal

Looking at a map of Yosemite National Park, you will notice a strange, narrow block of parkland stretching out several miles west beyond the regular park border. This block covers both sides of Highway 140—but not much else. That is where you find the tiny town of El Portal, neatly tucked away within park boundaries.

Chinquapin Falls ★

BEST SEASON: March–July
ELEVATION: 3900 ft
USGS QUAD: El Portal
CONTACT: Yosemite National Park; 209-372-0200

Chinquapin Falls is a relatively obscure 2000-foot cascade on Indian Creek, falling alongside Highway 140. How is such a tall waterfall so rarely spoken of? Well, Chinquapin Falls is proof that height alone does not make a spectacular waterfall. It is very narrow and tumbles down a distant mountainside rather than free-falling off a cliff into a gorgeous valley, like the more famous Yosemite Falls. Still, if you are traveling on Highway 140, keep your eyes peeled for it. It will be on the right side of the road shortly after El Portal if you are headed toward the park. Leaving the park on Highway 140, look for it on the left about 2.5 miles outside the Arch Rock entrance.

6 YOSEMITE VALLEY

This world-famous valley is nature's cathedral and showcase rolled into one. Words and pictures can never do it full justice. Bustling with tourists year-round, the park tries to limit cars on the roads by providing free shuttles while limiting parking spaces outside the main parking areas. You will save yourself a lot of hassles by taking the shuttle; you rarely have to wait more than a few minutes for the next bus. Before you leave, be sure to stop by Yosemite Village for a tour of the museum, the Ansel Adams gallery, and the Indian Village (behind the visitor center), which provides a glimpse of what Yosemite looked like in 1872.

Reach Yosemite Valley from the east by taking Highway 140 or 120 from Highway 99. You can also enter from the west by taking Highway 120 through Tioga Pass, but this entrance is often closed in the winter.

SILVER STRAND FALLS ★★★

BEST SEASON: March–June
ELEVATION: 6500 ft
USGS QUAD: El Capitan
CONTACT: Yosemite National Park; 209-372-0200

You may not hear the name Silver Strand Falls as frequently as, say, Yosemite Falls. Still this waterfall is one of the highest in the country, falling 1170 feet on a stream called Meadow Brook. The fall is more obscure because, like so many others in Yosemite, it sits near so many more spectacular falls that it tends to be overshadowed.

You can reach it by entering the park from the south and driving 24 miles. Park at the Wawona Tunnel View Area and Silver Strand Falls will be in the granite cliffs on your right. Do not confuse it with Bridalveil Falls, the most prominent fall visible here. You may have to study hard to find it if you visit in the spring before all the snow melts. Be sure to bring binoculars.

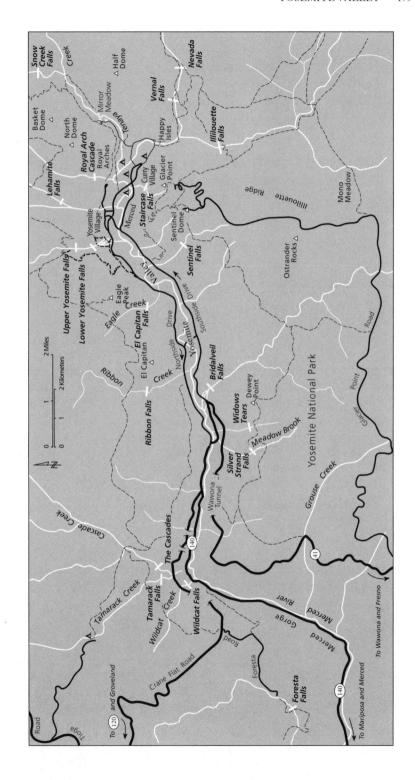

WIDOWS TEARS ★★

BEST SEASON: March–April
ELEVATION: 6600 ft
USGS QUAD: El Capitan (nl)
CONTACT: Yosemite National Park; 209-372-0200

Widows Tears has nearly 1100 feet in height, as it falls from an unnamed creek right beside Silver Strand Falls. The fall is also a favorite with ice climbers, since it freezes in the winter. View it from the same outlook as for Silver Strand.

TAMARACK FALLS ★★★

BEST SEASON: March–July
ELEVATION: 5500 ft
USGS QUAD: El Capitan (nl)
CONTACT: Yosemite National Park; 209-372-0200

Tamarack Falls is an often-overlooked 800-foot plunge on Tamarack Creek. It sits right near The Cascades, which are more impressive and closer to the road. When you enter from Highway 140, watch for an overlook after the first tunnel.

WILDCAT FALLS ★★★

BEST SEASON: March–June
ELEVATION: 4200 ft
USGS QUAD: El Capitan
CONTACT: Yosemite National Park; 209-372-0200

Wildcat Falls

Wildcat Falls is next to The Cascades. You can view it by walking along the road from The Cascades picnic area toward the Arch Rock Entrance Station. The waterfall is around 600 feet, but you can only see a small part from the road.

THE CASCADES ★★★★

BEST SEASON: March–July
ELEVATION: 3500 ft
USGS QUAD: El Capitan
CONTACT: Yosemite National Park; 209-372-0200

Sometimes called Cascade Falls, The Cascades is another of the best oft-overlooked waterfalls in Yosemite. Falling well over 1000 feet, it originates from a free fall on Cascade Creek as it merges with Tamarack Creek. The fall is spectacular during the snowmelt, and it takes little effort to reach it. If you enter Yosemite via the Arch Rock Entrance Station, you will pass Cascade

The Cascades

Falls on your way in on Highway 140. The fall is just less than 3 miles in from the entrance point. From Yosemite Valley, take Northside Drive to Highway 140 about 3 miles west of the Bridalveil Falls turnoff. Enjoy the fall from the parking area or follow a short trail to the fall's base. Expect to get drenched with mist if you visit during heavy flow season.

RIBBON FALLS ★★★★

BEST SEASON: April–June
ELEVATION: 6500 ft
USGS QUAD: El Capitan
CONTACT: Yosemite National Park; 209-372-0200

Ribbon Falls, gently trickling 1612 feet, is a sight to see if you get the chance. Called Lung-oo-too-koo-yah (the slender and graceful one) by the Native Americans, it is the tallest unbroken waterfall in the world. (Most other tall falls have tiered sections or cascades that make up the total height.) Unfortunately, Ribbon Falls is only visible for a short time and it dries up by the end of June. From Highway 41 north, enter the park and continue about 26 miles to Yosemite Valley. Look for a pullout near El Capitan and scan the cliffs for the falls, or gaze across the valley at it from the Bridalveil Falls Trail. Do not confuse Ribbon Falls with El Capitan Falls; Ribbon Falls is in the cliffs next to El Capitan.

EL CAPITAN FALLS ★★★★

BEST SEASON: February–March
ELEVATION: 4800 ft
USGS QUAD: El Capitan (ns)
CONTACT: Yosemite National Park; 209-372-0200

El Capitan Falls is also known as Horsetail Falls in some references. It drops 1500 feet off the eastern face of El Capitan into Yosemite Valley in the early spring during snowmelt. It is usually completely gone by late spring, so get here early if you hope to see it. You can view it from most good viewpoints of El Capitan; binoculars are helpful. The falls' claim to fame is that if you photograph it on a late night backlit by a sunset, many believe it looks like liquid fire pouring down the cliff.

SENTINEL FALLS ★★★★

BEST SEASON: April–June
ELEVATION: 5900 ft
USGS QUAD: Half Dome
CONTACT: Yosemite National Park; 209-372-0200

Another very high fall, Sentinel Falls is very much overshadowed by nearby Yosemite Falls. It plummets nearly 2000 feet in a tiered form, falling down the cliffs near Sentinel Rock. Visit the park early in the season to see Sentinel Falls. The best viewpoint is near the Fourmile Trailhead. The falls usually dry up by late June.

BRIDALVEIL FALLS ★★★★★

BEST SEASON: Year–round
ELEVATION: 4000 ft
USGS QUAD: El Capitan
CONTACT: Yosemite National Park; 209-372-0200

Bridalveil Falls may not be the highest in Yosemite National Park, but many consider it the prettiest. Falling 620 feet on Bridalveil Creek, Bridalveil Falls is a major

Bridalveil Falls in summer

tourist attraction and the subject of many a photograph. The flow is most powerful in the spring but has more of a bridal veil appearance in the summer when the lighter flow scatters in the wind. You can see the falls from numerous points throughout the park, but the best place to take it in is at the end of this short trail. Look for Bridalveil Falls parking lot near the western edge of Yosemite Valley, by following signs from the park's western entrance. The trail is about a quarter mile long.

UPPER YOSEMITE FALLS ★★★★★

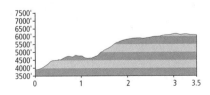

BEST SEASON: March–July
ELEVATION: 6500 ft
TRAIL LENGTH: 7 miles
USGS QUAD: Yosemite Falls
CONTACT: Yosemite National Park; 209-372-0200

Together, Upper and Lower Yosemite Falls plunge nearly 2500 feet and together they make the tallest waterfall in North America and fifth tallest in the world. They are also a major tourist destination, forming a view that few forget as it regally pours into the valley.

Upper Yosemite Falls

With Upper Yosemite Falls being as high as it is, you can get great views from points all around the park. Park your car at any of the spots along the road into Yosemite Village and gaze at the waterfall. Adventurous hikers can also take a 7-mile round-trip hike to the top for a breathtaking view of the whole valley. It is a tough hike though, gaining nearly 3000 feet in elevation. The trail is at the east end of the Yosemite Falls parking lot.

LOWER YOSEMITE FALLS ★★★★★

BEST SEASON: March–July
ELEVATION: 4400 ft
USGS QUAD: Yosemite Falls
CONTACT: Yosemite National Park; 209-372-0200

Although the upper falls are higher, Lower Yosemite Falls is just as picturesque. A 320-foot plunge, the waterfall picks up with surprising vigor where Upper Yosemite Falls leaves off. The trail to get there is a paved, quarter-mile walk from the parking lot. You will get a great view where you can see both the upper and lower falls together a short way along the trail, but continue onward to get an up-close look at the lower falls. Expect crowds; this is one of the most popular locations in the park.

Opposite: Lower Yosemite Falls

LEHAMITE FALLS ★★★

BEST SEASON: February–May
ELEVATION: 6800 ft
USGS QUAD: Yosemite Falls
CONTACT: Yosemite National Park; 209-372-0200

Lehamite Falls cascades over 1000 feet down the granite cliffs near Yosemite Falls, fed by Indian Canyon and Lehamite Creek. If you want to see it, park alongside Northside Drive next to Cook's Meadow near Yosemite Lodge. Look for it next to Yosemite Falls.

SNOW CREEK FALLS ★★★★★

BEST SEASON: March–July
ELEVATION: 5600 ft
TRAIL LENGTH: 8 miles
USGS QUAD: Yosemite Falls
CONTACT: Yosemite National Park; 209-372-0200

Snow Creek Falls is the second highest waterfall in Yosemite National Park, falling 2140 feet from Snow Creek, which originates at May Lake. You have to take a somewhat strenuous 8-mile round-trip hike to get anything more than a far-off view of it in the distance.

If you are up for it, however, it is one of the more rewarding hikes in the park. The trip passes several small, unnamed waterfalls and interesting flows along the way. Take the parking lot shuttle to stop number 17. Follow the trail toward Mirror Lake and continue to a bridge. Pick up the Snow Creek Falls Trail, which will lead you to the best viewpoints of the falls. Hikers frequently miss the waterfall since trees block the view. Look for it at the point where Tenaya Creek merges into Snow Creek, because the best view is off the trail.

TENAYA FALLS (U) ★★★

BEST SEASON: March–July
ELEVATION: 800 ft
TRAIL LENGTH: 4 miles
USGS QUAD: Yosemite Falls (ns)
CONTACT: Yosemite National Park; 209-372-0200

This lovely waterfall is private and serene. You can take the Snow Creek Falls Trail from the junction with the Mirror Lake Trail and continue about 0.75 mile upward. The trip passes some spectacular views of the Tenaya Canyon. You will need to use your navigational skills and you may need to hike off-trail.

TANECHKA FALLS ★★

BEST SEASON: April–May
ELEVATION: 4000 ft
TRAIL LENGTH: 3.5 miles
USGS QUAD: Yosemite Falls (ns)
CONTACT: Yosemite National Park; 209-372-0200

Hike any other time of the year than early spring, and you will not even notice that Tanechka Falls exists. If you do go in early spring, you will see it trickling down next to the Bridlepath Trail about a half mile past Mirror Lake on the south side of Tenaya Creek. Start from shuttle stop 17 and hike toward the lake.

ROYAL ARCH CASCADE ★★★

BEST SEASON: February–April
ELEVATION: 5400 ft
USGS QUAD: Half Dome
CONTACT: Yosemite National Park; 209-372-0200

The Royal Arch Cascade is another waterfall for which timing is key. This fall is a glorious sight when active, but it flows more commonly as a faint trickle. Go during snowmelt or after heavy rains and look for it tumbling 1250 feet from a very small watershed atop the Royal Arches. Stop next to Stoneman Meadow just past Curry Village for the best view.

STAIRCASE FALLS ★★

BEST SEASON: February–May
ELEVATION: 4300 ft
USGS QUAD: Half Dome
CONTACT: Yosemite National Park; 209-372-0200

Staircase Falls sits opposite the Royal Arch Cascade in Yosemite Valley, plunging down more than 1200 feet in a thin ribbon. The water skips down the rocks rather than flowing or tumbling in a continuous motion. This is not a waterfall that will get your heart pounding, however, being very thin and far off in the distance. You can view it from the meadows around Curry Village or atop Glacier Point.

Staircase Falls

7 MIST TRAIL

Mist Trail is an offshoot of the southeastern part of Yosemite Valley near shuttle stop 16. Don't worry about getting lost—just follow the crowd! Those who enjoy the peace and quiet as much as the waterfall itself may be frustrated by the abundance of fellow hikers on the trail, but that should go away once you reach the actual falls. After a short but fairly steep ascent you reach the first bridge, which gives you a view of Vernal Falls. From a distance, it may seem pretty ordinary. As you get closer you will change your opinion, but if you linger too long you'll have to change your clothes too since you'll be completely soaked from the mist. Shortly after Vernal there is a fork in the trail; stay left and you will see Nevada Falls straight ahead. Note: This trail is closed in the winter, so check with a ranger before heading there in the early spring to be sure it is open.

VERNAL FALLS ★★★★★

BEST SEASON: March–July
ELEVATION: 4700 ft
TRAIL LENGTH: 3 miles
USGS QUAD: Half Dome
CONTACT: Yosemite National Park; 209-372-0200

People have varying taste in waterfalls, but for those who prefer block-shaped powerful waterfalls rather than narrow tall waterfalls, Vernal Falls is arguably

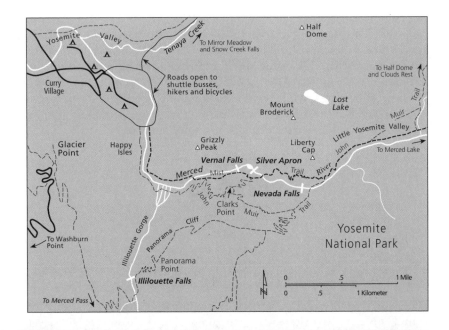

Vernal Falls

the best waterfall in all of Yosemite National Park and possibly all of northern California. This 317-foot giant roars on the Merced River along the Mist Trail. At peak flow, it stretches 70 to 80 feet across, but it slows to a relative trickle in the autumn months. Start hiking the Mist Trail from the bottom at shuttle stop 16, and you will reach the top of Vernal Falls in about 1.5 miles with just over 1000 feet in elevation gain. For hikers without the stamina to continue all the way to the top of the falls, you can see Vernal Falls from a bridge about a mile up the trail, but the view is far more spectacular if you continue upward.

SILVER APRON ★★

BEST SEASON: March–July
ELEVATION: 5100 ft
TRAIL LENGTH: 3.5 miles
USGS QUAD: Half Dome
CONTACT: Yosemite National Park; 209-372-0200

The Silver Apron is a unique water flow over a granite rock formation on the Mist Trail. The Merced River streams over the granite formations in a very thin layer before heading down toward Emerald Pool, and it includes a few short drops that form a pretty sight along the way to Nevada Falls. Find the Silver Apron about a quarter mile past Vernal Falls, but use caution since hikers have fallen to their deaths on these slick rocks.

GLACIER POINT FALLS ★★

BEST SEASON: April–May
ELEVATION: 4200 ft
TRAIL LENGTH: 4 miles
USGS QUAD: Half Dome (ns)
CONTACT: Yosemite National Park; 209-372-0200

Glacier Point Falls is not actually located on the Mist Trail, but its best viewing point is on the way to Nevada Falls. If you take the John Muir Trail as part of your loop to or from Nevada Falls, look toward Glacier Point in the early spring to see a thin, trickling waterfall making its way down the south side.

NEVADA FALLS ★★★★★

BEST SEASON: March–July
ELEVATION: 5900 ft
TRAIL LENGTH: 5 miles

Nevada Falls (Photo courtesy of Kevin Gong kevingong.com)

USGS QUAD: Half Dome
CONTACT: Yosemite National Park; 209-372-0200

Nevada Falls is another spectacular sight at peak flow, boasting 594 feet in height and a powerful roar as the Merced River pours down its waters. To see it, you face a 5-mile round trip with almost 2000 feet in elevation gain. Once you pass Vernal Falls, continue climbing upward. You will reach a junction from which you can continue to follow the Mist Trail or switch to the John Muir Trail. Either one will offer you a fine view of the fall.

8 MERCED LAKE

The Merced Lake area contains many long crisscrossing backpacking trails. Much of the national park is inaccessible by car, since building roads would harm

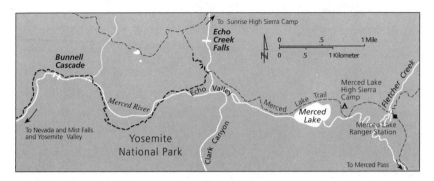

the environment and the natural beauty of the land. Among these trails lie a few interesting, relatively unknown waterfalls.

ECHO CREEK FALLS ★★

BEST SEASON: March–July
ELEVATION: 7000 ft
TRAIL LENGTH: 20–22 miles
USGS QUAD: Merced Peak
CONTACT: Yosemite National Park; 209-372-0200

Echo Creek Falls is a pretty cascade on Echo Creek, sitting very near the Merced Lake Trail. When hiking from Merced Lake or coming in from Yosemite Valley, you will pass Echo Creek. Take a side trip and head upstream about 1000 feet and you will find the fall. The trail length to reach the fall varies depending on your planned route. From Yosemite Valley, follow the Mist Trail to Nevada Falls and continue around 7 or 8 miles farther, then turn to follow Echo Creek. This route would be about 20 to 22 miles round trip.

BUNNELL CASCADE ★★

BEST SEASON: March–July
ELEVATION: 6400 ft
TRAIL LENGTH: 14–15 miles
USGS QUAD: Merced Peak
CONTACT: Yosemite National Park; 209-372-0200

Bunnell Cascade is a roughly 40-foot cascade on the Merced River. It has had several previous names, including Washburn Cascade, Diamond Shower Falls, and Little Grizzly Fall. See it late spring to early summer around the time of snowmelt near Bunnell Point alongside the Merced Lake Trail, or follow the trail along the Merced River about 4.5 miles past Nevada Falls.

9 FORESTA

The small town of Foresta is just northeast of El Portal on the western edge of the park. It is one of the few regions with privately owned property in Yosemite National Park. Unlike the larger Wawona, Foresta is more of a cluster of houses in the woods than anything else. A severe fire ravaged the area in 1990, which burned some 90 percent of the trees and destroyed property. Today, you can still see the remnants of fire, although the lush green foliage is slowly reconquering the landscape. The town is located some distance into the woods between Highways 120 and 140; you do not have to go on hour-long detours to avoid the crowds. From Highway 140, exit on Granite Court, and take an immediate right on Foresta Road. From Highway 120, exit on Foresta Road and turn right on Old Coulterville after just under a mile.

FORESTA FALLS ★★

BEST SEASON: March–June
ELEVATION: 4000 ft
USGS QUAD: El Portal
CONTACT: Yosemite National Park; 209-372-0200

Foresta Falls is a 40-foot cascade on Crane Creek in a hidden corner of Yosemite National Park. The trip is fairly easy. Take Big Oak Flat Road to the turnoff for Foresta, and then drive to the fork in the road, staying left on Foresta Road. Continue about a mile and a half to the fall. Park along the road in the pullout past the falls.

10 TIOGA PASS

Highway 120 through Yosemite, also called Tioga Pass Road, is a winding but spectacular drive. Be prepared to crawl; the many RVs on the road and the limited passing opportunities are almost blessings in disguise that give you time to take in the magnificent views. In addition to the numerous turnoffs and vista points, there are some really nice waterfalls tucked away along the road. Watch for seasonal falls along the road during snowmelt. Be advised, however, that Tioga Pass is frequently closed because of poor weather conditions even after it opens for the season. Be sure to check conditions before hitting the road if you are planning a spring trip, as temperatures at these altitudes can be significantly lower than the surrounding areas. The California Department of Transportation provides continual updates for Highway 120 at *www.dot .ca.gov/hq/roadinfo/sr120.*

Yosemite Creek Falls ★★

BEST SEASON: April–June
ELEVATION: 7400 ft
USGS QUAD: Yosemite Falls (ns)
CONTACT: Yosemite National Park; 209-372-0200

Here is a lovely 25-foot cascade on Yosemite Creek. It is not a particularly large waterfall, but if you are going to be in the area, it is definitely a waterfall worth seeing. Call in advance to verify the road is open. Take Highway 120 to the point at which it becomes Tioga Pass Road, then turn left and head about 20 miles to the Yosemite Creek Picnic Area. The waterfall is about 0.3 mile past the picnic area on the left.

---

11 Wawona

Wawona is a small community in the southwesternmost corner of the park with a school, post office, a hotel complex, and a few stores. Like Foresta, it is one of the few spots within park limits with privately owned houses—a remnant from the era before the park was established. Anyone entering the park through the

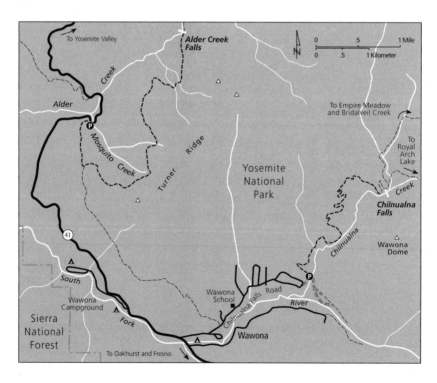

south entrance (Highway 41) will pass right through town. The elevation and climate in this region are about the same as in Yosemite Valley, which can best be summed up as mild and pleasant year-round.

CHILNUALNA FALLS ★★★★★

BEST SEASON: April–June
ELEVATION: 6400 ft
TRAIL LENGTH: 8 miles
USGS QUAD: Mariposa Grove
CONTACT: Yosemite National Park; 209-372-0200

Chilnualna Falls is nearly 700 feet tall as it falls on Chilnualna Creek. You'll face an 8.2-mile hike with a 2500-foot elevation gain in order to reach it, but you will be glad you made the trip be-

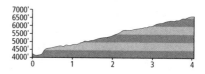

cause this is easily one of the best waterfalls in Yosemite. To top it off, the difficult trail scares off lots of tourists, so it tends to be more secluded.

From Highway 41 heading north, drive to Chilnualna Falls Road and turn right, then drive about 2 miles to the parking lot. From there, look for a trail leading uphill. The trail will pass several small cascades on Chilnualna Creek, but you will reach the falls in just over 4 miles.

ALDER CREEK FALLS ★★★

BEST SEASON: April–July
ELEVATION: 5700 ft
TRAIL LENGTH: 8 miles
USGS QUAD: Wawona (nl)
CONTACT: Yosemite National Park; 209-372-0200

As its name suggests, Alder Creek Falls, sometimes called Alder Falls, is a 250-foot fall on Alder Creek. It is not one of the most well known waterfalls

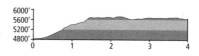

in the park because it involves an 8-mile round-trip hike. Still, for seclusion this may be the waterfall you want. Heading north on Highway 41, go just over 4 miles north of the turnoff for Chilnualna Falls Road. There will be a pullout for Mosquito Creek. (If you reach a signed pullout for Alder Creek, you have gone too far.) Park in the Mosquito Creek pullout and pick up the trail, which will not have a sign. Hike uphill for about 0.75 mile, and then turn left at the junction and follow the trail up to the falls.

ILLILOUETTE FALLS ★★★★★

BEST SEASON: May–July
ELEVATION: 5600 ft
TRAIL LENGTH: 4 miles
USGS QUAD: Half Dome
CONTACT: Yosemite National
Park; 209-372-0200

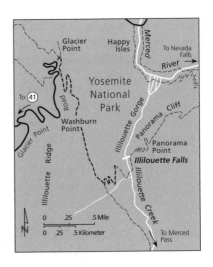

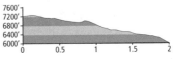

Illilouette Falls is a famous 370-foot drop on Illilouette Creek. For the best view, you will want to hike the Panorama Trail from Glacier Point for a 4-mile round trip with more than 1200 feet in elevation loss. This is the best way to see the fall up close, but you can also view it at a distance from various other trails throughout the park, including the Snow Creek Falls Trail and the Mist Trail. There is also a pullout with a good view of Illilouette Falls along the road about a mile before Glacier Point at Washburn Point. Remember that roads to Glacier Point will be closed until late spring.

PYWIACK CASCADE ★★★★

BEST SEASON: May–August
ELEVATION: 7300 ft
USGS QUAD: Tenaya Lake
CONTACT: Yosemite National Park; 209-372-0200

The Pywiack Cascade is a 660-foot drop on Tenaya Creek. It is technically possible to hike to its base, but it is very difficult to find, and there are no major established trails that lead to a good viewpoint. If you are an experienced off-trail hiker, check with a park ranger to discuss a route. The fall's GPS coordinates are 27.78712N, 119.48778W. For everyone else, the best place to view the Pywiack Cascade is from the outlook at Glacier Point, from which many other major Yosemite waterfalls are also visible.

---

12 FISH CAMP

Fish Camp, located a few miles south of Yosemite National Park along Highway 41, is a small town with a genuine, rustic feel to it. The area, which includes Oakhurst and surrounding towns, has a rich native heritage from the Mono

Fish Camp Falls at low flow

Indian culture that populated these parts. Some 600 Mono and Mi Wok Indians still live in the area, and you can get a better idea of its rich history by stopping by the Sierra Mono Museum in North Fork.

Fish Camp Falls ★★

BEST SEASON: April–September
ELEVATION: 5400 ft
TRAIL LENGTH: 1 mile
USGS QUAD: Fish Camp (ns)
CONTACT: Sierra National Forest; 559-683-4636

Fish Camp Falls is a series of three small waterfalls on Big Creek, with the tallest being about 25 feet. Despite their small size, the falls are very pretty and make a wonderful picnic destination. Beware of mosquitoes, which were out in full force when we visited the falls. Take Highway 41 north to Big Sandy Road (just under 15 miles north of Oakhurst), then turn right on Big Sandy Road. Then drive 2.7 miles on Big Sandy Road until you reach a dirt parking area. Take the trail heading to the left of the road. You should pass a picnic table and cabin, and then reach the falls in 0.5 mile.

Big Creek Falls ★

BEST SEASON: April–July
ELEVATION: 6300 ft
TRAIL LENGTH: 0.5 mile
USGS QUAD: Fish Camp (ns)
CONTACT: Sierra National Forest; 559-683-4636

Big Creek Falls is a relatively unspectacular 50-foot cascade on Big Creek. It lies outside the boundaries of Yosemite and involves a major detour off the road. If you are just looking for peace and quiet, it can be a nice place to relax and enjoy the fresh air. The creek is stocked with fish so it is a favorite for fishing. To get here, take the Big Sandy Road exit north of Oakhurst from Highway 41 and drive to Big Sandy Campground. Expect a creek crossing. After that, continue to Little Sandy Campground and look for a dirt pullout just under 0.5 mile farther where you can park and follow the creek to the waterfall. The road is slow and winding, so be prepared to drive slowly even though it is only about 8 miles to the falls.

EASTERN SIERRA REGION

Some areas of the Sierra Nevada, particularly those at high altitudes, are temperate and lush with patches of snow even in summer. Other areas are arid with bountiful rocks and shrubs but few trees. Yet, even the dry areas manage to surprise with

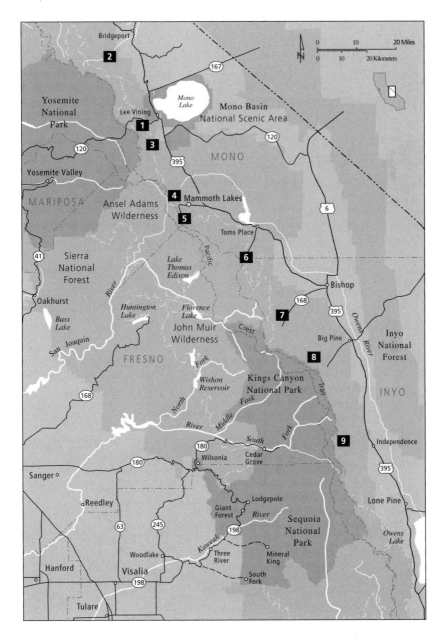

nice waterfalls where you least expect them, thanks to snowmelt runoff from surrounding mountains.

You might assume the majority of this region's towns are old mining centers. Upon closer inspection, however, you will find that not all these towns found their origins in gold mining. Bishop, for example, started as a supplier to the surrounding mining towns. As the saying goes, "Gold miners may strike it rich one day, but the guys who sell the pans strike it rich every day."

This region is also home to Bodie, one of the most famous ghost towns in the west. Once a rowdy place with an estimated 10,000 people and sixty-five (!) saloons, the town is now in a state of "arrested decay" as declared by the state when it took over and made it a national park in 1962. The town is just a short drive from the Twin Lakes and Lee Vining waterfalls, so be sure to stop by as you pass through. Take the Highway 270 exit off Highway 395 a few miles south of Bridgeport, and follow signs eastward.

1 LEE VINING

After your hike, be sure to stop by Nicely's Restaurant in the town of Lee Vining for a slice of their famous pie.

ELLERY LAKE FALLS ★★

BEST SEASON: May–July
ELEVATION: 9500 ft
USGS QUAD: Mount Dana (nl)
CONTACT: Inyo National Forest; 760-647-3044

Ellery Lake Falls lies outside the boundaries of Yosemite National Park. There is a sprinkling of falls around the lake, including one on the west side. The main one is roughly 300 feet high and trickles down into the lake area from Lee Vining Creek. Watch for it as you drive along Highway 120 at the eastern edge of

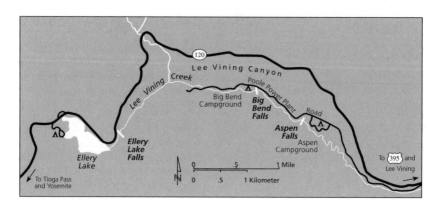

Ellery Lake. It is easiest to see from the road heading west; you may miss it when heading east.

BIG BEND FALLS ★★★

BEST SEASON: May–November
ELEVATION: 7700 ft
USGS QUAD: Mount Dana (nl)
CONTACT: Inyo National Forest; 760-647-3044

Big Bend Falls is a 35-foot cascade on Lee Vining Creek. It sits near Big Bend Campground along Poole Power Plant Road, just outside the eastern Highway 120 Entrance Station for Yosemite National Park. View the falls from your car, or stop for a very short scramble to its base. From the junction of Highway 395 and Highway 120, take 120 west to Poole Power Plant Road. Turn left, then drive 2.5 miles to the campground. The fall will be on your left.

ASPEN FALLS ★★

BEST SEASON: May–November
ELEVATION: 7500 ft
USGS QUAD: Yerington (nl)
CONTACT: Inyo National Forest; 760-647-3044

Aspen Falls is a 30-foot cascade on Lee Vining Creek. It will not have you gaping in wonder, but you can get up close to it. Take Highway 120 from the junction with 395, then turn left on Poole Power Plant Road and continue for 1.5 miles to Aspen Campground. Follow your ears to find the falls at the end of the campground.

Aspen Falls

LUNDY CANYON FALLS ★★★★

BEST SEASON: June–September
ELEVATION: 8200 ft
TRAIL LENGTH: 3 miles
USGS QUAD: Lundy (ns)
CONTACT: Inyo National Forest; 760-647-3044

The Lundy Canyon Trail offers some interesting choices. The waterfall can be impressive in the spring, but a trip in the fall offers a spectacular trek through plentiful aspens exploding with color. It's like a piece of New England scenery transplanted into California, the likes of which you won't find anywhere west of the Sierras. To get to the trail, look for signs to Lundy Canyon off Highway 395 a few miles north of where Highway 120 from Yosemite connects with 395. The exit is on your left; just follow the signs to the trailhead. You should be heading west on Lundy Lake Road.

The Lundy Canyon Falls are a series of spectacular cascades on two separate creeks. They are visible from the Lundy Canyon Trail. Budget a chunk of time to explore; this is time well spent for the waterfall lover. From the trailhead, continue along the creek about 1.5 miles to the falls' base. The falls are about 500 feet tall.

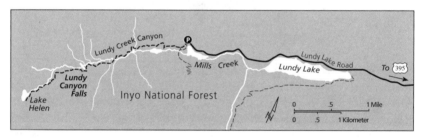

2 TWIN LAKES

Several areas in California bear the name Twin Lakes. This one is just northeast of Yosemite National Park, though you can only access it from Highway 395. Turn west at the Twin Lakes turnoff from Highway 395 near the town of Bridgeport and head to the western end of the lake to find the trailhead. The trails around Twin Lakes into the Hoover Wilderness—particularly the Horse Creek Trail and Twin Lakes Loop trails—are very busy in early summer.

HORSE CREEK FALLS ★★

BEST SEASON: June–August
ELEVATION: 8300 ft
TRAIL LENGTH: 4 miles

USGS QUAD: Buckeye Ridge
CONTACT: Humboldt-Toiyabe National Forest; 760-932-7070

The Horse Creek Trail is a popular place to hike in the Hoover Wilderness of Inyo and Humboldt-Toiyabe National Forests. The trail starts at the 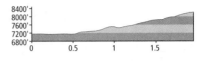 far end of Twin Lakes, so head to the western end and look for the trailhead. Once you start hiking the trail, you will pass several cascades, but the most impressive waterfall comes in about 2 miles in a beautiful valley—after a lot of climbing!

VIRGINIA PEAK FALLS ★

BEST SEASON: May–August
ELEVATION: 11,700 ft
TRAIL LENGTH: 14+ miles
USGS QUAD: Dunderberg Peak (ns)
CONTACT: Humboldt-Toiyabe National Forest; 760-932-7070

Virginia Peak Falls is a familiar sight to backpackers who head toward the inner Hoover Wilderness. It falls in a canyon on the north side of Virginia Peak, and long-distance hikers regularly climb it to pass over the mountain. There is a large lake atop the mountain from which the fall drains, which makes a nice spot to stop and rest after ascending the slabs beside the waterfall. The exact trail length will depend on your route.

BUCKEYE HOT SPRING FALLS ★

BEST SEASON: June–December
ELEVATION: 7000 ft
USGS QUAD: Twin Lakes
CONTACT: Humboldt-Toiyabe National Forest; 760-932-7070

This waterfall feeds into a popular hot spring as a thin cascading creek of one or two dozen feet. It is a warm fall that attracts swimmers from the summer through the winter. To get there, take Twin Lakes Road west from Bridgeport until you reach Forest Service Road 017 on the right. Turn right on FS 017 and continue until you reach the parking lot. Do not turn at the sign for Buckeye Campground.

3 JUNE LAKE

This offshoot of Highway 395 is a 14-mile loop that takes you past four lakes. June Lake is actually among the smallest! Despite its world-famous trout fishing, the

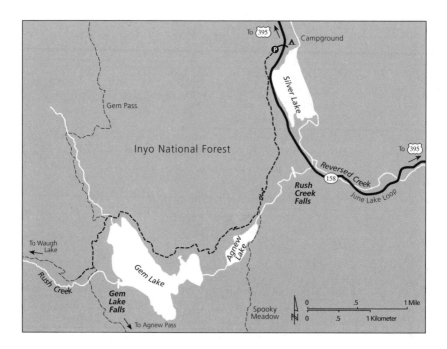

area is surprisingly peaceful and does not have too many tourists on the roads. The loop's official name is Highway 158 and it is found on the west side of Highway 395 a few miles south of the considerably larger Mono Lake.

Rush Creek Falls ★★

BEST SEASON: April–July
ELEVATION: 7400 ft
USGS QUAD: June Lake (ns)
CONTACT: Inyo National Forest; 760-924-5500

Rush Creek Falls is a double waterfall visible from the road around the June Lake Loop on the eastern side of Yosemite. The view is far off in the distance and the waterfall's flow and shape changes throughout the season. Look for it in the mountains above Silver Lake, about 5.5 miles in from the southernmost June Lake Loop entrance, which is also Highway 158.

Gem Lake Falls ★★

BEST SEASON: June–August
ELEVATION: 9000 ft
TRAIL LENGTH: 9 miles

Rush Creek Falls at low flow

USGS QUAD: Koip Peak (ns)
CONTACT: Inyo National Forest; 760-924-5500

Gem Lake Falls is a 50-foot cascade that falls on Rush Creek as it makes its way past the major lakes in the region. The hike to reach it involves significant elevation gain but can be accomplished

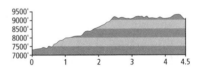

within a day at 9 miles round trip. Drive 1.5 miles past the viewpoint for Rush Creek, and then find the trail near Silver Lake. Follow the trail for 4.5 miles, continuing straight at the junction after 4 miles.

GLASS CREEK FALLS ★★★

BEST SEASON: May–July
ELEVATION: 8200 ft
TRAIL LENGTH: 4 miles
USGS QUAD: June Lake (ns)
CONTACT: Inyo National Forest; 760-924-5500

Glass Creek Falls is a large cascade totaling over 100 feet falling on Glass Creek and easily visible from the trail to the beautiful Glass Creek Meadows. The waterfall is 2 miles in from the trailhead. To get there, head west on Obsidian Dome Road from Highway 395 south of the June Lake Loop. You will find the trailhead after 2 miles.

4 DEVILS POSTPILE NATIONAL MONUMENT

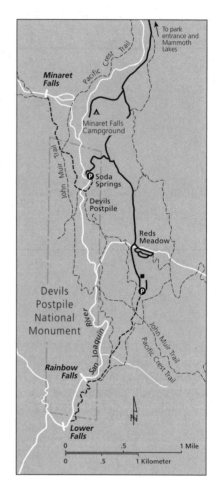

Devils Postpile National Monument is a beautiful alpine recreation area near Mammoth Falls. It was established in 1911 by presidential proclamation in an effort to preserve the postpile, Rainbow Falls, and the other parts of this small but truly unique part of the Eastern Sierras.

While the waterfalls of Devils Postpile National Monument offer stiff competition, the postpile itself steals the show by merit of its sheer uniqueness. Fortunately, the longer hike to Rainbow Falls will take you right by the postpile with its 60-foot tall, symmetrical columns. The postpile originated in an eruption of basalt lava that filled the area less than 100,000 years ago. As the lava cooled, it started to crack. With the help of unusual environmental conditions, the postpile we see today was shaped. Fast-forward to about 10,000 years ago: a glacier swept away a lot of the fractured pieces, polished and exposed the columns.

To visit Devils Postpile National Monument, start in Mammoth Lakes and drive up Highway 203 to a large parking lot. Park your car and pay the admission fee to the park and take a shuttle bus. Cars are not permitted to enter the park except in the very early morning and late evening. If you will be camping in the park, pay an access fee and campground fee here before proceeding.

RAINBOW FALLS ★★★★★

BEST SEASON: May–October
ELEVATION: 7400 ft
TRAIL LENGTH: 2.5 miles

Rainbow Falls

USGS QUAD: Crystal Crag
CONTACT: Devils Postpile National Monument; 760-934-2289

If it weren't for the postpile, this might be called Rainbow Falls National Monument. This San Joaquin River waterfall is that neat. It is only about 100 feet, which might sound puny if you have just come from Yosemite, but this waterfall is all about power. It has a pure block shape and at full force it is nothing less than impressive. Watch for its namesake rainbows in the mist at the bottom of the falls.

There are two ways to reach Rainbow Falls. From the shuttle, you can take the main stop for the Devils Postpile, then you can hike to the falls for a 5-mile round trip that involves a steep climb up the postpile. You can also ride to shuttle stop 9 for a shorter and easier walk to Rainbow Falls (1.25 miles each way), but you miss the postpile that way.

LOWER FALLS ★★★

BEST SEASON: May–October
ELEVATION: 7200 ft
TRAIL LENGTH: 3.5 miles
USGS QUAD: Crystal Crag
CONTACT: Devils Postpile National Monument; 760-934-2289

Lower Falls is a roughly 40-foot drop, also on the San Joaquin River. It is an interesting waterfall in its own right, although you might not guess it by the name. To reach it, continue hiking less than a mile past Rainbow Falls. You should reach it in about fifteen to twenty minutes. It is possible to get right up next to this waterfall, so expect to see fishers and swimmers.

MINARET FALLS ★★★

BEST SEASON: June–July
ELEVATION: 7900 ft
TRAIL LENGTH: 2 miles
USGS QUAD: Crystal Crag
CONTACT: Devils Postpile National Monument; 760-934-2289

Minaret Falls is the northernmost waterfall in Devils Postpile National Monument. It is another major attraction within the park, although not nearly as spectacular as Rainbow Falls. The falls tumble about 300 feet from Minaret Creek into the San Joaquin River. It is a 1-mile hike each way. Start from the main stop for the visitor center and hike as if approaching the postpile. Turn north on the John Muir Trail and follow signs to Minaret Falls.

SOTCHER LAKE FALLS ★★

BEST SEASON: June–September
ELEVATION: 7600 ft
TRAIL LENGTH: 0.75 mile
USGS QUAD: Crystal Crag
CONTACT: Devils Postpile National Monument; 760-934-2289

Sotcher Lake Falls is a 25-foot cascade falling into Sotcher Lake, which is hidden in Reds Meadow. It is not a postcard-worthy fall, but it does provide a nice, quiet place to enjoy a waterfall with only a very short hike. Take the shuttle bus operated by Devils Postpile into Reds Meadow, and then locate Sotcher Lake. Hike the Sotcher Lake Nature Trail around the lake, and then cross a stream on the west shore to view the falls.

---

5 MAMMOTH LAKES

Mammoth Lakes was once a geographically isolated area that got little attention from the gold bugs swarming other areas of the Sierras. That all changed in 1858 when miners found large amounts of silver east of Lake Tahoe, some ways up north from Mammoth Lakes. Fueled by rumors, prospectors flooded into the area in search of more precious metals. In 1878 the Mammoth Mining Company formed under famed Civil War general George Dodge. The company embarked on an ambitious mining project, which brought in thousands of people virtually overnight. Unfortunately, it was a bust and the company shut down just two years later. However, the natural beauty of the area saved the town from becoming another gold rush ghost town, as it attracted a small but continuous stream of wilderness enthusiasts in the summers.

As time went by, skiing became a winter attraction, and in later years a large mountain bike park with over 50 miles of dedicated trails was added. The town of Mammoth Lakes is a few miles west off Highway 395 (look for Highway 203). It is a great launching pad for a number of lovely falls—as well as nearby Devils Postpile National Monument.

TWIN FALLS ★★★★

BEST SEASON: May–August
ELEVATION: 8500 ft
USGS QUAD: Crystal Crag
CONTACT: Inyo National Forest; 760-924-5500

Twin Falls is a very nice 250-foot cascade into the Twin Lakes near Mammoth Lakes. It is easy to get a good view from the parking lot near the campground; you can take a short trail to get in closer to the falls. From Mammoth Lakes, take Highway 203

Twin Falls at low flow

west to the intersection with Lake Mary Road, then continue on Lake Mary Road for 2 miles before turning right on Twin Lakes Road. Follow the road another 0.5 mile to the viewpoint for the falls. The trail leading to the falls is less than a 0.5-mile round trip.

MAMMOTH CREEK FALLS ★★★

BEST SEASON: May–September
ELEVATION: 8200 ft
TRAIL LENGTH: 0.5 mile
USGS QUAD: Crystal Crag (ns)
CONTACT: Inyo National Forest; 760-924-5500

Mammoth Creek Falls is a pretty 40-foot drop in the same area as Twin Falls, but for some reason it is much less known. Follow the directions toward Twin Falls, but after turning on Lake Mary Road, look for a pullout after almost 2 miles. Pick up a use trail heading down to the creek while listening for the sound of falls.

Garnet Lake Falls ★★★

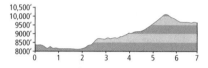

BEST SEASON: June–September
ELEVATION: 9700 ft
TRAIL LENGTH: 14 miles
USGS QUAD: Mount Ritter (ns)
CONTACT: Inyo National Forest; 760-924-5500

The trail to Garnet Lake is one of the most popular long distance trails in the region, and it just so happens that there is a 50-foot waterfall pouring into the lake too. The round trip is just over 14 miles and involves over 1200 feet in elevation gain, so bring plenty of water or plan to camp at the facilities near Garnet Lake. You will need a wilderness permit in order to camp anywhere in the Inyo National Forest.

To reach the trailhead, take Mammoth Lakes Road west from Highway 395, then turn right on Minaret Road for 8 miles to the trailhead, which will be on your right. The roads usually open in mid-June, but are subject to the same rules as Devils Postpile National Monument and are only accessible by shuttle except in early morning and late evening. Unless you enter during those hours, you will have to stop at the parking area for Devils Postpile's shuttle and pay the fee for a shuttle pass. Hike from the Agnew Meadows Trailhead to the Shadow Lake Trail, then take the Shadow Lake Trail toward Ediza Lake. Turn left on

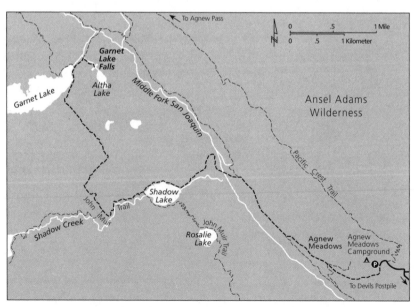

the John Muir Trail past the lake and follow it 2.5 miles uphill to Garnet Lake's outlet. As you approach Altha Lake, leave the John Muir Trail and follow your ears to find the falls tumbling out of Garnet Lake's outlet.

Shadow Lake Falls ★★★

BEST SEASON: June–August
ELEVATION: 8800 ft
TRAIL LENGTH: 6 miles
USGS QUAD: Mount Ritter (ns)
CONTACT: Inyo National Forest; 760-924-5500

The waterfall at Shadow Lake is about 70 feet tall, but it consists of multiple tiers. This waterfall is a great one to visit if you do not have the stamina (or time) to do a long backpacking trip, but you would still like to get out in the wilderness away from the tourists. Follow the directions outlined in the description for Garnet Lake Falls, and then start hiking at the Agnew Meadows Trailhead. Turn left on the Shadow Lake Trail after about 2 miles. The total trip is 6 miles, there and back.

Upper Nydiver Lakes Falls ★★

BEST SEASON: June–August
ELEVATION: 10,000 ft
TRAIL LENGTH: 11 miles
USGS QUAD: Mount Ritter (ns)
CONTACT: Inyo National Forest; 760-924-5500

The Nydiver Lakes are another picturesque mountain hideaway in the eastern Sierras—so pretty you will barely believe they are real. Upper Nydiver Lakes Falls, a 40-foot cascade, is the first of three waterfalls near the lakes. The whole trip takes 11 miles of difficult trekking with significant elevation gain, beginning at the same Agnew Meadows Trailhead as for Garnet Lake Falls. Follow the directions to Shadow Lake Falls, then after passing the falls, continue on the Shadow Lake Trail to the northern end of Shadow Lake. You will reach a junction; go right on the John Muir Trail for about a mile to another junction, at which point you should head left on the Ediza Lake Trail. Hike along Shadow Creek, passing another small waterfall. You will have to climb up two hills with numerous switchbacks, until you reach a stream crossing. This will be Nydiver Creek. Turn and follow the creek toward the lake. After about a quarter mile, there will be a fork in the stream, which will lead you toward the three Nydiver waterfalls.

MIDDLE NYDIVER LAKES FALLS ★★

BEST SEASON: June–August
ELEVATION: 10,000 ft
TRAIL LENGTH: 11.5 miles
USGS QUAD: Mount Ritter (ns)
CONTACT: Inyo National Forest; 760-924-5500

Middle Nydiver Lakes Falls is a 20-foot cascade on Nydiver Creek that drops over some interesting granite boulders. Walk downstream a bit from the upper falls to find the middle falls.

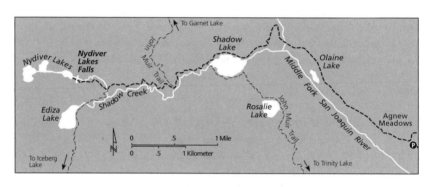

LOWER NYDIVER LAKES FALLS ★★

BEST SEASON: June–August
ELEVATION: 10,000 ft
TRAIL LENGTH: 12 miles
USGS QUAD: Mount Ritter (ns)
CONTACT: Inyo National Forest; 760-924-5500

The lower falls at Nydiver Lakes are a pretty neat 30-foot horsetail, plunging out and away from the rocks. From the middle falls, follow the creek downstream another quarter mile.

6 TOMS PLACE

Toms Place is a small town right off Highway 395 a few miles south of Crowley Lake, another famed fishing destination.

ROCK CREEK LAKE FALLS ★★

BEST SEASON: May–August
ELEVATION: 9700 ft
TRAIL LENGTH: 0.5 mile
USGS QUAD: Mount Morgan (ns)
CONTACT: Inyo National Forest; 760-873-2500

Rock Creek Lake Falls is a thin drop of about 25 feet on Rock Creek. It provides a nice getaway for hikers planning to be in the area for camping or other recreational activities. From Toms Place, head west from Highway 395 on Rock Creek Road and follow it 8 miles to the Rock Creek Campground. Start hiking on an unmarked trail across from the resort and you will reach the fall in about a quarter mile.

HORSETAIL FALLS ★★

BEST SEASON: May–August
ELEVATION: 9000 ft
TRAIL LENGTH: 4 miles
USGS QUAD: Convict Lake
CONTACT: Inyo National Forest; 760-873-2500

Horsetail Falls is a 70-foot plunging drop on an offshoot of McGee Creek. The view is distant and it is tough to see the entire waterfall, thus earning it two stars instead of three or more. Turn west on McGee Creek Road about 6 miles north of Toms Place on Highway 395. Find the McGee Creek Trailhead after 3 miles; it is about 2 miles of hiking before you reach the viewpoint for the falls.

---

7 BISHOP CREEK

The town of Bishop is in relatively dry Owens Valley some 4100 feet above sea level at the intersection of Highways 395, 16 and 168. Unlike most towns in this region, Bishop Creek, as it was originally named, started out as a cattle market rather than a gold mining operation. Recognizing the need for fresh meat in the surrounding mining towns, the cattlemen of Bishop did brisk business. The original Bishop family was among the first to settle in the area with some 600 head of cattle in 1861, but the family eventually moved on. The town, however, continued to grow and prosper despite bloody skirmishes with natives that continued for decades.

NORTH LAKE FALLS ★★

BEST SEASON: April–July
ELEVATION: 9300 ft
USGS QUAD: Mount Thompson (ns)
CONTACT: Inyo National Forest; 760-873-2500

North Lake Falls is a tall, thin cascade stretching down the hillside near the Bishop Creek Outfitters. From Bishop, turn west on Highway 168 from Highway 395 and drive to North Lake Road, which should be about 18 miles. Turn right and go 1.5 miles to the Bishop Creek Outfitters, then turn right and continue until you see the falls near North Lake.

BISHOP CREEK FALLS ★★★

BEST SEASON: April–September
ELEVATION: 8500 ft
USGS QUAD: Mount Thompson (ns)
CONTACT: Inyo National Forest; 760-873-2500

Bishop Creek Falls is a 150-foot cascade on Bishop Creek, fairly easy to access but surprisingly not very well known. View it on the way back from North Lake

Bishop Creek Falls

Falls, looking down at Bishop Creek near the intersection with Highway 168. Alternatively, you can park in the pullout near the turnoff for North Lake Falls and follow a path down to the falls.

GOLDMINE FALLS ★★★

BEST SEASON: May–July
ELEVATION: 7100 ft
USGS QUAD: Mount Thompson (ns)
CONTACT: Inyo National Forest; 760-873-2500

Goldmine Falls is a 40- to 50-foot cascade on the North Fork of Bishop Creek. It is easily visible from Highway 168 heading west of the town of Bishop. Look for it on the right after about 16 or 17 miles.

SCHOEBERS FALLS ★★

BEST SEASON: April–July
ELEVATION: 8600 ft
USGS QUAD: Mount Thompson (ns)
CONTACT: Inyo National Forest; 760-873-2500

This falls is also called Habeggars Falls and Misty Falls. It is a thin, pretty sheet of mist that trickles down the face of a rocky cliff. It falls on private property, but it can be viewed from the road. Take Highway 168 from Highway 395 in Bishop, and then turn left on South Lake Road after nearly 15 miles. Continue to the Bishop Creek Lodge, and look for the waterfall about a half mile past the lodge.

Goldmine Falls

Schoebers Falls

SOUTH FORK OF BISHOP CREEK FALLS ★★

BEST SEASON: May–September
ELEVATION: 9400 ft
TRAIL LENGTH: 0.25 mile
USGS QUAD: Mount Thompson (ns)
CONTACT: Inyo National Forest; 760-873-2500

The waterfall on the South Fork of Bishop Creek is not spectacular in itself, but it provides a nice backdrop for fishing. It is a 30-foot cascade on a creek stocked with trout. Turn left on South Lake Road after traveling about 15 miles on Highway 168 from Bishop. Drive 6 miles to the parking area. The waterfall is just over 100 feet from a nice picnic area.

---

8 BIG PINE

Big Pine, located at the intersection of Highway 395 and 168, was not always this dry. The area used to be a rich agricultural center until the Los Angeles Department of Water and Power started siphoning off water around the turn of the last century. This led to the slow but steady transformation into the arid semidesert you see today, explaining the seemingly bizarre irrigation canals scattered around the town.

FIRST FALLS ★★

BEST SEASON: April–July
ELEVATION: 8100 ft
TRAIL LENGTH: 0.5 mile

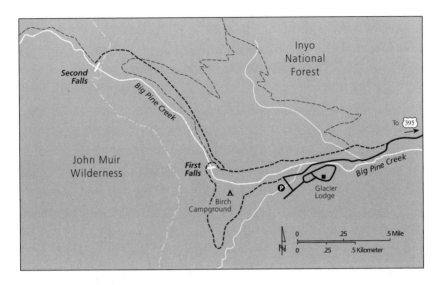

USGS QUAD: Coyote Creek
CONTACT: Inyo National Forest; 760-873-2500

First Falls is a 200-foot cascade on Big Pine Creek. It is accessible via a fairly easy hike, only a half-mile round trip for hikers who choose to turn back after the first fall. (Another option is to continue on toward Second Falls.) To view First Falls, turn west on Glacier Lodge Road from Highway 395 in Big Pine. Go about 10 miles to a day-use area near the end of the road. Hike along the dirt road that follows along the creek.

SECOND FALLS ★★

BEST SEASON: April–July
ELEVATION: 8850 ft
TRAIL LENGTH: 2.5 miles
USGS QUAD: Coyote Flat
CONTACT: Inyo National Forest; 760-873-2500

Second Falls is another 200-foot cascade on Big Pine Creek, like First Falls. After passing First Falls, turn left to stay on a dirt road that parallels the creek. After approximately 1.25 miles of hiking, you will get a view of Second Falls. From here, you can turn and head back or continue onward for a more sightseeing-filled backpacking trip.

9 INDEPENDENCE

This small town east of Kings Canyon National Park was almost entirely wiped out by a major fire in 1886 that took away everything from the courthouse and the saloon to

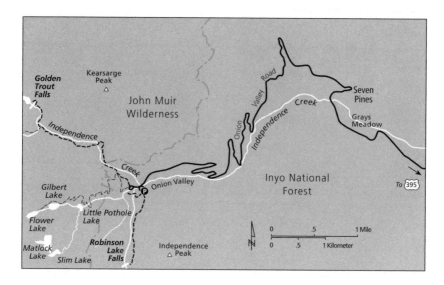

warehouses and residential houses. Fortunately, enough of the town remained so that the residents, with the help of supportive neighbor towns, were able to rebuild it.

Golden Trout Falls ★★

BEST SEASON: May–July
ELEVATION: 9200 ft
USGS QUAD: Kearsarge Peak (ns)
CONTACT: Inyo National Forest; 760-876-5542

This 50-foot plunge falls from a creek running out of Golden Trout Lake north of Onion Valley. From Highway 395 in Independence, turn west on Onion Valley Road and follow it for 13 miles to reach the parking area in Onion Valley. The waterfall is visible from the parking area. Off-trail hikers can try to get in closer to this fall, but there is no maintained trail.

Robinson Lake Falls ★★

BEST SEASON: May–July
ELEVATION: 9200 ft
USGS QUAD: Kearsarge Peak (ns)
CONTACT: Inyo National Forest; 760-876-5542

A creek from Robinson Lake forms this waterfall, cascading 200 feet down the mountain. View it from the Onion Valley parking area as described above. A trail does lead in closer to the base, but it is not maintained.

KINGS CANYON REGION

Located smack in the middle of California, Kings Canyon and Sequoia National Parks are easily accessible both from the San Francisco Bay Area and from the Los Angeles area. While these are technically two separate parks, they sit back to back

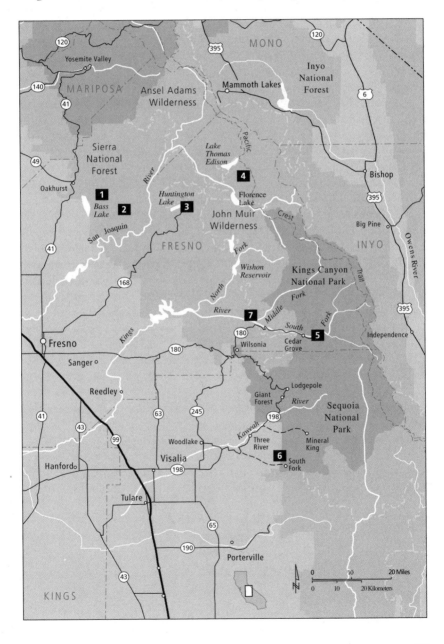

and are managed as one. You will drive through both as you take the Highway 180 to 198 loop, which is the most common visitors' route.

In addition to visiting the spectacular waterfalls, plan to stop at the General Sherman tree. It is the largest living thing on earth, and while not the tallest, it is certainly the biggest tree you will ever see in your life. Watch for the pullout next to the road in the Sequoia portion of the park. It is also possible to hike to the tree, passing through some other magnificent sequoias in the Giant Forest.

But there is more to this region than just the twin parks. Almost immediately as you travel east from Fresno, whether it is on Highway 198 or 41, you will be in the Sierra foothills. Soon, you replace the heat, dust, and vineyards with snowcapped mountains, pine forests, and more picturesque little alpine lakes than you can shake a stick at. In other words, we are talking prime waterfall hunting grounds.

While we have tried to include the most important falls in this book, keep in mind that an exploratory spring excursion will net you dozens if not hundreds of seasonal waterfalls, many of which can be seen right off the road. As a bonus, going in April or May means you will have the roads mostly to yourself, before the crowds clog up the roads and trails (and all the seasonal falls dry up).

Last, a note on the weather. Coming from a lower elevation, you may be surprised just how different the weather is "up there." You can start out in shorts and tee shirt in Fresno, only to find yourself surrounded by 2 feet of snow a couple hours later. The roads to Cedar Grove and Mineral King, where many major waterfalls are located, are usually closed until late spring or early summer—which may seem overly cautious until you come up here and experience the climate firsthand.

The bottom line: if you come in spring or early summer, bring warm clothes, snow chains, and the road-update hotline number so you can keep up with the latest developments (559-565-3341, then press 4). Weather can change suddenly, and you do not want to get stuck on a back road because you forgot the snow chains. As always, when in doubt, consult with a ranger before hitting the trails.

---

1 OAKHURST

Like many other towns in the Sierras, Oakhurst started during the California gold rush. A group of Texans hit the jackpot in nearby Coarsegold around 1850, but Oakhurst struck gold in another way. It focused on becoming the primary source of supplies, tools, and other merchandise needed by the numerous fortune-seekers swarming the region. As it turns out, this highly profitable strategy paid off no matter who struck it rich and who had to head back home with empty pockets.

BASS LAKE FALLS ★

BEST SEASON: March–August
ELEVATION: 3400 ft
USGS QUAD: Bass Lake
CONTACT: Sierra National Forest; 559-877-2218

This waterfall is a 20-foot dump into Bass Lake on Willow Creek. Local youth and tourists love this waterfall, and visitors commonly use it as a nature-made waterslide. It is also a nice picnic background, and the park has ample room for children to play. To get there, take Highway 41 through Oakhurst, and then turn right on Road 222. Drive 4 miles to Road 432 and turn left. Park at "The Falls" parking area.

ANGEL FALLS ★★

BEST SEASON: March–August
ELEVATION: 3600 ft
TRAIL LENGTH: 1 mile
USGS QUAD: Bass Lake
CONTACT: Sierra National Forest; 559-877-2218

Bass Lake Falls

Like Bass Lake Falls, Angel Falls appeals to local residents on warm summer days. This fall is a segment of Willow Creek that runs down a roughly 45-degree angle and has multiple cascades. To get there, follow Road 222 off Highway 41, and then turn left on Road 274 after 3.5 miles. Drive another mile to a dirt road just before the bridge. Follow the highest trail upstream along the creek to reach the falls in under a half mile.

DEVILS SLIDE FALLS ★★

BEST SEASON: April–July
ELEVATION: 4000 ft
TRAIL LENGTH: 4 miles
USGS QUAD: Bass Lake
CONTACT: Sierra National Forest; 559-877-2218

Devils Slide is a fun cascade, roughly 50 feet high on Willow Creek. It holds more attraction for swimmers than sightseers, but it makes a great place to have a family picnic. To get there, follow the directions to Angel Falls. Once you reach Angel Falls, keep hiking upstream another 1.5 miles to reach Devils Slide.

Lower cascades of Angel Falls

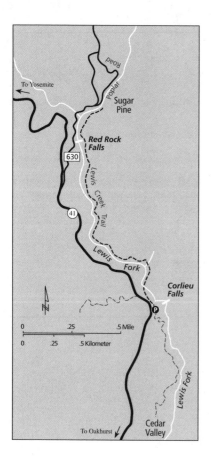

CORLIEU FALLS ★★★

BEST SEASON: January–August
ELEVATION: 3700 ft
USGS QUAD: White Chief Mountain
CONTACT: Sierra National Forest; 559-683-4636

Corlieu Falls is a lovely 40-foot plunge on Lewis Creek. View it from an overlook off Highway 41, or take a short hike to its base. Be ready for a steep scramble to get in close. If you have some time, hike the Lewis Creek National Recreation Trail to reach Red Rock Falls. To reach Corlieu Falls, take Highway 41 north to the sign for the Lewis Creek National Recreation Trail on the right about 8 miles north of Oakhurst.

RED ROCK FALLS ★★

BEST SEASON: February–July
ELEVATION: 4200 ft
TRAIL LENGTH: 3 miles
USGS QUAD: Fish Camp
CONTACT: Sierra National Forest; 559-683-4636

Red Rock Falls is about 20 feet high and stretches the width of Lewis Creek. You can use the Lewis Creek National Recreation Trail to reach it from the turnoff for Corlieu Falls. After viewing the latter, cross the creek and head left on the trail to reach the falls in just over 1.5 miles. Look for a junction with a sign for Red Rock Falls, then head to the left and reach the falls in a short distance. You can also take Highway 41 to Sugar Pine Road and pick up Lewis Creek National Recreation Trail from its northern end for a 1-mile round trip.

Corlieu Falls

2 NORTH FORK

North Fork is a small town with just over 3000 inhabitants, located at the intersection of Road 200, Malum Ridge Road, and Auberry Road between Highways 41 and 168. Be sure to double-check your map when driving in this area, as roads often have more than one name and may change without warning. For those interested in the native heritage of the region, it should be noted that North Fork held a breakthrough conference about California Indian education with 180 Indians from all over the state in 1967. The conference spawned the California Indian Education Association and is seen by some as a key moment in Indian educational history.

WHISKY FALLS ★★

BEST SEASON: May–July
ELEVATION: 5900 ft
USGS QUAD: Shuteye Peak
CONTACT: Sierra National Forest; 559-877-2218

Whisky Falls is sometimes spelled Whiskey. This is a tiered cascade of about 30 feet on Whisky Creek. Although it is accessible by car, the drive is long and slow. From the town of North Fork, head east on Road 225. After a mile, turn left on Road 233 (Cascadel Road). Go 2 miles, and then turn left onto Road 8S09. Continue for 7 miles before turning right on Road 8S70. It is 2 additional miles to the Whisky Falls Campground.

CHIQUITO FALLS ★★★

BEST SEASON: May–July
ELEVATION: 3700 ft
TRAIL LENGTH: 0.25 mile
USGS QUAD: Mammoth Pool Dam (ns)
CONTACT: Sierra National Forest; 559-877-2218

This waterfall is a roaring section of Chiquito Creek with a rocky 70-foot cascade. It is a very long drive, but makes a great attraction for those visiting Sweetwater Campground. From Highway 41 north, turn east on Road 200 toward North Fork. Pass through North Fork (about 20 miles from Highway 41) and turn east on Minaret Road. Drive 37 miles, and then turn right on Mammoth Pool Road and follow it 2 more miles to the campground. Look for a pullout on the left past the campground. It will be a 0.25-mile round-trip hike to the falls.

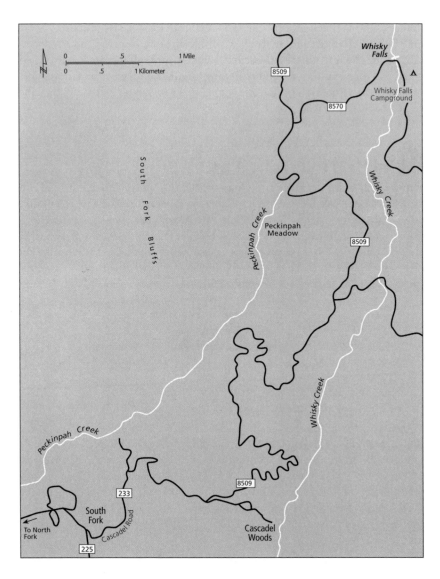

JACKASS FALLS ★★★★

BEST SEASON: December–June
ELEVATION: 6200 ft
USGS QUAD: Squaw Dome (ns)
CONTACT: Sierra National Forest; 559-877-2218

Jackass Falls is a two-part cascade on Jackass Creek that falls close to 100 feet combined. It is visible right from the road. Before making the trip, it is a good idea to check with a ranger to verify that the roads are open. Take Road 200 northeast off Highway 41 until you reach the town of North Fork. Near the center of town, take Road 225 (clearly marked) east. It becomes Road 81 after about 5 miles. Keep going past a fire station and a bunch of campgrounds until you reach the turnoff for Mammoth Pool Reservoir (clearly marked). Go about 6 miles and the falls should be clearly visible from the road.

3 HUNTINGTON LAKE

Huntington Lake is a nice High Sierra vacation spot hidden away from the crowds at about 7000 feet over sea level. It snows a lot here in the winter, but that only means more water to feed Rancheria Falls and other, smaller seasonal falls. You find Huntington Lake by taking Highway 168 northeast from Fresno. After about 50 miles, just after you pass Shaver Lake, Huntington Lake Road splinters off from Highway 168. Turn left onto Huntington Lake Road and keep going for another 11 miles until you reach the lake.

RANCHERIA FALLS ★★★

BEST SEASON: April–June
ELEVATION: 7500 ft
USGS QUAD: Kaiser Peak (ns)
CONTACT: Sierra National Forest; 559-855-5355

Rancheria Falls is a 150-foot seasonal waterfall on Rancheria Creek. At its peak flow, it is about 50 feet wide and visible from the road with a few options to reach its base. Drive to Huntington Lake on Highway 168, and then at the east end, turn east on Kaiser Pass Road and drive about a mile to a pullout on the left. Get in closer by following the Rancheria National Recreation Trail, which can be accessed from the Rancheria Campground. It is a roughly 2-mile round-trip hike to the falls.

4 JOHN MUIR WILDERNESS

This wilderness covers over half a million acres of heavy forests, deep canyons, steep mountain ridges, lush meadows, and countless lakes. For scenic nature sights with minimal human presence to spoil the experience, this is a good place to go. John Muir Wilderness stretches almost 100 miles along the Sierra Nevada range, more or less encapsulating the northern part of Kings Canyon National Park. Highway 395 between Mammoth Lakes and Lone Pine runs parallel to the wilderness and offers numerous inroads.

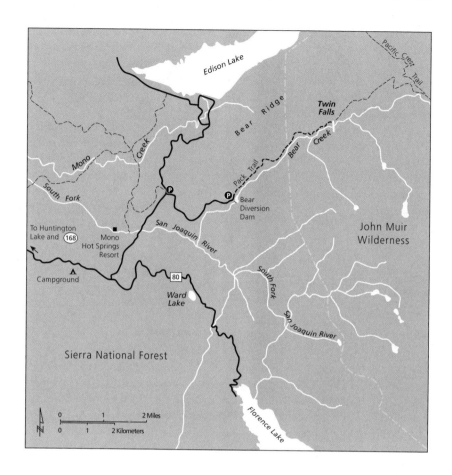

TWIN FALLS ★★★

BEST SEASON: June–September
ELEVATION: 8300 ft
TRAIL LENGTH: 8 miles
USGS QUAD: Florence Lake (ns)
CONTACT: Sierra National Forest; 559-855-5355

Twin Falls is a 20-foot fall in the John Muir Wilderness along Bear Creek. The trail is not too tough, but the drive to get there will be easier for high-clearance vehicles. Take Highway 168 east from Fresno all the way to the end at Huntington Lake (there is a junction—the road continues, but "Highway 168" ends). There, at the northeast corner of the lake, pass a bridge over a large creek and make a right toward Edison and Florence Lakes on Road 80. Go about

18 miles on what is an increasingly rough but paved road past a ranger station and Mono Hot Springs Resort. There is one T-junction along the way; go left toward Edison Lake. Once you see the Mono Lake Hot Springs, go another mile and watch for a dirt road on your right. This is a rough road, four-wheel drive is recommended. You can park the car and make it a longer hike if you are unsure of your car's abilities.

After about 2 miles, the dirt road ends by a dam where you should watch for the Bear Creek Trailhead (there will be a sign). Stay on the trail for about 4 miles and you will reach the falls. There are alternate routes to this fall, but this is the easiest. Stop by the ranger station on the way to pick up a map and discuss the options. Also, since this is a wilderness area, no wheels of any kind are allowed on the trails.

ROCK CREEK FALLS ★★

BEST SEASON: June–August
ELEVATION: 6800 ft
USGS QUAD: Dinkey Creek (ns)
CONTACT: Sierra National Forest; 559-855-5355

Rock Creek Falls is a 20-foot drop on Rock Creek in the Dinkey Lakes region. To get there, take Highway 168 east from Fresno for one and a half to two hours until you see Dinkey Creek Road near a sign for Shaver Creek. Go about 13 miles down the road and turn onto Rock Creek Road. The fall is clearly visible from the road about four miles down.

5 KINGS CANYON NATIONAL PARK

This is one of two separately established national parks, Sequoia and Kings Canyon, but they border one another and are managed as one. Both are home to sequoias large enough to humble the most jaded outdoor enthusiast, but there's more to this fascinating region than giant sequoias. With elevations ranging from 1500 feet to 14,491 feet, you will find vastly different environments throughout the two parks. If there ever was a place to study the many faces of The Great American Outdoors, this is it. As a bonus, there are more than 200 marble caverns scattered underground, some of which can be toured as a neat side trip from your waterfall hunting. You reach the Kings Canyon entrance by taking Highway 180 east from Fresno for just over an hour until you reach the park. For all waterfalls within Kings Canyon National Park, use 559-565-3341 for more information.

GRIZZLY FALLS ★★★★

BEST SEASON: May–June
ELEVATION: 4400 ft
USGS QUAD: Cedar Grove
CONTACT: Sequoia National Forest; 559-338-2251

Grizzly Falls sits just outside the boundary of Kings Canyon National Park in the Sequoia National Forest, but you still have to enter the park to view it. It is one of the easiest waterfalls to access, situated right off the road. The plunge is a two-tiered drop of 80 to 90 feet falling on Grizzly Creek near the junction with the Kings River. You can see it out your car window, or you can stop and walk up to its base. To reach it, take Highway 180 east from Fresno for about 53 miles. Stop at the entrance kiosk and pay the fee, then at the fork approximately 1.5 miles in, head left toward Cedar Grove and continue another 27 miles.

UPPER TENMILE CREEK FALLS ★★

BEST SEASON: May–July
ELEVATION: 3800 ft
USGS QUAD: Hume (ns)
CONTACT: Sequoia National Forest; 559-338-2251

As you drive down Highway 180 toward Cedar Grove, to the right you will catch a glimpse of Tenmile Creek cascading down the hillside. Although the view of

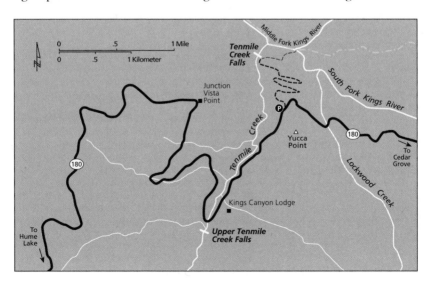

the entire falls is perhaps better from your car, it is also possible to hike in to get a closer look at part of the waterfall. After crossing a bridge just before Kings Canyon Lodge, look for a place to pull out on the right just next to the lower portion of the falls. Hike in about a 0.25 mile to find a 30-foot drop.

TENMILE CREEK FALLS ★★★

BEST SEASON: May–July
ELEVATION: 2900 ft
TRAIL LENGTH: 3.5 miles
USGS QUAD: Hume (ns)
CONTACT: Sequoia National Forest; 559-338-2251

Tenmile Creek Falls is a cascade of over 200 feet on Tenmile Creek near the Yucca Point Trail. It is one of the tallest waterfalls in Kings Canyon National Park, but it requires a 3.5-mile round-trip hike with 1200 feet of elevation loss. After passing through the Grant Grove area of Kings Canyon National Park along Highway 180, continue about 15 miles east to the Yucca Point Trailhead on the left. Follow the Yucca Point Trail just over 1.5 miles to an offshoot trail that will take you to Tenmile Creek Falls.

MIST FALLS ★★★★

BEST SEASON: May–July
ELEVATION: 5800 ft
TRAIL LENGTH: 8 miles
USGS QUAD: The Sphinx
CONTACT: Kings Canyon National Park; 559-565-3341

There is a reason why Mist Falls is called what it is. The 45-foot waterfall on the South Fork of the Kings River is not exceptionally high, but it is famous 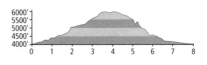 for its powerful flow, creating a huge cloud of mist as it smashes into the rocks during its peak flow. In lesser-flow seasons, it looks like an ordinary waterfall, but there is something unforgettable about seeing Mist Falls at its finest. It drowns out the surrounding scenery (and any attempt at communication). To reach Mist Falls, follow the directions to Grizzly Falls but continue another 11 miles, passing Cedar Grove Campground, to the trailhead parking lot. The hike is 8 miles there and back, involving a few sections of steep uphill hiking. Overnight camping is available in designated areas in Paradise Valley, but bear canisters are required for an overnight stay.

Mist Falls (Photo courtesy of Kevin Gong kevingong.com*)*

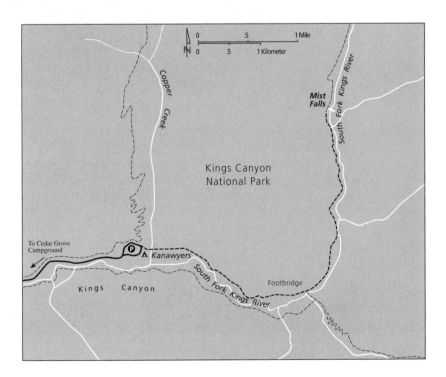

ROARING RIVER FALLS ★★★

BEST SEASON: May–July
ELEVATION: 5300 ft
TRAIL LENGTH: 0.4 mile
USGS QUAD: The Sphinx
CONTACT: Kings Canyon National Park; 559-565-3341

Roaring River Falls is a 40-foot tiered plunge that widens at the base as it pours
from the Roaring River into the Kings River. Some visitors like to swim at its
base, and it is easily accessible via a brief 0.4-mile round-trip hike on a wheelchair-
friendly paved trail. Follow the directions to Grizzly Falls, but continue 8 miles
past to a parking area for Roaring River Falls.

Roaring River Falls (Photo courtesy of Yen-Wen Lu)

Silver Spray Falls ★★★★★

BEST SEASON: May–July
ELEVATION: 5000 ft
TRAIL LENGTH: 30 miles
USGS QUAD: Tehipite Dome
CONTACT: Kings Canyon National Park; 559-565-3341

Seeing Silver Spray Falls is not an easy endeavor. The trip to reach it is about 15 difficult miles each way, but it traverses through breathtaking areas of Kings Canyon National Park that rival Yo-

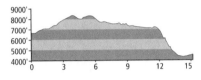

semite in beauty. Most backpackers agree that the Tehipite Valley area would be swamped with visitors were it not for the grueling trip to get there. Silver Spray Falls itself is hundreds of feet tall, pouring down Crown Creek into the valley.

The trailhead is outside the park in the Crown Valley region (Sierra National Forest). To get to the trailhead, take Highway 168 east to Dinkey Creek Road near

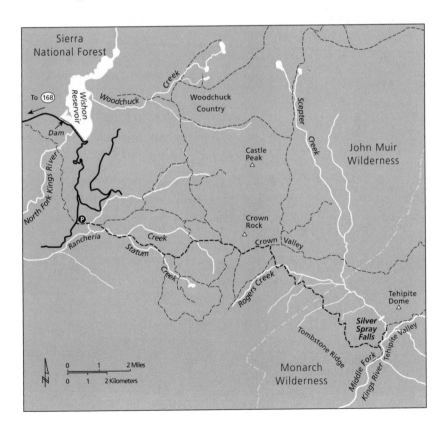

Shaver Lake. Take Dinkey Creek Road all the way to McKinley Grove Road and stay on the main road to the Wishon Reservoir. Cross over the dam and continue about 3 miles. There is a Y in the road; hang right and watch for the pullout after about a mile. The trail runs west to east, but you will turn south within a mile. After a while, look for a fork before Rogers Creek. Hang left (across the creek); do not follow the creek westward. Continue through Hay Meadow and descend into Tehipite Valley. Once you hit Crown Creek (first major creek), listen for the falls. You probably will not see the falls from the trail since the forest is very dense, so expect to do some exploring off the trail to get a good viewpoint.

Again, this is a very difficult backpacking trail. It is 10 to 11 miles to the valley floor, then another mile or two up the creek plus 0.25 to 0.5 mile off the trail to find a viewpoint for the falls. The best time to view the falls is probably spring, but getting there may be problematic due to snow and difficult creek crossings, so you may have to go in the fall and settle with less flow.

BLUE CANYON FALLS ★★★★★

BEST SEASON: May–July
ELEVATION: 4800 ft
TRAIL LENGTH: 31 miles
USGS QUAD: Slide Bluffs
CONTACT: Kings Canyon National Park; 559-565-3341

Blue Canyon Falls is another spectacular waterfall that stretches hundreds of feet. It falls down the Blue Canyon into the Kings River in the Tehipite Valley area, and hikers face a very strenuous backpacking trip to reach it. Follow the directions to Silver Spray Falls, and then continue about 3 miles northwest along the Kings River. It will be along the next major creek, falling on the left side of the river.

ELLA FALLS ★★★

BEST SEASON: May–July
ELEVATION: 5800 ft
TRAIL LENGTH: 3 miles
USGS QUAD: General Grant Grove
CONTACT: Kings Canyon National Park; 559-565-3341

Ella Falls is a 40-foot cascade on Sequoia Creek. The hike to reach it is just over 2 miles of downhill hiking with about 1000 feet of elevation loss, but it

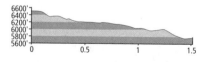

is worth the effort to see the scenery. From the park entrance on Highway 180, go 1.5 miles in, then turn left and continue another 1.5 miles to General Grant

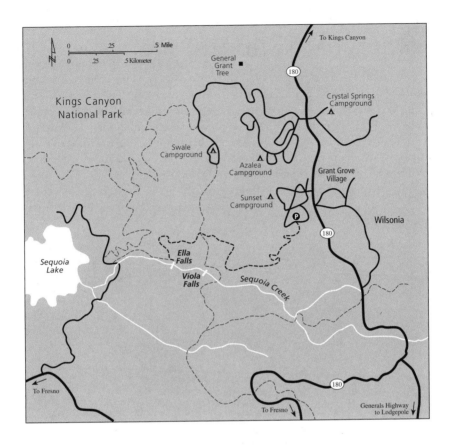

Grove. Start the hike at the bottom end of Sunset Campground, though you may have to park in Grant Grove Village. The area is often snow-covered until late spring, so call to check the weather before planning a trip here.

Viola Falls ★

BEST SEASON: May–July
ELEVATION: 5800 ft
TRAIL LENGTH: 3 miles
USGS QUAD: General Grant Grove
CONTACT: Kings Canyon National Park; 559-565-3341

Viola Falls is best seen as a side trip on the way to Ella Falls. It is a 5-foot drop on Sequoia Creek. A mile and a half into the hike to Ella Falls, turn left at the intersection with the South Boundary Trail and continue 0.25 mile to Viola Falls.

6 SEQUOIA NATIONAL PARK

As mentioned in the Kings Canyon entry, Sequoia and Kings Canyon are two separate parks, yet they are treated as one. As you move around the eastern part of the region, you will see Mount Whitney towering above. At 14,491 feet above sea level, Whitney is the highest mountain in the contiguous forty-eight states. Unfortunately, it hides behind a mountain chain (The Great Divide) so you cannot view it from the west. For the best angle, take Highway 395 (east of the park) to the town of Lone Pine and stop at the Interagency Visitor Center just south of town. To get to the Sequoia entrance, go to the town of Visalia 40 miles south of Fresno along Highway 99. Take Highway 198 east and go for about an hour until you reach the park.

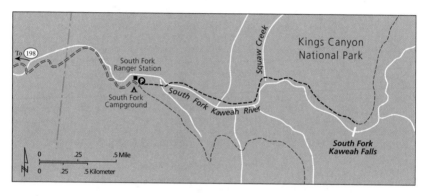

SOUTH FORK KAWEAH FALLS ★★★

BEST SEASON: April–September
ELEVATION: 4400 ft
TRAIL LENGTH: 3 miles
USGS QUAD: Moses Mountain (ns)
CONTACT: Sequoia National Park; 559-565-3341

South Fork Kaweah Falls is sometimes called Ladybug Falls. The falls are about 25 feet high, plunging on the South Fork Kaweah River. The hike follows the Ladybug Trail, which begins near South Fork Campground in the southernmost part of Sequoia National Park. From Highway 198, turn right on South Fork Drive in the town of Three Rivers about 8 miles west of the Ash Mountain entrance. Go about 14 miles to the South Fork Campground and park in the day-use area (unless you intend to camp, of course). Pick up the Ladybug Trail and hike just over 1.5 miles past the Ladybug Campground. You will need to leave the trail and scramble down to the river, passing a swimming hole along the way.

BLACK WOLF FALLS ★★★

BEST SEASON: June–July
ELEVATION: 7800 ft
USGS QUAD: Mineral King (ns)
CONTACT: Sequoia National Park; 559-565-3341

Black Wolf Falls is a 50-foot cascade on Monarch Creek. It is sometimes called Monarch Falls for this reason. You can view Black Wolf Falls from your car on the way to the parking area for the Farewell Gap Trail at the end of Mineral King Road. It is 0.5 mile before the parking area.

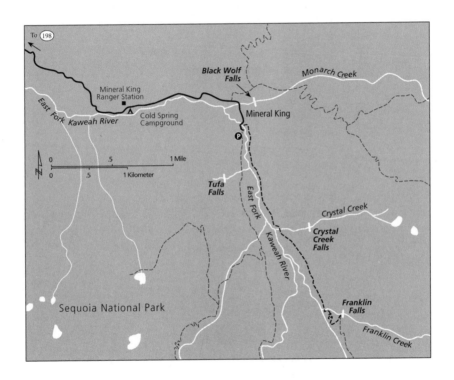

TUFA FALLS ★★

BEST SEASON: June–August
ELEVATION: 8000 ft
TRAIL LENGTH: 0.25 mile
USGS QUAD: Mineral King
CONTACT: Sequoia National Park; 559-565-3341

Tufa Falls is a cascade that pours 500 feet down Spring Creek into the East Fork Kaweah River. It is difficult to get a good view of it due to the number of trees growing on the mountainside, but the best place to see it is on the beginning of a hike on the Farewell Gap Trail (which also passes Crystal Creek Falls and Franklin Falls). From Highway 198, turn right on Mineral King Road before the Ash Mountain Entrance Station. Continue to the end of the road, about 25 miles, to the parking area. Because the road is narrow and winding, budget an hour for the 25-mile drive. To hike the Farewell Gap Trail, walk back up the road to the bridge over the river. Across it, turn right toward the Mineral King Pack Station and look for the trailhead. Tufa Falls is faintly visible near the beginning of the hike. A trail that begins in the parking lot also passes by Tufa Falls, but the view is slightly better from the Farewell Gap Trail. The road to the Mineral King area is generally closed until around Memorial Day weekend.

CRYSTAL CREEK FALLS ★★★

BEST SEASON: June–August
ELEVATION: 8000 ft
TRAIL LENGTH: 2 miles
USGS QUAD: Mineral King (ns)
CONTACT: Sequoia National Park; 559-565-3341

Crystal Creek Falls is another cascade that pours down along the Farewell Gap Trail. The view is better of Crystal Creek Falls than of Tufa Falls, so it is well worth continuing 0.75 mile past Tufa Falls to see it. Additionally, the hike is still very easy at this point. After viewing Crystal Creek Falls, you can turn back or continue onward to see Franklin Falls.

FRANKLIN FALLS ★★★

BEST SEASON: June–August
ELEVATION: 8400 ft
TRAIL LENGTH: 4 miles
USGS QUAD: Mineral King (ns)
CONTACT: Sequoia National Park; 559-565-3341

Franklin Falls is the final fall you will reach on the Farewell Gap Trail. It is a series of cascades on Franklin Creek down the slope near the trail. However, once you pass Crystal Creek Falls, the trip becomes somewhat more difficult although not strenuous. Hike uphill another mile past Crystal Creek Falls to find it. There are spectacular views of the surrounding scenery from this point on the trail.

MARBLE FALLS ★★★★

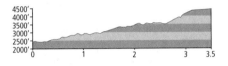

BEST SEASON: March–June
ELEVATION: 4300 feet
TRAIL LENGTH: 7 miles
USGS QUAD: Giant Forest
CONTACT: Sequoia National Park; 559-565-3341

Marble Falls is a series of cascades on the Marble Fork of the Kaweah River. It would be one of the highest waterfalls in California if it weren't that the cascades are not continuous. There are a series of individual drops of 30 to 40 feet. Unfortunately, the trail is somewhat difficult, with over 2000 feet of elevation gain over 3.5 miles. Entering from the Ash Mountain Entrance Station, drive north 4 miles on Highway 198 to Potwisha Campground. Park in the day-use parking area at the upper end of the campground, then look for the trailhead near site 16. The trail is hot and dry with little shade, so it might be difficult to hike in the summertime. No camping is allowed along this trail.

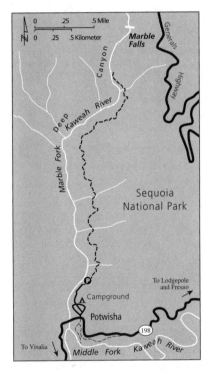

PANTHER CREEK FALLS ★★★

BEST SEASON: March–June
ELEVATION: 3800 ft
TRAIL LENGTH: 6 miles
USGS QUAD: Lodgepole (nl)
CONTACT: Sequoia National Park;
559-565-3341

Panther Creek Falls is a neat 150-foot downpour from Panther Creek into the Middle Fork Kaweah River. It requires a 6-mile round-trip hike on the Middle Fork Trail, which is a neat but relatively unshaded trek alongside the river. The hike starts near the Buckeye Flat Campground. Turn right about 6 miles in from the park entrance on Highway 198. Bear left at the fork just before the campground and continue 1.25 miles to the trailhead. You will reach the waterfall after almost exactly 3 miles of hiking. The road to the trailhead is closed to vehicles during wet weather since the clay surface can become quite slick.

EAST FORK KAWEAH FALLS ★★

BEST SEASON: May–July
ELEVATION: 6000 ft
TRAIL LENGTH: 4 miles
USGS QUAD: Silver City (ns)
CONTACT: Sequoia National Park; 559-565-3341

East Fork Kaweah Falls is a small, 20-foot cascade that pours down rocky boulders on the East Fork Kaweah River. The hike is just over 2 miles round trip, beginning at the Atwell Mill Campground. Heading north on Highway 198 from Visalia, turn right on Mineral King Road 2 miles west of the Ash Mountain Entrance Station. Continue about 20 miles to the parking area for the Atwell/Hockett Trail past the campground. Start hiking on the Hockett Trail for just over a mile, descending about 500 feet in elevation, to where the trail meets the river.

MIDDLE FORK KAWEAH FALLS ★★

BEST SEASON: May–July
ELEVATION: 3000 ft
TRAIL LENGTH: 0.5 mile
USGS QUAD: Giant Forest (ns)
CONTACT: Sequoia National Park; 559-565-3341

Middle Fork Kaweah Falls is a 20-foot cascade on the Middle Fork Kaweah River near Buckeye Flat Campground. In its peak season it has a considerable flow,

Middle Fork Kaweah Falls

making it interesting to waterfall seekers. The hike is also an easy 0.5-mile round trip. Enter Sequoia National Park from Highway 198 and drive 6 miles north to the campground, which will be on the right. Start hiking on the Paradise Creek Trail at the east end of the campground. After crossing a bridge over the river, leave the main trail and continue upstream about a tenth of a mile.

BIG FERN SPRINGS ★★★

BEST SEASON: March–July
ELEVATION: 3900 ft
USGS QUAD: Giant Forest
CONTACT: Sequoia National Park; 559-565-3341

Big Fern Springs has a pretty little waterfall that is easily accessible from the side of the road. It is between 30 and 50 feet of cascades and serves as a lovely spot

Big Fern Springs

to stop and get some fresh air while traveling through Sequoia National Park. Take Highway 198 3 miles north of Hospital Rock or just over a mile south of the Amphitheater Point outlook. Expect minimal flow in dry weather.

GRANITE SPRING ★★

BEST SEASON: March–July
ELEVATION: 4800 ft
USGS QUAD: Giant Forest
CONTACT: Sequoia National Park; 559-565-3341

This is a 60-foot plunge along the side of Highway 198. Look for it about a mile north of the Amphitheater Point lookout. It is best seen in the spring to assure that there will be a flow.

Granite Spring

PINEWOOD FALLS (U) ★★

BEST SEASON: March–June
ELEVATION: 6500 ft
USGS QUAD: Giant Forest (ns)
CONTACT: Sequoia National Park; 559-565-3341

As you drive north on Highway 198, look for this unnamed seasonal plunge near the Pinewood area a mile and a half south of the pullout for the General Sherman Tree. It is a 20-foot drop over a large, smooth rock on the east side of the highway.

CASCADE CREEK FALLS ★★

BEST SEASON: May–July
ELEVATION: 4600 ft
TRAIL LENGTH: 1 mile
USGS QUAD: Giant Forest (ns)
CONTACT: Sequoia National Park; 559-565-3341

This waterfall is only about 20 feet high, falling on Cascade Creek, but it is along the hiking trail to Crystal Cave and makes a nice stopping point for park visitors on their way to the cave. Purchase tickets for a guided tour of Crystal Cave at the park entrance, and then drive 15 miles north of the southernmost entrance on Highway 198. Turn left at the turnoff for Crystal Cave and continue another 7 miles. The waterfall is about 0.5 mile in on the trail to Crystal Cave. If you plan to travel here in May, be sure to call the park to verify that the area is open since it is frequently subject to road closures.

TOKOPAH FALLS ★★★★

BEST SEASON: May–July
ELEVATION: 7200 ft
TRAIL LENGTH: 3 miles
USGS QUAD: Lodgepole
CONTACT: Sequoia National Park; 559-565-3341

Tokopah Falls is a scenic 1200-foot cascade that pours majestically into the To-kopah Valley on the Marble Fork Kaweah River. Its size and power will surprise

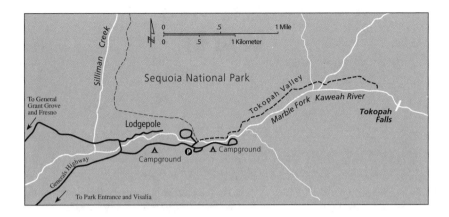

you, as will its volume. The hike is just over 1.5 miles each way on a relatively flat trail, so the trail tends to be quite popular. After entering the park from Highway 180 east of Fresno, continue 1.5 miles and turn right toward Sequoia National Park. Go 25 miles to the Lodgepole Campground turnoff and continue to the day-use area near the Marble Fork Kaweah River. Call the park ranger to check conditions before planning a springtime trip; the trail is occasionally covered in snow until June.

7 MONARCH WILDERNESS

With a regal name like this, you expect some majestic views. Don't worry—in Monarch Wilderness, you get them in spades. Covering almost 45,000 acres, elevations range from about 2000 feet to well over 11,000 feet, offering a rich variety of flora and wildlife. The bad news is that this is seriously rugged terrain. There are no trails here, and even seasoned off-trail hikers better be prepared for a real adventure heading into this place. Located at the western border of Kings Canyon–Sequoia National Parks, you actually drive through this wilderness when you travel on Highway 180 from Fresno.

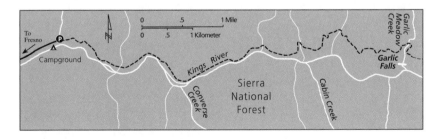

Opposite: Pinewood Falls near the General Sherman Tree

GARLIC FALLS ★★★★

BEST SEASON: May–July
ELEVATION: 2400 ft
TRAIL LENGTH: 10 miles
USGS QUAD: Hume
CONTACT: Sierra National Forest; 559-297-0706

Garlic Falls is a multitiered 640-foot fall on Garlic Meadow Creek leading into the Kings River. It is possible to get a distant view from Yucca Point along Highway 180 heading toward Cedar Grove from the park entrance, but the best way to view Garlic Falls is by backpacking along the Kings River National Recreation Trail. Take Highway 180 from Fresno, then turn left on East Trimmer Springs Road at Centerville and keep going until the road ends. The trailhead is at the very end of the road, past the toilets. The hike to the falls is 5 miles each way. The first 3 miles are national recreation trail, but the trail becomes less maintained for the last 2 miles until it ends in the falls. Due to the winding roads, the drive to the trailhead can be an hour and a half or more, especially when people are pulling boats.

APPENDIX A:
INDEX OF RECREATIONAL
AUTHORITIES AND LAND OWNERS

The following is a list of the contact information for the pertinent land management agencies and other owners that control the waterfalls mentioned in this book. Most state and national parks require entrance fees. Visit the park websites or call for current fee information.

ARMSTRONG REDWOODS STATE RESERVE
17020 Armstrong Woods Road, Guerneville, CA 95446
707-869-2015
www.parks.ca.gov/?page_id=450
Waterfalls: Armstrong Falls (San Francisco Bay Area)

AUBURN STATE RECREATION AREA
501 El Dorado Street, Auburn, CA 95604-3266
530-885-4527
www.parks.ca.gov/?page_id=502
Waterfalls: American Canyon Falls, Knickerbocker Falls, Lake Clementine Falls, Paradise Canyon Falls, Codfish Falls (Sacramento/San Joaquin Region)

BIG BASIN REDWOODS STATE PARK
21600 Big Basin Way, Boulder Creek, CA 95006
831-338-8860
www.parks.ca.gov/default.asp?page_id=540
Waterfalls: Berry Creek Falls, Sempervirens Falls, Golden Cascade, Silver Falls (San Francisco Bay Area)

BIG SPRINGS GARDEN
32613 Highway 49, Sierra City, CA 96125
530-862-1333
www.bigspringsgarden.com/
Waterfalls: Big Springs Garden Falls (Tahoe Region)

BUREAU OF LAND MANAGEMENT ARCATA
1695 Heindon Road, Arcata, CA 95521-4573
707-825-2300
www.ca.blm.gov/arcata
Waterfalls: Lost Coast Falls (North Coast)

BUREAU OF LAND MANAGEMENT ALTURAS
708 West Twelfth, Alturas, CA 96101
530-233-4666
www.ca.blm.gov/alturas
Waterfalls: Pit River Falls (Lassen Region)

BUREAU OF LAND MANAGEMENT FOLSOM
63 Natoma Street, Folsom, CA 95630
916-985-4474
www.ca.blm.gov/folsom
Waterfalls: Stevens Creek Falls (Sacramento/San Joaquin Region)

BUREAU OF RECLAMATION
16349 Shasta Dam Boulevard, Shasta Lake, CA 96019
530-275-1554
www.usbr.gov/mp/ncao/
Waterfalls: Shasta Dam (Shasta-Trinity Region)

CALIFORNIA DEPARTMENT OF FISH AND GAME
1100 Fortress Street Suite 2, Chico, CA 95973
916-445-0411
www.dfg.ca.gov/
Waterfalls: Upper Fairy Falls, Lower Fairy Falls, Coal Canyon Falls (Sacramento/San Joaquin Region)

CASTLE CRAGS STATE PARK
P.O. Box 80, Castella, CA 96017-0090
530-235-2684
www.parks.ca.gov/?page_id=454
Waterfalls: Burstarse Falls (Shasta-Trinity Region)

CASTLE ROCK STATE PARK
15000 Skyline Boulevard, Los Gatos, CA 95033-8291
408-867-2952
www.parks.ca.gov/default.asp?page_id=538
Waterfalls: Castle Rock Falls (San Francisco Bay Area)

CITY OF VACAVILLE PUBLIC WORKS
650 Merchant Street, Vacaville, CA 95688
707-449-5170
www.ci.vacaville.ca.us/departments/public_works/
Waterfalls: Creek Walk Falls (San Francisco Bay Area)

DEVILS POSTPILE NATIONAL MONUMENT
P.O. Box 3999, Mammoth Lakes, CA 93546
760-934-2289
www.nps.gov/depo/
Waterfalls: All Devils Postpile National Monument waterfalls (Eastern Sierra Region)

EAST BAY REGIONAL PARK DISTRICT
P.O. Box 5381, Oakland, CA 94605
510-562-PARK
www.ebparks.org/
Waterfalls: Abrigo Falls, Murietta Falls, Little Yosemite Falls (San Francisco Bay Area)

EDGEWOOD COUNTY PARK
Edgewood and Old Stage Roads, Redwood City, CA 94063
650-368-6283
www.eparks.net/
Waterfalls: Sylvan Trail Falls (San Francisco Bay Area)

EL DORADO IRRIGATION DISTRICT
2890 Mosquito Road, Placerville, CA 95667
530-622-4513
www.eid.org/
Waterfalls: Sly Park Falls (Lake Tahoe Region)

ELDORADO NATIONAL FOREST
www.fs.fed.us/r5/eldorado/

PACIFIC RANGER DISTRICT
7887 Highway 15, Pollock Pines, CA 95726
916-644-2347
Waterfalls: Bassi Falls, Horsetail Falls (Lake Tahoe Region)

PLACERVILLE RANGER DISTRICT
4260 Eightmile Road, Camino, CA 95709
530-644-2324
Waterfalls: Bridal Veil Falls, Buttermilk Falls (Lake Tahoe Region)

GEORGETOWN RANGER DISTRICT
7600 Wentworth Springs Road, Georgetown, CA 95634
530-333-4312
Waterfalls: Pilot Creek Falls (Lake Tahoe Region)

AMADOR RANGER DISTRICT
26820 Silver Drive, Pioneer, CA 95666
209-295-4251
Waterfalls: Caples Creek Falls (Lake Tahoe Region)

FOREST OF NISENE MARKS STATE PARK
Aptos Creek Road, Soquel Drive, Aptos, CA 95003
831-763-7062
www.parks.ca.gov/default.asp?page_id=666
Waterfalls: Five Finger Falls, Maple Falls (San Francisco Bay Area)

GOLDEN GATE NATIONAL RECREATION AREA
Fort Mason, Building 201, San Francisco, CA 94123-0022
415-561-4700
www.nps.gov/goga/
Waterfalls: Morses Gulch Falls (San Francisco Bay Area)

GROVER HOT SPRINGS STATE PARK
P.O. Box 188, Markleeville, CA 96120
530-694-2248
www.parks.ca.gov/?page_id=508
Waterfalls: Hot Springs Creek Falls (Lake Tahoe Region)

HUMBOLDT COUNTY VISITORS BUREAU
1034 Second Street, Eureka, CA 95501
800-346-3482
www.redwoodvisitor.org/
Waterfalls: Mill Creek Falls (North Coast)

HUMBOLDT REDWOODS STATE PARK
P.O. Box 100, Weott, CA 95571
707-946-2409
www.parks.ca.gov/?page_id=425
Waterfalls: South Fork Honeydew Falls (North Coast)

HUMBOLDT-TOIYABE NATIONAL FOREST
www.fs.fed.us/r4/htnf/

BRIDGEPORT RANGER STATION
HCR 1 Box 1000, Bridgeport, CA 93517
760-932-7070
Waterfalls: Leavitt Falls, Cascade Falls, Sardine Falls, Sardine Creek Falls
(Yosemite Region); Horse Creek Falls, Virginia Peak Falls, Buckeye Hot
Spring Falls (Eastern Sierra Region)

CARSON RANGER DISTRICT
1536 South Carson Street, Carson City, NV 89701
775-882-2766
Waterfalls: Llewellyn Falls, Carson Falls (Lake Tahoe Region)

INYO NATIONAL FOREST
www.fs.fed.us/r5/inyo/

MONO BASIN SCENIC AREA RANGER STATION
P.O. Box 429, Lee Vining, CA 93541
760-647-3044
Waterfalls: Ellery Lake Falls, Big Bend Falls, Aspen Falls, Lundy Canyon Falls (Eastern Sierra Region)

MAMMOTH LAKES RANGER STATION
P.O. Box 148, Mammoth Lakes, CA 93546
760-924-5500
Waterfalls: Rush Creek Falls, Gem Lake Falls, Glass Creek Falls, Twin Falls, Garnet Lake Falls, Mammoth Creek Falls, Shadow Lake Falls, Nydiver Lakes Falls (Eastern Sierra Region)

WHITE MOUNTAIN RANGER STATION
798 North Main Street, Bishop, CA 93514
760-873-2500
Waterfalls: Rock Creek Lake Falls, Horsetail Falls, North Lake Falls, Bishop Creek Falls, Goldmine Falls, Schoebers Falls, South Fork of Bishop Creek Falls, First Falls, Second Falls (Eastern Sierra Region)

MOUNT WHITNEY RANGER STATION
P.O. Box 8, Lone Pine, CA 93545
760-876-5542
Waterfalls: Golden Trout Falls, Robinson Lake Falls (Eastern Sierra Region)

JACKSON DEMONSTRATION STATE FOREST
802 North Main, Fort Bragg, CA 95437
707-964-5674
www.fire.ca.gov/php/rsrc-mgt_jackson.php
Waterfalls: Chamberlain Creek Falls (North Coast)

JEDEDIAH SMITH REDWOODS STATE PARK
1375 Elk Valley Road, Crescent City, CA 95531
707-464-6101 ext. 5112
www.parks.ca.gov/?page_id=413
Waterfalls: Fern Falls (North Coast)

KINGS CANYON AND SEQUOIA NATIONAL PARKS
47050 Generals Highway, Three Rivers, CA 93271-9700
559-565-3341
www.nps.gov/seki/
Waterfalls: All waterfalls within Kings Canyon and Sequoia National
Parks (Kings Canyon Region)

KLAMATH NATIONAL FOREST
www.fs.fed.us/r5/klamath/

HAPPY CAMP RANGER STATION
63822 Highway 96, P.O. Box 377, Happy Camp, CA 96039-0377
530-493-2243
Waterfalls: Ishi Pishi Falls, Ukonom Falls, Sheridan Falls, Twin Falls
(Shasta-Trinity Region)

LAKE TAHOE BASIN MANAGEMENT UNIT
P.O. Box 731002, 870 Emerald Bay Road, Suite 1, South Lake Tahoe, CA 96150
530-573-2600
www.fs.fed.us/r5/ltbmu/
Waterfalls: Cascade Falls, Upper Eagle Falls, Lower Eagle Falls, Upper
Glen Alpine Falls, Lower Glen Alpine Falls (Lake Tahoe Region)

LASSEN NATIONAL FOREST
www.fs.fed.us/r5/lassen/

ALMANOR RANGER DISTRICT
P.O. Box 767, Chester, CA 96020
530-258-2141
Waterfalls: Deer Creek Falls, Lower Deer Creek Falls (Lassen Region)

EAGLE LAKE RANGER DISTRICT
55 South Sacramento Street, Susanville, CA 96130
530-257-2151
Waterfalls: Upper and Lower Canyon Creek Falls (Lassen Region)

LASSEN VOLCANIC NATIONAL PARK
P.O. Box 100, Mineral, CA 96063
530-595-4444
www.nps.gov/lavo/
Waterfalls: Hat Creek Cascades, Kings Creek Cascades, Kings Creek
Falls, Mill Creek Falls, Bluff Falls (Lassen Region)

LAVA BEDS NATIONAL MONUMENT
1 Indian Well Headquarters, Tulelake, CA 96134
530-667-8104
www.nps.gov/labe
Waterfalls: Crystal Cave Falls (Lassen Region)

MALAKOFF DIGGINS STATE HISTORICAL PARK
23579 North Bloomfield Road, Nevada City, CA 95959
530-265-2740
Waterfall: Humbug Creek Falls (Sacramento/San Joaquin Region)

MARIN COUNTY OPEN SPACE DISTRICT
3501 Civic Center Drive, San Rafael, CA 94903
415-499-6387
www.marinopenspace.org/
Waterfalls: Cascade Falls, Dawn Falls (San Francisco Bay Area)

MARIN MUNICIPAL WATER DISTRICT
220 Nellen Avenue Corte, Madera, CA 94925
415-945-1455
www.marinwater.org/
Waterfalls: Little Carson Creek Falls, Cataract Falls, Cascade Falls,
Plunge Pool Falls (San Francisco Bay Area)

MAYACAMA MOUNTAINTOP RETREAT
1557 Los Alamos Road, Santa Rosa, CA 95409
707-538-8461
Waterfalls: Mayacama Retreat Falls (San Francisco Bay Area)

MCARTHUR BURNEY FALLS MEMORIAL STATE PARK
24898 Highway 89, Burney, CA 96013
530-335-2777
www.parks.ca.gov/?page_id=455
Waterfalls: Burney Falls (Lassen Region)

MEMORIAL COUNTY PARK
9500 Pescadero Creek Road, Loma Mar, CA 94021
650-879-0238
www.eparks.net
Waterfalls: Pomponio Falls, Upper Pomponio Falls (San Francisco Bay Area)

MENDOCINO NATIONAL FOREST
www.fs.fed.us/r5/mendocino/

COVELO RANGER STATION
78150 Covelo Road, Covelo, CA 95428
707-983-6118
Waterfalls: Rattlesnake Creek Falls, Balm of Gilead Falls (North Coast)

PASKENTA WORK CENTER
P.O. Box 227, Paskenta, CA 96074
530-833-5544
Waterfalls: Stony Creek Falls (Sacramento/San Joaquin Region)

MODOC NATIONAL FOREST
441 North Main Street, Alturas, CA 96101
530-233-5811
www.fs.fed.us/r5/modoc/
Waterfalls: Mill Creek Falls (Lassen Region)

MOUNT DIABLO STATE PARK
96 Mitchell Canyon Road, Clayton, CA 94517
925-837-2525
www.parks.ca.gov/default.asp?page_id=517
Waterfalls: Mount Diablo Falls (San Francisco Bay Area)

MOUNT TAMALPAIS STATE PARK
801 Panoramic Highway, Mill Valley, CA 94941
415-388-2070
www.parks.ca.gov/default.asp?page_id=471
Waterfalls: Steep Ravine Falls (San Francisco Bay Area)

PACIFIC GAS & ELECTRIC
Highway 49 and Coyote Street, Nevada City, CA, 95959
916-386-5164
www.pge.com/
Waterfalls: Bear River Falls (Lake Tahoe Region)

PLUMAS NATIONAL FOREST
www.fs.fed.us/r5/plumas/

FEATHER RIVER RANGER DISTRICT
875 Mitchell Avenue, Oroville, CA 95965-4699
530-534-6500
Waterfalls: Feather Falls, Upper Frey Creek Falls, Lower Frey Creek Falls, Milsap Bar Falls, Seven Falls, Curtain Falls (Sacramento/San Joaquin Region)

BECKWORTH RANGER DISTRICT
P.O. Box 7, Blairsden, CA 96103
530-836-2575
Waterfalls: Little Jamison Falls, Hawsley Falls, Frazier Falls, Fern Falls
(Lassen Region)

SUPERVISOR'S OFFICE
P.O. Box 11500, Quincy, CA 95971-6025
530-283-2050
Waterfalls: Indian Falls (Lassen Region)

MOUNT HOUGH RANGER STATION
39696 Highway 70, Quincy, CA 95971
530-283-0555
Waterfalls: Chambers Creek Falls (Sacramento/San Joaquin Region)

POINT REYES NATIONAL SEASHORE
1 Bear Valley Road, Point Reyes Station, CA 94956
415-464-5100
www.nps.gov/pore/
Waterfalls: Alamere Falls, Phantom Falls, Horsetail Falls (San Francisco
Bay Area)

PORTOLA REDWOODS STATE PARK
9000 Portola State Park Road, #F, La Honda, CA 94020
650-948-9098
www.parks.ca.gov/default.asp?page_id=539
Waterfalls: Tiptoe Falls (San Francisco Bay Area)

PRAIRIE CREEK REDWOODS STATE PARK
Prairie Creek Redwoods State Park, Orick, CA 95555
707-464-6101, Ext. 5301
www.parks.ca.gov/?page_id=415
Waterfalls: Gold Dust Falls, South Gold Bluffs Beach Falls, North Gold
Bluffs Beach Falls, Fern Canyon Falls, John Baldwin Falls (North Coast)

REDWOOD NATIONAL AND STATE PARKS
1111 Second Street, Crescent City, CA 95531
707-464-6101
www.nps.gov/redw
Waterfalls: Trillium Falls (North Coast)

RUSSIAN GULCH STATE PARK
P.O. Box 440, Mendocino, CA 95460
707-937-5804
www.parks.ca.gov/?page_id=432
Waterfalls: Russian Gulch Falls (North Coast)

SAMUEL P. TAYLOR STATE PARK
P.O. Box 251, Lagunitas, CA 94938
415-488-9897
www.parks.ca.gov/default.asp?page_id=469
Waterfalls: Stairstep Falls (San Francisco Bay Area)

SAN FRANCISCO RECREATION & PARK DEPARTMENT
501 Stanyan Street, San Francisco, CA 94117
415-831-2700
parks.sfgov.org/
Waterfalls: Rainbow Falls, Huntington Falls, Tea Garden Falls (San Francisco Bay Area)

SAN PEDRO VALLEY COUNTY PARK
600 Oddstad Boulevard, Pacifica, CA 94044
650-355-8289
www.eparks.net
Waterfalls: Brooks Falls (San Francisco Bay Area)

SEQUOIA NATIONAL FOREST
www.fs.fed.us/r5/sequoia/

HUME LAKE RANGER DISTRICT
35860 E Kings Canyon Road, Dunlap, CA 93621
559-338-2251
Waterfalls: Grizzly Falls, Tenmile Creek Falls, Upper Tenmile Creek Falls (Kings Canyon Region)

SHASTA-TRINITY NATIONAL FOREST
www.fs.fed.us/r5/shastatrinity/

MCCLOUD RANGER STATION
P.O. Box 1620, McCloud, CA 96057
530-964-2184
Waterfalls: Upper McCloud Falls, Lower McCloud Falls, Middle McCloud Falls, Upper Squaw Valley Creek Falls, Lower Squaw Valley Creek Falls (Shasta-Trinity Region)

MOUNT SHASTA RANGER STATION
204 West Alma, Mount Shasta, CA 96067
530-926-4511
Waterfalls: Mud Creek Falls, Ash Creek Falls, Whitney Falls, Coquette
Falls (Shasta-Trinity Region)

BIG BAR RANGER STATION
Star Route 1, Box 10, Big Bar, CA 96010
530-623-6106
Waterfalls: Grizzly Lake Falls, Schneiders Bar Falls (Shasta-Trinity Region)

WEAVERVILLE RANGER STATION
P.O. Box 1190, Weaverville, CA 96093
530-623-2121
Waterfalls: Swift Creek Falls, Canyon Creek Falls (Shasta-Trinity Region)

COFFEE CREEK RANGER STATION
Star Route 2, Box 4630, Trinity Center, CA 96091
530-266-3211
Waterfalls: Kickapoo Waterfall (Shasta-Trinity Region)

SHASTA LAKE RANGER STATION
14225 Holiday Drive, Redding, CA 96003
530-275-1587
Waterfalls: Montgomery Creek Falls, Lion Slide Falls (Shasta-Trinity Region)

FOREST SUPERVISOR
3644 Avtech Parkway, Redding, CA 96002
530-226-2500
Waterfalls: Potem Falls (Shasta-Trinity Region)

SIERRA NATIONAL FOREST
www.fs.fed.us/r5/sierra/

YOSEMITE VISITOR'S BUREAU
41969 Highway 41, Oakhurst, CA 93644
559-683-4636
Waterfalls: Fish Camp Falls, Big Creek Falls (Yosemite Region); Corlieu
Falls, Red Rock Falls (Kings Canyon Region)

BASS LAKE RANGER DISTRICT
57003 Road 225, North Fork, CA 93643
559-877-2218
Waterfalls: Bass Lake Falls, Angel Falls, Devils Slide Falls, Whisky Falls,
Chiquito Falls, Jackass Falls (Kings Canyon Region)

HIGH SIERRA RANGER DISTRICT
29688 Auberry Road, Prather, CA 93651
559-855-5355
Waterfalls: Rancheria Falls, Twin Falls, Rock Creek Falls (Kings Canyon Region)

SISKIYOU COUNTY VISITORS' BUREAU
P.O. Box 1138, Mount Shasta, CA 96067
530-926-3850
www.visitsiskiyou.org/
Waterfalls: Mossbrae Falls, Hedge Creek Falls, Sweetbriar Falls (Shasta-Trinity Region)

SIX RIVERS NATIONAL FOREST
www.fs.fed.us/r5/sixrivers/

SMITH RIVER NATIONAL RECREATION AREA
P.O. Box 668, Gasquet, CA 95543
707-457-3131
Waterfalls: Myrtle Creek Falls, Grassy Flat Falls, Madrona Falls, Little Spout Falls, Little Jones Creek Falls, Knopki Falls, Wilderness Falls (North Coast)

LOWER TRINITY RANGER DISTRICT
P.O. Box 668, Willow Creek, CA 95573
530-629-2118
Waterfalls: Gray Falls, Willow Creek Cascades, Willow Creek Falls (Shasta-Trinity Region)

SMITHE REDWOODS STATE RESERVE
69350 Highway 101 #4, Leggett, CA 95585
707-247-3318
www.parks.ca.gov/default.asp?page_id=427
Waterfalls: Dora Creek Falls (North Coast)

SOUTH YUBA RIVER STATE PARK
17660 Pleasant Valley Road, Penn Valley, CA 95946
530-432-2546
www.parks.ca.gov/default.asp?page_id=496
Waterfalls: Rush Creek Falls, Yuba River Falls (Sacramento and San Joaquin Valley)

STANISLAUS NATIONAL FOREST
www.fs.fed.us/r5/stanislaus/

SUMMIT RANGER DISTRICT
#1 Pinecrest Lake Road, Pinecrest, CA 95364
209-965-3434
Waterfalls: Blue Canyon Falls, Deadman Creek Falls, Kennedy Meadow
Falls, Niagara Creek Falls (Yosemite Region)

GROVELAND RANGER STATION
24545 Old Highway 120, Groveland, CA 95321
209-962-7825
Waterfalls: All West Highway 120 waterfalls (Yosemite Region)

SUGARLOAF RIDGE STATE PARK
2605 Adobe Canyon Road, Kenwood, CA 95452
707-833-5712
www.parks.ca.gov/?page_id=481
Waterfalls: Sonoma Creek Falls (San Francisco Bay Area)

SUNOL-OHLONE REGIONAL WILDERNESS
P.O. Box 82, Sunol, CA 94586
925-862-2244
Waterfalls: Murietta Falls, Little Yosemite Falls (San Francisco Bay Area)

SUTTER BUTTES TOURS
4949 West Butte Road, Live Oaks, CA 95933
530-696-2646
Waterfalls: The Falls (Sacramento and San Joaquin Valley)

TAHOE NATIONAL FOREST
www.fs.fed.us/r5/tahoe/

FORESTHILL RANGER STATION
22830 Foresthill Road, Foresthill, CA 95631
530-367-2224
Waterfalls: Grouse Falls (Lake Tahoe Region)

TRUCKEE RANGER STATION
10342 Highway 89 North, Truckee, CA 96161-2949
530-587-3558
Waterfalls: Webber Falls, Heath Falls (Tahoe Region)

NORTH YUBA RANGER STATION
15924 Highway 49, Camptonville, CA. 95922
530-288-3231
Waterfalls: Loves Falls, Pauley Creek Falls, Faucherie Lake Falls,
Bowman Lake Falls (Lake Tahoe Region)

SIERRAVILLE RANGER STATION
Highway 89, P.O. Box 95, Sierraville, CA 92126
530-994-3401
Waterfalls: Webber Falls (Lake Tahoe Region)

UVAS CANYON COUNTY PARK
8515 Croy Road, Morgan Hill, CA 95037
408-779-9232
www.parkhere.org/
Waterfalls: Granuja Falls, Black Rock Falls, Upper Falls, Basin Falls, Uvas Falls, Triple Falls (San Francisco Bay Area)

WHISKEYTOWN NATIONAL RECREATION AREA
P.O. Box 188, Whiskeytown, CA 96095
530-242-3400
www.nps.gov/whis/
Waterfalls: Boulder Creek Falls, Lower Brandy Creek Falls, Brandy Creek Falls, Crystal Creek Falls, Upper Crystal Creek Falls (Shasta-Trinity Region)

YERBA BUENA GARDENS
760 Howard Street, San Francisco, CA 94103-3119
415-541-0312
www.yerbabuena.org/
Waterfalls: Martin Luther King, Jr. Memorial Falls (San Francisco Bay Area)

YOSEMITE NATIONAL PARK
P.O. Box 577, Yosemite National Park, CA 95389
209-372-0200
www.nps.gov/yose/
Waterfalls: All waterfalls within Yosemite National Park boundaries (Yosemite Region)

APPENDIX B: FUN LISTS

There are so many waterfalls in California that it would be hard to name all the best ones. The following are a few of our favorites, grouped by category.

HIGHEST WATERFALLS

Obviously, the highest waterfalls are not a category open for interpretation. California is actually home to most of the highest waterfalls in the entire United States, although a few recently discovered waterfalls in other states may rival these. Not surprisingly, all the highest waterfalls in California are in Yosemite Valley.

Yosemite Falls. Renowned as the highest waterfall in the country and the fifth highest in the world, the combination of Upper and Lower Yosemite Falls, along with its middle cascades, stretches a whopping 2425 feet.

Snow Creek Falls. Hike a ways up from Yosemite Valley and you will reach this 2140 foot fall in a pretty, more remote part of the park.

Sentinel Falls. A lesser-known seasonal waterfall that sits near Bridalveil Falls, Sentinel Falls is 1920 feet tall. Be sure to visit in the spring for optimal flow.

Ribbon Falls. Another seasonal fall that you will only see in the spring, Ribbon Falls is a popular fall of 1612 feet.

El Capitan Falls. The mighty El Capitan is not particularly known for the seemingly tiny waterfall that pours off its cliffs in the summer, but this waterfall is actually one of the highest in the park at about 1400 feet. Be sure to bring binoculars to get the best view—unless you like rock climbing, of course!

MOST BEAUTIFUL WATERFALLS

Some waterfalls are just so pretty that they take your breath away. Being high is one thing, but it does not always make the fall the most picturesque. The following falls are a few of our favorites from our travels in compiling this book.

Burney Falls. Tucked away in a somewhat remote area of northern California, Burney Falls is widely considered one of the prettiest falls in the state. It may only be 129 feet tall, but it keeps a powerful flow year-round and is awe-inspiring from every angle. What do you expect from a waterfall that is the centerpiece of its own state park?

Vernal Falls. Vernal Falls is our favorite Yosemite waterfall. In its peak season, Vernal Falls has a strong, majestic, roaring flow that makes it a destination in its own right.

Rainbow Falls. One of the crown jewels of Devils Postpile National Monument in the eastern Sierra region, Rainbow Falls gets its name by casting rainbows toward its base.

Alamere Falls. Two significant waterfalls in California pour into the ocean. One is McWay Falls on the Big Sur Coast in Southern California, and the other is Alamere Falls. Few sights are grander than a waterfall pouring into the Pacific Ocean.

Mossbrae Falls. Mossbrae Falls is an extraordinary, wide waterfall that erupts as much from the hillside as it does from the creek that feeds into the river. This waterfall must be seen to be fully appreciated; no photos can do it justice.

BEST SHORT WATERFALL HIKES

The hikes in this book range from a few hundred feet to over a dozen miles. Here are a few of our favorite trails of 5 miles or less. All of these are easily completed in less than six hours.

Tueeulala and Wapama Falls. Many think the Hetch Hetchy Valley would have rivaled the Yosemite Valley had it not been flooded to create the reservoir. Yet, even with the environmental damage done, the hike around the water to reach these two falls is one of the most fun you will find anywhere.

Mist Trail to Vernal and Nevada Falls. The Mist Trail is certainly not an easy hike, but at just over a 5-mile round trip it is certainly one of the most rewarding. It takes you past two five-star falls with distant views of Illilouette Falls, and it is hard not to feel a sense of accomplishment after completing the hike.

Rainbow Falls. With two access possibilities, including a 5-mile hike past Devils Postpile or a 2-mile trek through the forests of the monument, whichever way you choose to reach Rainbow Falls will be memorable.

Lundy Canyon Falls. The entire eastern Sierras region is beautiful, but the Lundy Canyon hike is really special. It changes by the season and can have fall colors to rival New England. That plus the 500-foot waterfall make this a hike tough to beat.

Steep Ravine Falls. People around the world marvel at and admire the coastline of the Pacific Ocean. The hike to Steep Ravine Falls traverses the area just north of Point Reyes National Seashore, one of the most photographed sections of the California coast.

BEST LONG WATERFALL HIKES

Some waterfalls take a while to reach. The hikes below are some of the best for waterfall watchers that want to make a day of it.

Alamere Falls. For the same reasons the trip to Steep Ravine Falls made our list of the best short hikes, the hike to reach Alamere Falls is hard to beat as a long hike. It can be completed as a day trip or combined with additional hiking to make a backpacking trip.

Mist Falls. The hike to Mist Falls and back is just 8 miles, barely qualifying for this list, but it sure is a pretty trail. It traverses a popular area of Kings Canyon National Park through unforgettable scenery and ends in an impressive waterfall.

Feather Falls. Feather Falls has its own national recreation area. At the right time of year, when the waterfall is flowing at peak flow, hiking to Feather Falls makes a top-notch day trip on a not-too-hard trail.

Grand Canyon of the Tuolumne. For true waterfall enthusiasts, the trail through the Grand Canyon of the Tuolumne is an absolute must. It passes several falls, including California Falls, Le Conte Falls, and the fascinating Waterwheel Falls. Make it a day trip or hike farther for a multiday backpacking trek.

Lost Coast Falls. This hike must be done in the spring to assure that there will be waterfalls, but in the right season it is a peaceful stroll by the Pacific Ocean in a place that you are sure to have it all to yourself.

MOST UNUSUAL WATERFALLS

Tired of the same old routine cascades? Try some of the following falls for something out of the ordinary.

Waterwheel Falls. Waterwheel Falls gets its name because the strength of the fall and the orientation of the bedrock is such that you can actually spot wheels of water rolling along its flow.

Mossbrae Falls. The hike to reach Mossbrae Falls is unique in itself; it follows along a railroad, including some almost painfully narrow sections that will have you fearing an oncoming train. As described above, Mossbrae Falls has the unusual feature of having the water erupt from the hillside as well as the creek that feeds the falls.

Crystal Cave Falls. Does it get much more unusual than to find a frozen waterfall deep within a cave?

Stairstep Falls. A seasonal waterfall of Yosemite Valley, Stairstep Falls is often missed for its lack of grandeur. But be sure to travel over near Curry Village in the spring and take a look; this waterfall actually skips sideways along the rocks of a cliff.

Alamere Falls. Since there are so few waterfalls falling directly into the ocean, we felt Alamere Falls deserved a spot on this list.

BEST WATERFALLS TO PICNIC BESIDE

Some waterfalls are beautiful, but there's just no place to sit and enjoy them. If you are the type that likes to enjoy a picnic when you reach the falls, try some of these.

Crystal Creek Falls. This powerful waterfall in Redding, of all places, has a shaded picnic area just around the bend from the falls' viewpoint. Be sure to visit in the spring so it won't be too hot!

Burney Falls. It does not take much of a hike to view Burney Falls, but since the waterfall is so easy to get to, why not enjoy a picnic lunch in the area just next to the viewpoint?

McCloud Falls. There are great places to picnic in Fowlers Campground and sprinkled along the hiking trail that leads to Middle and Upper McCloud Falls. It is a wonderful place to bring the family.

Uvas Canyon County Park Falls. The picnic areas in Uvas Canyon County Park are not right next to the falls. Still, if you come in winter or springtime, the rushing creek is so loud that you will feel like the falls are right next to you even in the picnic area.

Upper Eagle Falls. A very popular destination in the Tahoe region, Upper Eagle Falls has a picnic area near the parking lot with the waterfall just a stone's throw away.

BEST WATERFALLS TO VISIT WITH KIDS

Some children like waterfalls, but if your kids are the type to think that waterfalls are boring, try some of these. Some may not be the most spectacular but your kids are sure to have a great time.

Bass Lake Falls. Bass Lake is a great park with lots of activities and recreational possibilities. The waterfall itself is not terribly tall and doubles as a waterslide during the summer months with lines of people waiting to slide down.

Frazier Falls. This is your chance to visit a truly impressive waterfall with a hike that is so easy that your kids won't be able to complain.

McCloud Falls. There is a ton to do along this trail—everything from swimming to fishing to just plain running wild. Middle McCloud Falls is sure to whet your waterfall appetite while keeping everyone happy.

Lower Yosemite Falls. The hike to reach Lower Yosemite Falls is easy enough for wheelchairs. To make it even better, you can get right up close to the waterfall and feel its spray by climbing on a huge pile of giant rocks.

Golden Gate Park Falls. Golden Gate Park is a favorite destination for families visiting San Francisco. Everyone is sure to enjoy a stroll past the waterfalls as a part of the visit.

BEST WATERFALL ROAD TRIPS

If you want to see a lot of waterfalls by car with a minimal amount of hiking, these are the places to go.

Sonora Pass. Also known as Highway 108, Sonora Pass is pretty for other reasons, but the sheer number of waterfalls along this way is astonishing. Most are drive-bys or very short hikes.

Yosemite Valley. In spring, Yosemite Valley is awash in waterfalls. You will see Yosemite Falls flowing at its peak flow, and then there are dozens of other seasonal waterfalls falling from various points throughout the valley. Be sure to bring your binoculars for the best views.

Highway 199 waterfalls. This trip must be done in the winter or spring, but for a guaranteed collection of pretty waterfalls, the drive is gorgeous with waterfalls aplenty falling right by the road.

Devils Falls. Some drivers may find this route a little scary during seasons when the road conditions are not so good, but Devils Falls in its peak season is possibly one of the best drive-to waterfalls anywhere. It pours down literally right next to the road. As a bonus, Mexican Gulch Falls is just a short drive farther.

Highway 299 waterfalls. This route in the Shasta-Trinity region is not quite as pretty as Highway 199, but you will find a large number of seasonal waterfalls pouring down the hills and into the Trinity River. Visit in winter or early spring for the best odds of seeing lots of falls.

BEST WHEELCHAIR-ACCESSIBLE WATERFALLS

Sadly, very few hikes are wheelchair-friendly. Luckily, there are still several spectacular falls that are accessible to folks in wheelchairs. These are the best ones, excluding pure drive-by waterfalls.

Bridalveil Falls. Renowned for its beauty, Bridalveil Falls is one of the most famous waterfalls in Yosemite. The short trail that begins in Bridalveil's parking lot is paved and easy for wheelchairs.

Yosemite Falls. The trail to Lower Yosemite Falls is paved, allowing waterfall watchers with physical disabilities to get an up-close look at the falls. There are also great views of Upper Yosemite Falls along the way.

Frazier Falls. Due to its more remote location, Frazier Falls is not as famous as numerous less spectacular falls. Still, this is a very pleasing, peaceful alpine trail that is paved. Individuals in wheelchairs may require some assistance on steeper sections, but the waterfall is still not difficult to reach.

Burney Falls. It does not really take much of a hike to reach Burney Falls, but there is a very easily accessible outlook point about a hundred yards from the parking lot. This waterfall is so pretty that it deserves a spot on almost every list.

Rush Creek Falls. The Independence Trail in Yuba River State Park is well-known for being an unpaved wilderness trail that is accessible to wheelchairs. While this waterfall is nothing spectacular, the trail is nice enough that it earns a spot on this list for allowing folks in wheelchairs to escape the feel of civilization for a little while. In addition, it is one of the only wheelchair-accessible trails longer than 0.5 mile, so there are possibilities for a day hike along it.

BEST UNKNOWN OR REMOTE WATERFALLS

Nearly all waterfall enthusiasts have heard of waterfalls like Yosemite Falls, Bridalveil Falls, and Burney Falls. However, there are some truly awesome waterfalls in California that get overlooked because they are not in heavily trafficked tourist destinations.

Silver Spray Falls. The trip to reach this Kings Canyon National Park waterfall is so overwhelming that few bother to make the trek. It cannot be completed as a day hike and requires a minimum of one night camping in a remote wilderness-like area. But some compare the beauty of Tehipite Valley to the more famous Yosemite Valley—Tehipite Valley just lacks the roads. Silver Spray Falls, as a result, may be the best "unknown" waterfall in the whole state.

Mill Creek Falls. Traveling to remote Modoc County in the northeastern corner of California requires some dedication. It is a very long trip from any metropolitan area. However, Modoc National Forest does have an easily accessible 100-foot waterfall with its own campground. To really get away and enjoy a pretty waterfall, but without the backpacking required for Silver Spray Falls, this may be one of your best bets.

Grouse Falls. Some waterfall enthusiasts in California are probably familiar with Grouse Falls, a 700-foot segmented plunge in Tahoe National Forest near Foresthill. This waterfall would surely be more popular were it not for the detour of 25 miles each way to reach it; it is a long drive for a 1-mile round-trip hike.

Upper Crystal Creek Falls. The lower fall on Crystal Creek is a familiar one and is very pretty. We did not know about the 400-foot upper cascade on Crystal Creek until we spoke to a Whiskeytown ranger, who gave us the directions and sent a photo.

Coal Canyon Falls. It is truly shocking how many waterfalls there are in the Sacramento/San Joaquin region. Coal Canyon Falls was another neat 150-foot waterfall that we had not heard of until we spoke with a ranger from the North Table Mountain Wilderness.

INDEX OF WATERFALLS BY NAME

ABOUT THE AUTHORS

Matt Danielsson works as an editor for a technology publisher while Krissi splits her time between freelance writing and being a mom. They have previously co-written *A Bark in the Park: The 45 Best Places to Hike With Your Dog in the Shasta/Rogue River Region*, a hiking book for dog owners in northern California and southernmost Oregon. In addition, they have authored a series of three guides for new parents on how to find the best websites for various parenting issues.

Did we get a junction mixed up somewhere? Is there a better route to a certain trailhead? Did we overlook a neat waterfall in your area? Try as we might to do careful research and consult with local rangers, there's always a chance we missed something. That's why we want to hear from you! Please send any comments, corrections, or suggestions you may have to: *waterfalls@danielssonarts.com* and we will do our best to get it right in the next edition of this book. Thanks in advance for your help!

THE MOUNTAINEERS, founded in 1906, is a nonprofit outdoor activity and conservation club, whose mission is "to explore, study, preserve, and enjoy the natural beauty of the outdoors...." Based in Seattle, Washington, the club is now the third-largest such organization in the United States, with seven branches throughout Washington State.

The Mountaineers sponsors both classes and year-round outdoor activities in the Pacific Northwest, which include hiking, mountain climbing, ski-touring, snowshoeing, bicycling, camping, kayaking, nature study, sailing, and adventure travel. The club's conservation division supports environmental causes through educational activities, sponsoring legislation, and presenting informational programs.

All club activities are led by skilled, experienced instructors, who are dedicated to promoting safe and responsible enjoyment and preservation of the outdoors.

If you would like to participate in these organized outdoor activities or the club's programs, consider a membership in The Mountaineers. For information and an application, write or call The Mountaineers, Club Headquarters, 300 Third Avenue West, Seattle, WA 98119; 206-284-6310. You can also visit the club's website at www.mountaineers.org or contact The Mountaineers via email at clubmail@mountaineers.org.

The Mountaineers Books, an active, nonprofit publishing program of the club, produces guidebooks, instructional texts, historical works, natural history guides, and works on environmental conservation. All books produced by The Mountaineers Books fulfill the club's mission.

Send or call for our catalog of more than 500 outdoor titles:

The Mountaineers Books
1001 SW Klickitat Way, Suite 201
Seattle, WA 98134
800-553-4453
mbooks@mountaineersbooks.org
www.mountaineersbooks.org

 The Mountaineers Books is proud to be a corporate sponsor of The Leave No Trace Center for Outdoor Ethics, whose mission is to promote and inspire responsible outdoor recreation through education, research, and partnerships. The Leave No Trace program is focused specifically on human-powered (nonmotorized) recreation.

Leave No Trace strives to educate visitors about the nature of their recreational impacts, as well as offer techniques to prevent and minimize such impacts. Leave No Trace is best understood as an educational and ethical program, not as a set of rules and regulations.

For more information, visit *www.LNT.org*, or call 800-332-4100.

OTHER TITLES YOU MIGHT ENJOY FROM
THE MOUNTAINEERS BOOKS

100 Classic Hikes in Northern California, 2nd Ed.
John Soares & Marc Soares

Best Hikes with Dogs: Bay Area and Beyond
Thom Gabrukiewicz

Best Short Hikes in Redwood National and State Parks
Jerry Rohde and Gisela Rohde

100 Hikes in the San Francisco Bay Area
Marc Soares

Best Hikes with Children in the San Francisco Bay Area, 2nd Ed.
Bill McMillon & Kevin McMillon

Trekking California
Paul Richins

75 Year-Round Hikes in Northern California
Marc Soares

Available at fine bookstores and outdoor stores, by phone at 800-553-4453 or on the web at *www.mountaineersbooks.org*

THE MOUNTAINEERS BOOKS